HEPHAISTION OF THEBES:

APOTELESMATICS

BOOK III: ON INCEPTIONS

TRANSLATED BY
EDUARDO J. GRAMAGLIA

EDITED WITH AN INTRODUCTION BY
BENJAMIN N. DYKES, PHD

The Cazimi Press
Minneapolis, Minnesota
2013

Published and printed in the United States of America
by The Cazimi Press
621 5th Avenue SE #25, Minneapolis, MN 55414

© 2013 by The Cazimi Press and Benjamin N. Dykes, Ph.D.

ISBN-13: 978-1-934586-40-2

ACKNOWLEDGEMENTS

I would like to thank the following friends and colleagues, in alphabetical order: Demetra George, Eduardo Gramaglia, and Deb Houlding. Special thanks go to Chris Brennan, for his commentary and discussion of many issues in Hephaistion.

Also available at www.bendykes.com:

 Designed for curious modern astrology students, *Traditional Astrology for Today* explains basic ideas in history, philosophy and counseling, dignities, chart interpretation, and predictive techniques. Non-technical and friendly for modern beginners.

 Two classic introductions to astrology, by Abū Ma'shar and al-Qabīsī, are translated with commentary in this volume. *Introductions to Traditional Astrology* is an essential reference work for traditional students.

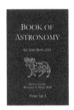 The classic medieval text by Guido Bonatti, the *Book of Astronomy* is now available in paperback reprints. This famous work is a complete guide to basic principles, horary, elections, mundane, and natal astrology.

 This first volume of the new medieval mundane series, *Astrology of the World I: The Ptolemaic Inheritance* describes numerous techniques in weather prediction, prices and commodities, eclipses and comets, and chorography, translated from Arabic and Latin sources.

 The largest compilation of traditional electional material, *Choices & Inceptions: Traditional Electional Astrology* contains works by Sahl, al-Rijāl, al-'Imrānī, and others, beginning with an extensive discussion of elections and questions by Benjamin Dykes.

The famous medieval horary compilation *The Book of the Nine Judges* is now available in translation for the first time! It is the largest traditional horary work available, and the third in the horary series.

The Search of the Heart is the first in the horary series, and focuses on the use of victors (special significators or *almutens*) and the practice of thought-interpretation: divining thoughts and predicting outcomes before the client speaks.

The Forty Chapters is a famous and influential horary work by al-Kindī, and is the second volume of the horary series. Beginning with a general introduction to astrology, al-Kindī covers topics such as war, wealth, travel, pregnancy, marriage, and more.

The first volume of the *Persian Nativities* series on natal astrology contains *The Book of Aristotle*, an advanced work on nativities and prediction by Māshā'allāh, and a beginner-level work by his student Abū 'Ali al-Khayyāt, *On the Judgments of Nativities*.

The second volume of *Persian Nativities* features a shorter, beginner-level work on nativities and prediction by 'Umar al-Tabarī, and a much longer book on nativities by his younger follower, Abū Bakr.

The third volume of *Persian Nativities* is a translation of Abū Ma'shar's work on solar revolutions, devoted solely to the Persian annual predictive system. Learn about profections, distributions, *firdārīyyāt*, transits, and more!

This compilation of sixteen works by Sahl ibn Bishr and Māshā'allāh covers all areas of traditional astrology, from basic concepts to horary, elections, natal interpretation, and mundane astrology. It is also available in paperback.

Expand your knowledge of traditional astrology, philosophy, and esoteric thought with the *Logos & Light* audio series: downloadable, college-level lectures on CD at a fraction of the university cost!

Enjoy these new additions in our magic/esoteric series:

Astrological Magic: Basic Rituals & Meditations is the first book in our new esoteric series. It thoroughly introduces a magical cosmology and shows how to perform ritual correctly, integrating Tarot and visualizations with rituals for all Elements, Planets, and Signs.

Available as an MP3 download or physical CD, *Music of the Elements* was composed especially for *Astrological Magic* by MjDawn, an experienced electronic artist and ritualists. Hear free clips at bendykes.com/music.php!

Nights is a special, 2-disc remastering by MjDawn of the album GAMMA, and is a deep and powerful set of 2 full-disc soundtracks suitable for meditation or ritual work, especially those in *Astrological Magic.* Hear free clips at bendykes.com/music.php!

Aeonian Glow is a new version of the original ambient work mixed by Steve Roach, redesigned by MjDawn and Vir Unis from the original, pre-mixed files. This album is entrancing and enchanting: hear free clips at bendykes.com/music.php!

TABLE OF CONTENTS

TABLE OF FIGURES

INTRODUCTION

I am pleased to introduce Book III of Hephaistion of Thebes's *Aposteles-matics*, or *Outcomes* (see below), an important (albeit late) ancient compilation on elections (or "inceptions"), event charts, and inquiries of many types. It is the first installment in my new Hellenistic series in astrology, which will include works by major and minor authors, including Theophilus, Valens, Manetho, Firmicus Maternus, and many more. It will be translated primarily by Eduardo Gramaglia, and published concurrently with a new Arabic series, translated by me from Arabic into English—again, with many major and minor authors.

Book III of the *Apotelesmatica* is the only part not already translated by Robert Schmidt for his Project Hindsight: Books I-II are on basic concepts in astrology, mundane techniques, and nativities.[1] As Book III is the first in this Hellenistic series, it gives me the opportunity to explain some vocabulary and our own approach to the (largely) Greek material, especially in relation to the large body of work already translated and discussed by Schmidt in his own books and audio workshops.

Before beginning, let us address the title of the work itself, an Anglicized form of the Greek (*Apotelesmatika*).[2] The core of the word is the verb *teleō*, which means to "fulfill, bring to an end, finish," and also "to perform sacred rites, initiate into the Mysteries." The prefix *apo* ("from, away from") yields *apotelesma*, which denotes some kind of full completion, finished product, or simply the "result" of some process or event. Thus, apotelesmatics or *apotelesmatica* means "referring to final results." Astrologically, this came to mean either the effects of the planets in human life, or the astrological practice of interpreting outcomes from a chart. For example, Valens refers to an *apotelesmatographia*,[3] literally the "writing of the final effects," but referring specifically to the natal chart: either the drawn-out chart itself or the interpretation made from its features. In sum, apotelesmatics is the study of outcomes based on astrological configurations (whether natal configurations or others), apart from any special theory as to whether the stars cause or only indicate those outcomes.

---

[1] In the future we hope to translate these as well, with all of Hephaistion to be published in a single volume.

[2] This comment was largely written by Gramaglia.

[3] See for example Valens's *Anth.* II, Introduction, which Schmidt translates as "effect-description."

§1: Pingree's introduction and edition

Let me introduce Hephaistion himself and his work; probably the best way to do this is simply to translate some of Pingree's own Latin introduction to his critical edition of Hephaistion (1973, pp. *vff.*), which we used for this translation. Following this, I will introduce some of our editorial devices, some vocabulary, glossaries, and so on.

"Hephaistio was born in Thebes, Egypt,[4] at midday on the 30th day of the month of Aethyr in the 97th year from Diocletian (November 26, 380), conceived by his mother (as he himself reckoned it) at the second hour of the night on the 26th/27th of the month of Mecheir (February 20, 380). About his life no other record comes forth, but we know that he dedicated three books of *Apotelesmatics*, composed for his friend Athanasius, around 415. There are those who, being misled by the words *With God* placed at the beginning of the work, believe that he was a Christian: but the Byzantine librarians often ornamented astrological works with such words, lest they be thought irreligious for writing down suspicious pagan works.

"The three books of Hephaistio's *Apotelesmatics* are comprised of three astrological categories: of which the first hands down to us the elements of this knowledge, especially excerpted from the work of Ptolemy, and from the writings of the ancient Egyptians which were derived from the Babylonian teaching of the Chaldeans; the second presents the study of nativities (particularly drawn from Ptolemy and Dorotheus); the third makes us more certain about elections, being especially taken from the fifth book of Dorotheus."

---

[4] Modern Luxor, Egypt.

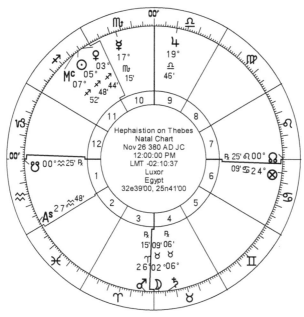

Figure 1: Hephaistion's nativity (tropical, modern calculation)

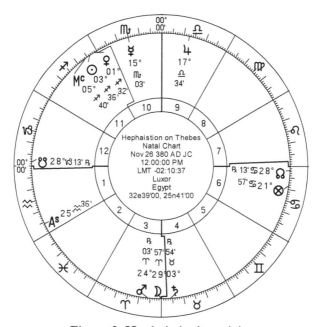

Figure 2: Hephaistion's nativity
(Fagan-Bradley sidereal, modern calculation)

"Hephaistio added little of his own, but he compiled, abridged, [and] mutilated the works of others, just as he preserved some things from the lost writings of the astrologers. We do not know for sure whether in fact he composed the book of astrological definitions *On the Dispositions of the Heavens*[5] (which is sometimes attributed to him in the manuscripts), but for certain we must deny that he was the author of the chapter *On Treasure* (furnished only with the name, "by Hephaistio" in codex **U**). Therefore, the remaining things edited here seem to be all of the genuine writings of Hephaistio. However, the witnesses of three books are weak, and so we should hope that stronger ones will be found.[6]

"Hephaistio seems to have written out the majority of the text of Ptolemy's *Apotelesmatics*, but we find the excerpts to be abridged here and there: see for example II.15.18. And who would affirm for certain whether Hephaistio himself has compressed the text, or he used a codex of Ptolemy which was already defective? But one may compare Hephaistio's readings with those of the codices of Ptolemy. Therefore, although we will enlarge our arguments about the Ptolemaic text in greater detail in another place, here we must explain certain judgments about the codex as read by Hephaistio, in a summary way…[7]

"Hephaistio even excerpted the majority of the work of Dorotheus—five books of a poem on astrology, I say—either retained in verse or rendered as prose. The hexameters of Dorotheus have perished most unhappily, except for those which Hephaistio preserves, and very few others—but by most benevolent Fortune, an Arabic translation by 'Umar bin al-Farrukhān [al-Tabarī] made in about 800 from the Pahlavi recension, has survived. We are now preparing an edition of the Arabic translation from two codices: Constantinople Yeni Cami 784, and Berlin or. Oct. 2663.[8] When the excerpts of Hephaistio are compared with the Arabic text, it is clear that he or the copyist has

---

[5] *Peri tēs ouranias diatheseōs.*

[6] This may be an ironic reference to *Deut.* 17.6-7 or 19.15, in which two or three witnesses are enough to ensure conviction.

[7] I omit here some technical discussions of the codices—but will include it in the complete Hephaistion volume. I also omit a table showing the correspondences between Hephaistion and Ptolemy in Books I-II.

[8] This was published in 1976: see Dorotheus in the Bibliography.

neither written out the complete chapters, nor preserved the order of sentences unchanged.

"However, here it seems useful to us to note the inscriptions of the chapters of the Arabic translation of Dorotheus, and the chapters of Hephaistio derived from them:"[9]

Hephaistion	Dorotheus
III.1	V.1: Introduction
III.1	V.2: On the straight and slanted signs
III.1	V.3: On the solsticial signs
III.1	V.4: On the signs of two bodies
III.1	V.5: On the corruption of the Moon
III.7	V.6: On those who wish to build
III.9	V.16: On marriage and sexual intercourse
III.11	V.17: On a woman's departure
III.12	V.18: On miscarriage/abortion
III.16	V.9: On trade
III.16	V.10: On buying land
III.16	V.11: On buying slaves
III.16	V.43: On the ascent and descent of the Moon
III.17	V.23: On the buying and construction of ships
III.19	V.12: On buying flock-animals
III.21	V.13: On the manumission of a slave
III.25	V.14: On seeking a gift
III.27	V.15: On letters
III.28	V.20: On debt
III.30	V.21: On journeys
III.30	V.22: On returning
III.30	V.25: On putting a ship into water
III.31	V.29: On the infirm
III.31	V.31: On the condition of an infirm person
III.32	V.39: On cutting and phlebotomy
III.32	V.40: On cutting an impediment of the eye
III.38	V.33: On those in litigation

---

[9] I include only the relevant parts of the table referring to Book III; see also Appendix F.

III.40	V.27: On those who are put in prison
III.41	V.32: On the condition of a boy and his wealth
III.42-46	V.35: On something looted or lost, if it would be gotten back
III.47	V.36: On fugitives
App. II	V.42: On a will

For his edition of Hephaistion, Pingree relied on three primary codices (along with some minor ones) and four Epitomes. The primary codices were as follows:

- **A** (Paris Gr. 2841), of the 13th Century. It is incomplete, and from it are based two other minor manuscripts, **a** (Paris Gr. 2415) and **N** (Madrid BN I 1525).
- **P** (Paris Gr. 2417), also from the 13th Century. It preserves the majority of Hephaistion, and from it come **P2** and **p**.
- **L** (Laurentianus 28, 34), from the 11th Century and therefore the oldest.

As for the Epitomes (which Pingree printed in their entirety in his Volume II), Pingree argued that they derive from other Greek manuscripts which were at the same level of transmission and authority as **P**'s and **A**'s sources (see his p. *xxi*).

Now, from these passages and tables above we can see that the work of Dorotheus[10] was crucial for the composition of Hephaistion's Book III, not to mention Book II's treatment of nativities. Hephaistion's work is an important check on 'Umar's Arabic of the Pahlavi version of Dorotheus (late 700s AD), as well as the parallel passages found in Arabic works of people like Māshā'allāh, Sahl ibn Bishr, al-Khayyāt, and compilations by al-Rijāl and al-Imrānī.[11] This is especially due to the fact that he preserves many original Greek verses from Dorotheus. As such, Book III acts as an important first step in producing a reconstructed Dorotheus, which I am currently working on and hope to publish in a few years.

---

[10] Hephaistion Book III also refers to Nicaeus Protagoras, Petosiris, and Manetho.
[11] For translations of many of these from Latin, see my *Choices & Inceptions: Traditional Electional Astrology* (2012), available on my own site (www.bendykes.com).

As a contribution to that future project, I have also included Dorothean *Excerpts* and *Fragments* in the Appendices, as well as a table (based on Pingree) showing correspondences between Book III and the Arabic Dorotheus, as well as some other works. These *Excerpts* and *Fragments* require some explanation:

- *Excerpts* refer to a list of 69 Greek passages of material by (or rather, summarized from) Dorotheus, identified by Pingree within *Vaticanus Graecus* 1056, ff. 238-41. Pingree and Charles Burnett printed them as Appendix II of the Latin *Book of Aristotle* (1997), recently translated by me into English as *The Book of Aristotle*, in my *Persian Nativities I* (2009). Again, I have included the ones relevant to the material in Hephaistion's Book III.
- *Fragments* are Greek and Latin passages explicitly mentioning or attributed to Dorotheus, many of which can be directly correlated with al-Tabari's Arabic version of Dorotheus. These were originally published in the Appendices of Pingree's 1976 translation of al-Tabari's version, and I have included the ones relevant to Book V of Dorotheus. They often act as supplements to Hephaistion's versions of the same passages.

§2: Editorial conventions

As Eduardo Gramaglia and I worked with Pingree's critical edition, we decided upon the following conventions for indicating his own changes as well as our own ways of making the text clear:

- ( ) Rounded parentheses indicate our own way of indicating parenthetical comments and clarifications in the translation. Pingree did sometimes add parentheses in this way to the Greek, but since we did not always agree with them, they should all be considered our own.
- < > Pointed brackets indicate additions by Pingree in Greek, either based on material from some of the Epitomes or other sources. Sometimes these are only individual words (which we rarely comment on), or even the chapter numbers; but some are substantive

sentences and passages. We indicate the sources for these longer additions in the footnotes.

- [ ] Square brackets are additions by us in order to make the *English* presentation of the Greek clearer. For example, if the Greek speaks of the Moon and Venus (both feminine), but then resorts to pronouns ("she") to discuss them further, we might replace "she" with the name of the relevant planet in square brackets so as to help the reader.

Footnotes. Footnotes which are only transliterations of a Greek word (with suggested alternatives) are unattributed, as are all substantive comments and explanations by Dykes. Commentary by Gramaglia is marked with (**EG**), and where both Dykes and Gramaglia make comments, they are distinguished by (**BD**) and (**EG**).

Sentence numbers. Finally, I have continued my decision (begun in my *Astrology of the World I*) to number sentences in boldface within the text itself (following Pingree's numbers) for easier reference. Thus, to refer to Book III, Chapter 47, sentence 5, the convention is: III.47, **5**.

§3: What is distinctive in Hephaistion?

There are several special items of interest in Book III, which to our knowledge are not at all, or hardly, represented elsewhere in Hellenistic astrology. Perhaps the most important is the matter of how Book III illuminates the history of horary astrology, which I will address in the next section. There are three other noteworthy topics:

*Chapter III.6, **7-17**: Animal sacrifices.* In this chapter, Hephaistion presents a couple of remarkable ways in which astrologers apparently usurped the traditional practice of the priestly reading of entrails—made even more interesting due to the fact that he was writing as late as the 5th Century AD. First (**8-10**), since the Moon affects the internal composition of bodies, it is important to elect a proper time (with proper sect conditions) for opening the animal—not for a positive interpretation, but to make the entrails *readable*. Then (**11-16**), Hephaistion offers an angular template along with zodiacal attributions—not for reading the entrails themselves, but for reading the *chart* of the sacrifice. In this way, the sacrifice and entrails become only the occasion for performing an *astrological* interpretation of what they represent. One may easily imagine that this was a stepping-stone for the later cessation of haruspexy altogether, because once the divinational aspect is transferred over to the chart, the angles (at least) can become a general template for the time of *any* kind of sacrifice or offering. See also below, where Hephaistion's Ch. III.4 provides a generic template for interpreting thoughts and predicting outcomes.

*Chapter III.7, **13-17**: Consecrating statues and other objects.* In this chapter, Hephaistion gives some general instructions for the creation and consecration of statues and other objects, particularly when the Moon is in the sign relevant to the divinity which is the object of the consecration.

Fifteenth-parts. Finally, in a few places Hephaistion divides the signs into two halves of 15° apiece, with different electional interpretations for each (although some of the signs are explicitly divided into decans or faces): Chs. III.9, **7** and **12**, and III.5, **62ff**. Dividing the signs in half can also be seen in Pingree's translation of the *Yavanajātaka* Ch. 1, **39** and Ch. 2, but in the former case the division pertains to the rulership of those parts, and in the latter case the halves there are assigned anthropomorphic figures much like the faces or decans are—without any clear interpretive meaning.

§4: Questions (horary), thought-interpretation, and inceptions

In my *Choices & Inceptions* (2012) I discussed the theory of elections at length, as well as the fact that many Dorothean texts on elections and event charts were later turned into a distinct branch of astrology called "questions"—also known in English as "horary," presumably because they deal with pressing questions of the moment, of the "hour." In this place I would like to address the issue of how far back the practice of questions goes, in the context of Hephaistion Book III. The origin of questions has been the subject of controversy, with some claiming it is one of the earliest practices, but others claiming it was a later development.[12] I addressed some of the literature on this in my translation of Hermann of Carinthia's *Search of the Heart* (2011), in which I also discussed "thought-interpretation," the practice of casting a chart to identify the client's concern astrologically before the consultation properly begins. In general, thought-interpretation seems to have been a preliminary to the question, i.e., interpreting broadly the topic of the question, before it is verbally stated or before the exact question has been

---

[12] See for example Brennan 2007.

narrowed down. In some cases, thought-interpretation moved directly into predicting the outcome of the matter. (It can also be about guessing the object held in a client's hand: see *Search* Appendices I-J.)

I should state my own approach to this matter. In a broad sense, I think the issue of "how far back" horary goes is not the right question to ask, or rather it is not the most interesting question. For to be sure, anyone who consults an astrologer has a question in mind, about matters past, present, or future. Now, I take it for granted that questions, elections, and event charts (under certain conditions) are all valid, so the real issue is this. No ancient Greek sources we know of have an explicitly developed branch called "questions," but in the 8th Century, Arabic writers suddenly appeared with full-blown manuals on the subject, with standard lists of typical questions and procedures for answering them. So, *what is the difference between Greek and Arabic texts, and what could account for them?*

First, we can say generally that later, medieval works on questions were either reworked from Greek texts on elections and event charts, or were modeled on them. For example, an election for the proper time to make a business deal appears later as the question, "Will a business deal be successful?" And other questions such as "How long will the king reign?" are often modeled on elections for the event of acceding to the throne (see my translation of *The Book of the Nine Judges* for examples of this). Second, medieval texts included techniques of thought-interpretation (and its outcomes), which are already shown explicitly in older texts such as Hephaistion Book III and the *Yavanajataka.*

But in order to ask more pointedly about horary questions in Hephaistion, let us first look at instances of two sets of Greek terms in Book III. These are important because the use of "question," "inquiry," and so on are repeated almost ritually at the beginning of each question in later Arabic and Latin horary texts. If there were a smooth overlap or transition between Hephaistion and the explicit horary texts of the Middle Ages, we should expect to find their technical use in Book III.

Punthanomai, peusis. These words mean to "ask, inquire," and "inquiry, question," respectively: they are about getting information. Interestingly, the derived noun *peustēria* (not used in Hephaistion) specifically means a ritual sacrifice for *learning the will* of the gods. They are used 9 times in Book III, as follows:

- Ch. III.6, **3**; III.23, **2** (twice). These three instances refer to the topic being discussed by the client and astrologer, without any technical astrological meaning.
- Ch. III.7, **18**. This refers to the client's own ritual petition to the gods, for which the astrologer is asked to design an election. That is, it means the action which the client will undertake *after* consulting with the astrologer.
- Ch. III.11, **2**. This refers to the client's asking about the outcome of a past event (i.e., an event chart). This case is ambiguous and will be discussed below.
- Ch. III.4, (title), **8, 20, 22**. All four instances pertain to the practice of thought-interpretation and predicting outcomes, and will be discussed below.

Here, only the occurrences in Ch. III.4 could refer to what we would call a straightforward "horary" question, but we will see below that they do not, exactly. Ch. III.11, **2** does indeed seem to indicate something like horary, but only through the instructions Hephaistion gives, not through the use of *peusis/punthanomai* themselves.

Zēteō, zētoumenon. These words mean to "seek," and "the thing sought," and are exactly parallel to the Latin *quaero, quaesitum*, whence we get our English "question," "querent," and "quaesited" in later horary texts. These occur 14 times in Book III, as follows:

- Ch. III.42, **24** and **27** (twice); III.45, **20**; III.47, **14, 37, 81, 97** (twice). These nine instances refer to actually going out and seeking a runaway or thief or stolen goods. They are not astrological.
- Ch. III.2, **3**; III.5, **59**. These two instances refer to what the *astrologer* does when examining a chart: for instance, seeking out the Ascendant to see what it tells us.
- Ch. III.4, **4, 9** (twice). These three instances refer to the object of the client's inquiry (*peusis*), and so do seem to have a technical meaning.

Again, only the occurrences in Ch. III.4 seem to affect the issue of horary, because they are explicitly tied to a client's inquiry or *peusis*.

In short, only a few instances of these apparently technical terms (whose equivalents feature so prominently in medieval horary texts) are suggestive of question charts, and they are all included in either Ch. III.4 or III.11, **2**. Let us examine these passages, along with others which do not use these words but which do suggest something other than "standard" elections: thought-interpretation, predicting outcomes, event charts, and horary (or proto-horary). I will proceed in the order of increasing pertinence—that is, going from passages which seem to indicate some kind of proto-horary but do not (or are ambiguous), to the more suggestive and clear cases (including those which contain the technical terms above).

Chapter III.4, **19ff.**: *Thought-interpretation through twelfth-parts.* In this portion of III.4, Hephaistion presents a list of twelfth-parts for the Ascendant, by which the astrologer is supposed to have "foreknowledge." But the list does not pertain to outcomes, only the *content* of the inquiry. This is an unambiguous use of thought-interpretation, which later medievals attributed to the Indians (*Search*, I.9.3). It is not a case of classical horary questions.

Chapter III.3: "Irrational" inceptions. In this chapter, Hephaistion discusses the inceptions of people who are "irrational" (*alogos*, lit. "without reason"). He explicitly links the considerations there to accounts of "monstrous" nativities and even of animals (**1**), and in the natal context the astrologer presumably examines the chart to see if the native is irrational, or perhaps has birth defects or mental illness, and so on. What is unusual about this chapter is that Hephaistion says *if* one sees indications of irrationality in the inception, *then* it is the inception of an irrational person (**2-3**). Now, if this chapter were simply about *planning* an inception for an irrational person, then we would not be using the chart to find irrationality: that is, if the client were planning a marriage, then the astrologer would simply plan a future inception using the normal rules for marriage. But here, the astrologer is *finding* irrationality through the "inception." To me this only makes sense if the astrologer is casting a consultation or thought-interpretation chart (as with Ch. III.4, see below), and *then* realizing that the client is irrational after examining it. Based on his descriptions (**4**), he seems to mean that the astrologer is using a consultation chart or thought-interpretation approach, to identify a client whose *mind or proposed action* is irrational, uncivilized, erratic, or dangerous. In this case, the "inception" or consultation chart would be an early warning sign, leading the astrologer to decide whether to take the client. As written, it is not itself an indication of classical horary in used by Hephaistion—but it could be *used by* a horary astrologer to find indications of mental difficulties in a question chart.[13]

*Chapter III.41, **1-2**: Natal consultation.* This passage is interesting in part because of its placement in Book III. Here, the client is asking about possibilities for wealth. But instead of casting an inception chart for something like a business partnership or specific future venture, Hephaistion proceeds directly to a combination of natal analysis, profection, and transits. We would expect this kind of delineation to be found in the book on nativities (Book II), not in a book on inceptions and event charts. For natal delineations tend to deal with general possibilities for things like wealth. And in a strictly natal reading, we might expect the astrologer to predict general periods which are useful for wealth, but not predictions about specific months or days. But in this case the client is asking about wealth *now*, such as over the upcoming year or even months. This is indeed a "question," but also something that could also be done in a natal context, using solar revolutions, profections, and so on. So we have a situation where the client has a pressing need to know about wealth now (which sounds like a question), but without a specific object in mind (which we would want in a question), answered through an application of normal *natal* predictive techniques, in a book that is generally on inceptions and event charts. To me these ambiguities rule it out as an example of full-blown horary.

*Chapter III.4, **1-4** and **7-8**: Thought-interpretation, outcomes.* Now we come to more interesting cases, which include passages using the technical terms above. These parts of III.4 are clear instances of thought-interpretation (including the predicting of outcomes), with some horary elements. The purpose of **1-2** is to say that one may know beforehand what the inquiry (*peusis*) of the client is, based on the "inception" chart (*katarchē*). Obviously, if the inception were a normal election, one would not have to foretell what the inquiry is, since the client has already described it. Instead, the astrologer casts the "inception," and from it determines what the nature of the inquiry is, and its likely outcome. In **3-4**, Hephaistion uses the cadent and succeedent places around the Midheaven to determine what has already happened and will happen, much in the way that one might normally look at the separations and applications of the Moon.

---

[13] Chris Brennan has kindly pointed out that this could be a version of the later "considerations before judgment" in horary.

In **7-8**, Hephaistion then supplies an alternative way of looking at the angles, in which the Ascendant describes the nature of the inquiry, the Midheaven the action, the Descendant the outcome, and the fourth place things which are hidden or unknown. This last point is intriguing, because it seems designed to warn the client about things which he has not fully considered or should be aware of: this is clearly a general template for thought-interpretation or some kind of horary question, not the explicit planning of an electional chart.

These parts of Ch. III.4 are very interesting for its evidence of thought-interpretation and the outcomes of events. But they do not adhere to what we might consider the "classical" horary question: "Where is my lost cow?" "Will I marry X?" Of course, classical horary also includes what we might call event charts: upon hearing some news (an event), a general might ask his astrologer, "Is the news accurate?" But in these archetypal horary questions, while the querent is in the midst of a flow of events, he is asking about something not immediately in his control, and for which he is not already *undertaking or planning an action*. Put differently, a classical question is usually of the form, "How will things come about (apart from a deliberate action I am already undertaking or plan to)?"[14] But a classical election is of the form, "I want to do X, pick a good time for me to do it." It seems to me that these portions of Ch. III.4 are about something else that may bridge these two: identifying the content and outcome of an action *already being undertaken or planned*. This is a combination of thought-interpretation and outcomes, *about* an action already somehow in play and initiated by the client.

*Chapter III.4, **14-18**: Foreknowledge through the Lot of Fortune*. After these examples of thought-interpretation and possible proto-horary, Hephaistio provides yet again another way of having foreknowledge, "once the inception [chart] is established." This is a more ambiguous situation. In the whole context of Ch. III.4, it seems to be a way of judging the outcomes of a thought, *once* the thought or matter has been identified via the methods just mentioned above. Hephaistion first imagines that the placement of the Lot of Fortune could show how relationships with friends might be affected by the matter (**15-17**). But he then argues that a certain position of the Lot could show that the action is "utterly useless" (**18**). Does this mean that he is dealing with the

---

[14] Some horary texts do also talk about the answer to a question in terms of the client's action: "Yes, it will happen—but only if you do X." But in these cases, the client has not already done X and does not know if he should do X.

nature of the proposed action ("the client is thinking of a useless matter"), or that the *outcome* of the thought will be useless? Unfortunately, his descriptions and two examples are so limited in scope that it is hard to be sure. It could also be a series of stray observations about an election once it is planned, or even a proto-horary question (see previous paragraph).

Chapter III.11, **2** *(a runaway wife); Chapter III.47,* **51** *(a runaway thief or slave).* Finally, these two passages pose similar issues, and should be read together. In the case of the wife, the text provides two choices for casting the chart. If the husband knows the actual time the wife left (an event chart), then the chart should be cast for that time; but if he does not know when it was, the majority of the manuscripts[15] allow that it can be cast for the moment of the consultation: in this latter case, it would appear to be a straightforward example of a question or "horary" chart.

In the case of theft, the text likewise offers two possibilities. The preferred option is to cast the chart for the time the theft actually occurred (an event chart), but the second option is to cast it for the time *the client first heard about it.* Now, the real problem is the theft itself—for property is missing. But it only became a problem *for the client* when he heard about it. This is a bit different from the situation with the runaway wife, because presumably the husband did not need to hear about it: he was there when it happened, or knew approximately when it did, even if he does not know the exact time.

In these passages, there is clearly some leeway involved in the casting of the chart. We prefer the event chart, or at least the chart for the time when it became a problem *for the client*: this is the same in both cases. But for the runaway wife, the time of the consultation is allowed. Is this evidence of the practice of horary questions? Perhaps, but it is not evidence of a *developed branch* called "questions," as we see in the later tradition. Actually, it resembles something called a "universal question" in later horary, in which a client

---

[15] One manuscript (Vaticanus Graecus 297) omits the entire phrase "or else....from you." Obviously, without this phrase the sentence is purely about an event chart and there can be no suggestion of it being a question (horary). But if this phrase *is* valid, it allows a question chart that is akin to casting a "universal" question for someone who does not know their nativity. In this case, the preference would be for the event chart of the moment the wife left; but if the client did not know the time, one would resort to a question chart cast for the time of the consultation. One important argument against omitting the phrase is that Vaticanus Graecus (labeled **X**) contains only "little bits" (*frustulas*) of Hephaistion in it anyway: indeed, it appears as a short passage in the middle of a copy of Valens, and so in no way represents a sustained treatment of Hephaistion.

asks for a horary chart about something that would normally pertain to the nativity. That is, a client with an unknown birth date comes to the astrologer and asks "universal" or "general" questions about life: "Will I marry? Will I be successful?" Without a nativity, the astrologer has no choice but to cast a question chart for the time of the consultation. Just as the nativity would normally act as a root chart for finding the answer, but without one we may cast a universal question, so Hephaistion seems to imply that without an accurate event chart (in the case of the wife), we have no choice but to cast the only chart possible: the time of the consultation.

Let us now summarize what we can say about the general relationship between elections, thought-interpretation, event charts, and proto-horary, as they are presented in texts like Hephaistion Book III:

- "Inception" (*katarchē*) is a general term that *normally* covers standard elections and event charts, but in a few cases (III.4) is used to denote thought-interpretation (through a consultation chart), as well as the outcome of thoughts which are already being put into action, or are intended to be.
- Terms like "inquiry," "question," "seek," and "the thing sought" are for the most part used *non-technically*, and apparently technical uses of these terms must be considered in context: they are not consistent terms of art, and their occurrences contain ambiguities. As a corollary, the current academic use of the term "katarchic astrology" to include all of these types should be abandoned, because it uncritically groups different assumptions and procedures together. That is, to the extent that Hephaistion uses *katarchē* ambiguously, "katarchic astrology" also partakes of this ambiguity, and conceals more than it reveals. Academics and professional astrologers should use more accurate, distinguishing terms in understanding this field, in line with later astrological practice: "elections/inceptions," "thought-interpretation," "event charts," and "questions/horary."
- In one case (III.3), inceptions are examples of thought-interpretation but could be *used* by a horary astrologer to diagnose a querent's situation. Likewise, the use of thought-interpretation in consultations (such as III.4) could be the first stage in identifying a horary question (and was so in the medieval period), but Hephaistion's text does not state this.

- Where inceptions seem to clearly indicate horary questions (III.11, 2; perhaps III.47, **51**), they are second-best alternatives, used when the client does not know the time of the preferred event chart. These may be similar to the later practice of "universal" questions, when a horary chart is cast as a second-best alternative for a querent who does not know his own nativity.

On the whole, our examination of Hephaistion Book III yields a negative answer when it comes to evidence of a clear tradition of full-blown horary, at least by the 5th Century AD—despite the lone passage at III.11, **1**. Of course, clients come to astrologers with all sorts of inquiries, and astrologers undoubtedly felt the need for a developed branch of astrology called "questions." And in practice they may have adopted what we would call horary to deal with complex client situations. But there is no evidence that astrology was taught or studied in just this manner, through instructional texts in Hephaistion or those available to him. Until further evidence emerges, we should consider Persian and Arabic writers (or those writing in Greek within their milieu)[16] the founders of proper classical horary astrology.

§5: Useful and important terms in Hephaistion Book III

In this section I will introduce a number of important terms and concepts which are prominent in Book III, and in Hellenistic astrology generally. I proceed in alphabetical order:

Additive, subtractive (*prostithēmi, aphaireō*). As in medieval texts, Hephaistion speaks of planets being "additive" (or "adding") and "subtractive" (or "subtracting") in several ways. But unlike medieval texts, Hephaistion does not seem to be interested in the Ptolemaic astronomical notion of adding and subtracting referring to the use of planetary tables. That is, in Ptolemaic tables certain numbers used to determine planetary positions are listed in columns which either increase or decrease in value, and so medievals sometimes refer to these as either adding (i.e., increasing) or subtracting (i.e., decreasing). For Hephaistion on the other hand, these terms refer to the astrologically significant motions of the planets: i.e., moving direct or

---

[16] For example, Theophilus of Edessa may have written proper classical horary texts in Greek, but these were within the Persian milieu of the 8th Century. We intend to translate the works of Theophilus for our forthcoming Hellenistic series.

retrograde, or moving faster or slower than average, or (in the case of the Moon) waxing and waning, or moving northerly or southerly in ecliptical latitude. Following is an exhaustive list of these terms in Book III, the Appendices, and Dorotheus *Fragments*.

Of the 12 instances of "additive" (*prostithēmi*) and 7 instances of "subtractive" (*aphaireō*), 4 refer to a planet being either direct or retrograde;[17] 2 are ambiguous as to being direct, or else moving faster (perhaps even faster than average);[18] 1 probably means being retrograde, but perhaps moving slowly around the first station;[19] and 6 definitely refer to a planet moving faster or slower (perhaps even faster or slower than average).[20] Six others combine different types of adding and subtracting, with reference to the Moon: in 2 cases, the Moon should be adding in numbers and light or phase, which means moving faster and waxing;[21] in 3 others, the Moon should be adding (or subtracting) in numbers with respect to longitude and latitude, which means moving faster (or slower) and moving northerly (or southerly) in ecliptical latitude;[22] finally, 1 instance has the Moon subtracting in light, which means waning.[23]

Assembly, connection, adherence. The definitions of Antiochus and its commentaries,[24] and later Arabic texts, distinguished between different types of sign-based and degree-based configurations which planets may have. The following three are the most important, but they are defined in various ways in different texts and languages—and we cannot assume that Hephaistion (who offers his own version of the definitions) always means them in the same way, borrowing as he does from multiple sources.

Assembly (Gr. *sunodos*, Lat. *conventus*). The Greek word literally means to be "on the same path" or to "travel together," but is the same word for used for an "assembly" or meeting of people: thus the English "synod," as in a meeting of Church bishops. At a bare minimum, this simply means that two or more planets are in the same sign,[25] and so is the loosest kind of relationship by body one may have: it is not quite the same as what we would normally

---

[17] III.9, **34** (twice); III.47, **23** and **94**;

[18] III.27, **1**; III.30, **67**.

[19] III.30, **5**.

[20] III.16, **11**; III.43, **8** (twice); Appendix B, **2**; *Frag.* V.41, **1-34**, sentences **20-21**.

[21] III.6, **10**; III.7, **10**.

[22] III.1, **7**; III.16, **11**; III.30, **2**.

[23] III.6, **5**.

[24] See Schmidt 2009, pp. 150-67. My references to Porphyry come from these passages.

[25] Again, the ideal case is when the lighter planet is applying to the heavier one.

call a bodily conjunction. Antiochus goes further and specifies that they must be between 3°-15° apart. One complication with this word is that Hephaistio's Greek uses *sunodos* to refer also to the bodily conjunction of the New Moon, which is obviously a more tightly-defined situation. I have opted for the looser word "assembly" (rather than "meeting"), due to the greater distance that is allowed in this configuration. The parallel Arabic *muqāranah*, which is usually understood as a "comparison" or "association," also implies something looser, as though two things are side-by-side for comparison but with some distinction between them.

Connection (Gr. *sunaphe*, Lat. *coniunctio*, Ar. *ʾittiṣāl*). This is a degree-based aspect, which Antiochus says must be within 3° or less for most planets, but in the case of the Moon it begins at 13°.

Adherence (Gr. *kollēsis*, Lat. *coniunctio*, Ar. *ʾittiṣāl*). This is a degree-based bodily conjunction, which again begins when the planets are 3° apart. Rhetorius implies that for the Moon it begins at 13°, since he says it involves "a day and a night"—that is, a 24-hour period of the Moon's standard motion, which is approximately 13°. Some Latin authors picked upon the meaning of *kollēsis* to imply gluing or sticking together, and used *adhaero* ("to adhere") or similar terms.

Eastern/western, rising/setting (*anatolē, dusis*). Over the centuries, astrologers have defined different ways for a planet to be either "eastern," "arising," or "oriental," and "western," "setting/sinking," or "occidental." Unfortunately, there is no clear consistency in these terms, whether in Greek, Arabic, or Latin. The reason is that, in many ancient languages, to be "eastern" or "arising" generally refers to the eastern horizon, where the Sun rises (and the opposite for "western" or "setting/sinking")—as well as the fact that at certain positions, planets can be seen either emerging from the Sun's rays or setting/sinking under them, especially at dawn (when the Sun is actually in the east), or at dusk (when he is actually in the west). And since the planets can be at such positions relative to the Sun anywhere in the chart, there is a fundamental ambiguity as to what each astrologer means. If a planet is eastern, does it mean it is in the eastern quadrant of the chart (where the Sun rises, no matter where he happens to be in the chart), or arising from the rays of the Sun (either later or earlier in the zodiac), or some other meaning? For the most part in Book III, Hephaistion and his sources mean that a planet is eastern or arising if it is in a position to be emerging from the rays of the Sun, probably within 15° of him: this can take place no matter where the Sun happens to be. Likewise, if the planet is setting or sinking, it usually means it is going under the rays, no matter where the Sun happens to be. In yet other cases, Hephaistion seems to mean that the planet is actually on the Ascendant (probably close to the horizon) or on the Descendant (again, close to the horizon). In each case, we have placed in footnotes what we believe the sense of the term is.

Fixing (Gr. *pēxis*, Ar. *ʾaṣl*, Lat. *radix*).[26] The verb *pēgnumi* ("to stick in, fix") yields the noun *pēxis*, which primarily means to fix something in place or put something together, often in the context of woodworking. It also denotes solidity and coagulation. On the one hand, Valens (*Anth.* V.6) uses it to refer to stationing planets as being "fixed" in place, but in Hephaistion it refers generally to a "root" chart: a chart which is the basis for other charts. In most cases, this fixing (or in Arabic and Latin, the "root" or "foundation") is the nativity itself: in that case, we are looking for an election or event chart or ongoing transits which bear some relation to the nativity. In other cases, Hephaistion seems to mean the inception chart itself, as the basis for ongoing transits or other techniques. In a related way, Hephaistion sometimes refers to the "fixing of the beginning" (*archē*) or the "fixing from the beginning": in this case, the "fixing" is the establishment of the planets as being in this place or other, at the "beginning" (the nativity). This latter use of *archē* to denote the nativity nicely illustrates the point I made in *Choices & Inceptions* (2012), that an "inception" chart is a secondary beginning (*katarchē*) relative to the original nativity or original beginning (*archē*).

Hour (*hōra*), **Hour-marker** (*hōroskopos*), **Hour-divider** (*hōronomos*). These terms refer to the Ascendant. In some cases they may refer to the precise degree of the Ascendant or horizon itself, but more often they refer to the rising sign as a whole: such as when a planet is in aversion to the Hour-marker by being in the twelfth sign, or speaking of the lord of the Hour-marker or Hour. "Hour" should not be confused with the lord of the *planetary* hour (a division of daylight and nighttime hours into twelve, assigning planets to each hour).[27] I have capitalized Hour so as to help make this clear.

House, domicile (*oikos*). We use "house" instead of "domicile," as the Greek (and Arabic) does. Most Latin texts use *domus* (house), but sometimes employ *domicilium* ("domicile, house") when referring to house ownership or rulership.

---

[26] The grammatical content of this comment was largely written by Gramaglia.
[27] For these, see *Introductions to Traditional Astrology* (2010, V.13).

Lord, master, ruler, host (*Kurios, despotēs, oikodespotēs, oikodektōr*). All of these terms are equivalent to the lord or ruler of a sign, apparently varied for literary style. All of them imply some kind of ownership or management responsibility for the sign (or the topics of the place which falls on it), but "host" (*oikodektōr*) has an extra connotation: since a planet may be in a sign ruled by another planet, the first planet is (as it were) a guest in that sign, and the ruler its host. Many traditional astrologers pointed out the interpretive importance of this relationship, from its relationship to "mixing" (see below), to its effect on the condition of the guest: see for example Firmicus Maternus II.20.[28]

Maltreatment, harm (Gr. *kakōsis*). Although Antiochus does define the maltreatment and harm of planets with a list of specific configurations (such as having one's domicile lord poorly situated, or being besieged),[29] we cannot always presume that Hephaistion means this particular list whenever he uses *kakōsis* and its variants:[30] he or his sources may have something broader in mind. For example, the standard list of impediments or hindrances or types of misfortune in medieval texts generally includes being burned under the rays of the Sun, being in one's fall or descension, being in a conjunction or bad aspect with the malefics, being retrograde, *etc.* The Greek-English glossary below lists how we have translated this and related terms.

Mixing (*sugkerannumi*). Medieval Arabic and Latin texts often speak of planets mixing, commixing, or commingling. In most cases this seems to refer to planets aspecting each other: so that if Venus is configured to Mars by sign or degree, she "commingles" with him. Hephaistion uses this term as well, but is clear that it refers to the mixture resulting from *being in another planet's sign.* Thus if Mars is in Virgo, he does not become Virgoan, but rather mixes with *Mercury's* qualities, since Mercury rules Virgo. For an example of this, see III.45, **6-7**. If this is a standard way of referring to mixing (and I am not sure it is), it should force a re-appraisal of Arabic and Latin texts, since presumably some of their sources would have referred to this kind of mixing, and not mixing by configuration or aspect.

Pre- and post-ascending (*apoklima, epanaphora*). These terms refer to places which are "declining" or "cadent" from the angles or pivots, or "suc-

---

[28] In Holden's recent translation (2011), this is listed as II.22.
[29] See Schmidt 2009, pp. 266-74.
[30] There is also some controversy over the precise members of the list, which comes in various forms: see Schmidt pp. 266-74, which lists about 6 types of maltreatment.

ceedent" to them. Thus, each angle can be grouped into a triad of places, with the angle or pivot in the center, the pre-ascending or cadent place to its right, and the post-ascension or succeedent place to its left.

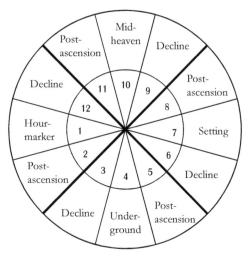

Figure 3: Angular triads: pre- and post-ascending places

Predictive methods. Throughout Book III, Hephaistion also shows how to apply various timing techniques to electional or event charts, as follows:

- Profections: III.20, **3**; prob. III.31, **13**; III.41, **1-2**.; *Excerpt* XIX, **4**.
- Primary directions: III.31, **13**.
- Ascensional times of signs: III.5, **53**; III.39, **2**.
- Time lords generally: III.39, **2**.
- Transits: throughout; see also *Excerpts* XXI-XXII.

Rejoicing houses. As in many Hellenistic texts, Book III makes relatively frequent reference to the planets' rejoicing houses. Each planet rejoices in a particular house, which itself has a special title (as may be seen in the figure below). The possible meanings embedded in this scheme are very intriguing, and I will likely write on them at another time;[31] but for the moment note that each category of the planets forms its own axis: the luminaries' rejoicing houses are opposed, as are those of the benefics and malefics. Mercury, who

---

[31] See also Brennan 2013, some of which presents ideas developed in conversation with me.

does not naturally belong in any of these categories, rejoices in the Ascendant. In Hephaistion and the verses by Dorotheus, the titles seem only to indicate the relevant house, without revealing any special doctrine or significations. For example, Chapter III.4, **17** speaks of the lord of the Lot of Fortune being in the Bad Spirit, which is the twelfth: whatever the ultimate origin and meaning of the rejoicing places are, Hephaistion's use of "Bad Spirit" does not suggest anything other than the usual twelfth-house meanings.

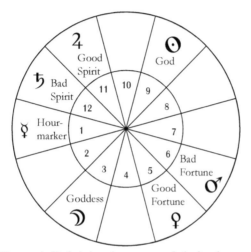

Figure 4: Rejoicing houses and their planets

Seeing, looking, *etc.* Those familiar with traditional texts (especially from Greek) know that a variety of configurations between planets are indicated by words for seeing and looking. In Arabic and Latin these were later distilled into just a few terms: most often *naẓara* ("look at") in Arabic, and *aspicio* ("look at," "aspect") or *respicio* ("regard") in Latin. But Greek authors employ many different words, and it is not always clear if they have distinct meanings from one another. It would be hard indeed to know this from something like Book III, since both Hephaistion and the versified Dorotheus use a variety of words in apparently identical ways. In fact, Dorotheus acts as a special case here: since his verse structure requires lines with a precise number of vowels and syllables on each line, it would be difficult indeed for him to use each word in only one way while still keeping to the verse structure. Indeed, it is typical for ancient didactic poems to use synonyms for the sake of structure as well as literary variety. So we should not read too much into words like "see, look at, look upon, contemplate," *etc.* It is most likely that in using these terms, Hephaistion or Dorotheus simply means that some planet is configured to another sign or planet, whether by sign alone or by a certain number of degrees. (And they rarely indicate any difference between sign- and degree-based relations.) Nevertheless we indicate the verbs in footnotes. See also the discussion of testimony and witnessing below.

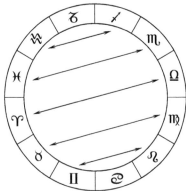

Figure 5: Seeing signs
(Dor. *Excerpt* XVIII, 1;
Heph. II.23)

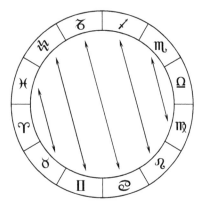

Figure 6: Hearing signs
(Dor. *Excerpt* XVIII, 1;
Heph. II.23)

Seeing and hearing signs. Just as signs are grouped by triplicity, quadruplicity, ascensional times, and in other ways, ancient astrologers identified what they called the "seeing" and "hearing" signs. These are used by Hephaistion and Dorotheus to identify signs which show personal compatibility—for example, in friendships and romantic relationships. Not all astrologers agreed on these definitions, including the so-called "commanding and obeying" signs. The signs which "see" one another (not to be confused with aspects, which also connote seeing), are those which are equidistant from the tropics (Cancer, Capricorn).[32] Thus, Gemini and Leo see each other, and so on as shown in the figure below. I have not found a text which says whether Capricorn and Cancer themselves see each other. The signs which "hear" each other are those which are equidistant from the equi-

---

[32] See Heph. II.23, and *Excerpt* XVIII, **1**.

noxes (Aries, Libra).[33] Thus Pisces and Taurus hear each other. Hephaistion says that according to Thrasyllus, Aries and Libra themselves do *not* hear each other—which leads me to think that Capricorn and Cancer likewise cannot see each other.

Testimony, witnessing (*marturia, epimarturia*). In medieval texts, "testimony" or "witnessing" has a couple of standard uses. First, it seems simply to mean that two planets "see/aspect" each other, and so testify or bear witness *to each other*. Second, that within a chart these planets offer testimony *to the astrologer* about their respective importance. As an example of the latter, medieval astrologers regularly looked for a planet which was "strongest" or "conquered" in the chart, and a planet might have several possible testimonies which indicated this: perhaps being angular or pivotal, coming out of the rays, being in one or more of its own dignities, and so on.

Only a couple of Greek texts ever define what testimony or witnessing is. The *Definitions* of Antiochus was apparently an early example, with Hephaistion (in Book I) and Porphyry offering later and substantially similar accounts (probably based on Antiochus himself).[34] It is worth speaking about Antiochus and the others here, because recently Robert Schmidt has argued[35] that testimony and bearing witness have a special, limited meaning. In the definitions, two planets are said to bear witness to one another when they are configured with each other according to the standard classical aspects or configurations: a hexagon, square, triangle, or a diameter (the opposition). Thus each planet must at least be in a sign which is configured in an acceptable way: so, Mars in Aries is configured by a hexagon or sextile to Venus in Gemini. This should mean that Mars and Venus are testifying to each other or are bearing witness to one another.

But then Antiochus and the others point out that these figures can occur in two ways: by sign alone, or by degree. Antiochus says they are "brought to completion" in both ways, while Porphyry says that one must see whether they "complete" the figure by degree and "not only/merely" by sign. Later definitions likewise discuss planets in various states of degree-based configurations (see **assembly** above), including two versions of besieging—one based on sign, one based on degrees. Schmidt, however, argues against these plain statements that there are *not* two types of testimony or witnessing, and

---

[33] See Heph. II.23, *Excerpt* XVIII, **1**, and Paul of Alexandria Ch. 8.
[34] Or more probably the *Summary* of Antiochus; see Schmidt 2009.
[35] See Schmidt 2009, pp. 127-31.

that in fact testimony *does not* take place by sign alone. What the authors really mean (he argues) is that when the planets are in the properly configured signs, testimony only takes place if they perfect their degree-based aspect before one of them changes signs. So, if Mars in Aries is configured by a hexagon to Venus in Gemini, they will only bear witness or give testimony to each other if their aspect is completed by degree while they are in their respective signs.

Now, it is true that in certain charts especially it is of interest whether the planets complete a degree-based aspect. Indeed, Arabic-speaking astrologers defined every way in which planets might fail to complete them, along with interpretations for each.[36] And it may be that Antiochus's preferred model for these configurations was applying aspects, which will ideally become exact. But I see no direct evidence that Schmidt's interpretation is correct in the definitions themselves, and certainly not in Hephaistion Book III. For one thing, the texts say that *there are two* ways to have testimony, and *one* of them is by sign alone. Mentioning that it can also happen by degree, does point forward to further types of degree-based configurations, but not that only a completed, degree-based aspect counts. For his argument, Schmidt seems to rely mainly on Porphyry's statement that one *ought to see whether* planets complete a figure by degree: but these words are more in the character of an instruction, not a definition. The word for witnessing or testimony is only given once at the head of the definition, and everything else that follows discusses and distinguishes the two types of configuration: by sign and by degree. Thus the first medieval view of testimony between planets is in line with the ancient statements. In the future I will write about this at greater length. For now, I think we can be safe in saying that *when* planets are configured, whether by sign alone or by degree (within appropriate signs), they will bear witness and testify to each other, even if we prefer that they also complete the aspect by degree.

Triangle, square, hexagon, diameter. Configurations between signs and planets are determined by three shapes (and one semi-shape) which can be drawn between signs: triangles, squares, hexagons, and signs which are opposed (i.e., where the circle is divided in half along its diameter). In these texts we will stick to these normal English terms for the shapes even though they are not as familiar to readers of medieval texts (who might see "trine,"

---

[36] See for example my *Introductions to Traditional Astrology: Abū Ma'shar & al-Qabīsī* (2010), Part III. A table of these failed connections is in Appendix B of that book.

"sextile," "quadrature" or "quartile," and "opposition"). These terms differ slightly from Schmidt's and others' use of "trigon" and "tetragon" for the triangle and square.

Triangle (triplicity). Related to this use of polygons, traditional texts distinguished linguistically between signs related by polygons for the sake of aspects (e.g., trine, square), and the groups of multiple signs forming those angles (e.g., triplicity, quadruplicity). Thus Latin texts distinguish between a trine (*trinus*) and a triplicity (*triplicitas*). Greek does not seem to have distinguished these in the case of *trigōnon*, which can mean either signs related by a trine (such as Aries-Leo) or the three signs forming a triangle or triplicity (Aries-Leo-Sagittarius). In most cases, it is easy to tell the difference between a triangular aspect or configuration, and a triplicity and its lords; but in other cases it is unclear. We have decided to follow the Greek in calling all of these "triangles," and offer clarifications in footnotes where it seems ambiguous.

§6: Table of planetary names

In this volume we have used the usual Latin names for the planets and signs where they appear in Hephaistion's prose: for instance, Aries instead of *Krios*. But we have retained Dorotheus's Greek names and epithets in order to retain the flavor of his verses.

- Aegis-bearing One (*Aigiochos*): Jupiter.[37]
- *Aigiochos* (Aegis-bearing One): Jupiter.
- *Aphroditē*: Venus.
- *Aphrogeneia* (Foam-born One): Venus.
- *Arēs*: Mars.
- *Brotoloigos* (Plague of Mortals): Mars.
- *Dios*: Jupiter (genitive of *Zeus*).
- *Enualios* ("Warlike One"): Mars.
- Fiery One (*Pyroeis*): Mars.
- Foam-born One (*Aphrogeneia*): Venus.
- Glittering One (*Stilbōn*): Mercury.
- *Hēlios*: the Sun.
- *Hermēs*: Mercury.
- Horned One (*Keroessa*): the Moon.
- Impetuous[38] One (*Thouros*): Mars.

---

[37] The *aigis* was a shield of Zeus, derived from the verb "to rush, move violently" (*aissō*).
[38] Or, "rushing."

- *Keroessa* (Horned One): the Moon.
- *Kronos*: Saturn.
- *Kypris*: Venus.
- *Kythereia* (*Kythereia*): Venus.
- *Kythereia, Kythērē* (or Cytherea, Kythereia): Venus.
- *Mēnē*: the Moon.
- *Paphiē*, the Paphian: Venus.
- *Phainōn* ("Shining One"): Saturn.
- Plague of Mortals (*Brotoloigos*): Mars.
- *Pyroeis* ("Fiery One"): Mars.
- *Selēnē*: the Moon.
- Shining One (*Phainōn*): Saturn.
- Son of Maiā: Mercury.
- *Stilbōn* ("Glittering One"): Mercury.
- Swift-begotten of Maiā: Mercury.
- *Thouros* ("Impetuous One"): Mars.
- Warlike One (*Enualios*): Mars.
- *Zeus*: Jupiter.

§7: Greek-English glossary

This glossary is a guide to how we have translated certain key Greek terms, especially for those who are familiar with Hellenistic texts translated by Schmidt (many of whose translations I follow). In each case I give our preferred English translation, sometimes with an explanation. Boldface words direct the reader either to other Greek entries in this list, or to explanatory entries in my astrological Glossary at the end of the book.

- *Agathos* (referring to benefic planets). "Good one."
- *Aktinobolia*. "Hurling of rays." This refers to a planet in a later sign than another (especially by square), so that when moved by clockwise primary motion, its ray or aspect comes up to meet and strike the second planet: for example, Mars at 15° Cancer hurls a ray at Jupiter in 10° Aries.
- *Allotrioō*. To be "estranged," "alienated," equivalent to **Aversion**.
- *Anatolē*. "East," or "rising." As the "east," (equivalent to Lat. *oriens* and *ascendens*), it indicates the Ascendant (either the rising sign itself, or its degree). As "rising," it generally refers to emerging out of the Sun's rays. See *dusis* below, and §5 above.

- *Aphaireō*. "Subtractive" or decreasing, typically referring to being retrograde or slowing down in speed. See §5 above.
- *Apoklima*. "Decline," referring to places **cadent** from the angles. See also §5 above.
- *Aporria*. "Flowing away," functionally equivalent to **separation**.
- *Apostrophē*. "Aversion" (lit. "to be turned back/away"). See **Aversion**.
- *Asundetos*. "Unconnected." see A**version**.
- *Blaptō*. To "harm" or hinder, but also to mislead and distract, thus "harry" or "harrass." In Heph. III.40, **30**, it seems to be the equivalent of **Besieging**.
- *Blepō*. "Look at, see."
- *Chrēmatizō*. To be "busy" or carry out business, with the connotation of being active, busy, successful. For the busy or advantageous houses, see **Advantageous places** and the footnote to III.6, **3**.
- *Derkomai*. To "look on at."
- *Despotēs*. "Master," equivalent to the **Lord** of a sign.
- *Dōdekatēmorion*. "Twelfth-part"; see **Twelfth-parts**.
- *Dusis*. "Setting" or "sinking." As "setting," it generally refers to the western or setting point of the chart (the Descendant); as "sinking" (but sometimes rendered as "setting"), it refers to going under the Sun's rays. See *anatolē* above, and "eastern" in §5 above.
- *Emperischesis*. "Enclosure," a form of **Besieging**: in Antiochus, it indicates besieging by degrees rather than merely by sign (*perischesis*).
- *Epanaphora*. "Post-ascending," "post-ascension." Equivalent to **Succeedent**.
- *Epeidon* (related to *ephoraō*). To "look on, look upon, behold."
- *Epembasis* (lit. "advance, step, commencement"). "Ingress," but in Heph. III.41, **2** it seems to be equivalent to a **Profection**.
- *Ephoraō, epeidon, epidein.* To "look upon, observe."
- *Epiblepō*. To "look upon, regard."
- *Epidekateuō*. To "decimate," equivalent to making a superior square (at least by sign, if not by degree) from the tenth sign from a

place.[39] For example, a planet in Scorpio decimates a planet in Aquarius. Decimation is a special example of **Overcoming**.

- *Epimartureō.* To "bear witness, witness."
- *Epitheōreō.* To "contemplate, examine."
- *Epopteuō.* To "oversee." In Heph. III.2, **11**, it may be a synonym for **Overcoming**.
- *Hōroskopos.* "Hour-marker," indicating either the degree of the Ascendant itself, or the entire rising sign.
- *Kakōsis.* "Maltreatment." See §5 above. We also translate *kakōtos*, *akakōtos* as "harmed, unharmed."
- *Katarchē.* "Inception." Used for the undertaking of an election, or an event chart, or perhaps the consultation chart from which thoughts are interpreted. See my Introduction.
- *Kathupertereō.* To "overcome." See **Overcoming**. Heph. III.2, **1** allows overcoming by a **diameter**. Overcoming from a superior **square** is a special instance of overcoming, called **decimation** (see *epidekateuō*).
- *Kentron.* "Pivot." See **Pivot**.
- *Klima.* "Clime." In general, this refers simply to a "region" of the earth which is ruled by some planet or sign; but in more mathematical accounts (such as in Ptolemy or al-Bīrūnī), it refers to a line or band of latitude on the earth, likewise ruled by some planet or sign. See *Astrology of the World I*, Part IV.
- *Kollaō, kollēsis.* To "adhere," "adherence." See my Introduction.
- *Koruphē.* "Peak," normally referring to the Midheaven ("the sign at the peak," Heph. III.9, **21**).
- *Ktisis.* A "foundation" chart, normally indicating a **root** chart such as the nativity.
- *Kurios.* "Lord," equivalent to the **Lord** of a sign.
- *Martureō, marturia.* "Testify, testimony." See my Introduction.
- *Oikodektōr.* "Host" (lit., "house-receiver"), equivalent to the **Lord** of a sign, but considered as a host because other planets may be in that sign.
- *Oikodespotēs.* "Ruler," equivalent to the **Lord** of a sign.

---

[39] I follow Schmidt's translation of this work, which could also be termed "being upon the tenth." Chris Brennan has kindly pointed out that the negative connotations of "decimation" can be misleading, especially since benefics can have this relation to each other, with positive meanings.

- *Oikos*. "House." Equivalent to a planet's **Domicile**.
- *Paradosis*. Lit. "handing over," often referring to **profections**.
- *Parodeuō, parodos*. "Transit" (lit., to "pass by").
- *Parousia*. "Presence," normally referring to where a planet's body is.
- *Perischesis*. "Surrounded," a form of **Besieging** (translated by Schmidt 2009 as "containment"). In Antiochus, it indicates besieging by sign as opposed to besieging by degree (*emperischesis*).
- *Peusis, punthanomai*. "Inquiry, question," and "to inquire, ask."
- *Pexis*. "Fixing," referring to a **root** chart such as a nativity or inceptional chart on which other charts or techniques are based. See *ktisis* above.
- *Pragma*. "Deed, action, matter."
- *Prattomena*. "Dealings," referring to human actions or interactions between planets.
- *Prattomenon*. "Affair, matter."
- *Praxis*. "Work, doing, business."
- *Proairesis*. "Choice."
- *Prostithēmi*. "Additive," normally referring to a planet moving direct or fast. See §5 above.
- *Schēma*. "Figure," referring to the geometric figures (and the **Diameter**) which define **Aspects**.
- *Sunaptō, sunaphē*. To "connect," a "connection." See my Introduction.
- *Sundesmos*. "Node," but lit. "bond, ligament."
- *Sunodos*. "Assembly, meeting" (lit., "on the same path." This is also used for the conjunction of the Sun and Moon at the New Moon.
- *Suschēmatizō*. To be "configured": that is, to assume a **Figure**.
- *Telos*. "End," in the sense of "completion."
- *Thema*. A "chart," particularly a nativity.
- *Theōreō*. To "behold, look at, contemplate."
- *Zeteō, zētoumenon*. To "seek," "what is sought."

HEPHAISTION OF THEBES

APOTELESMATICS
BOOK III: ON INCEPTIONS

[Proem]

1 Together with the two books from the compilation of what the ancients have concisely said,[1] let me set forth this third and most useful one, about all kinds of inceptions, oh most virtuous and pious among my friends, Athanasius, utmost lover of learning.

2 It will be possible for you, with great easiness, to successfully learn from this book things about human nature and all matters pertaining to it, as well as that which results from their choices,[2] thus being able to fix well-established and correctly-arranged inceptions, as far as possible. On the other hand, you will also be able to observe what falls to each one's lot through Fortune and on its own.[3] And by examining the arrangement of planets in the inception, we shall see how each one will turn out and what kind of end it will have.

3 In relation to the computation of the inception, we examine the disposition of the stars just as in every nativity: it is therefore necessary to accurately determine the time of the inception on every matter, by means of an articulated marking of the Hours, as accurately as possible, and thus establish the pivots, in the same way as in a nativity. **4** Once we have found out the longitude and latitude of both luminaries and the five wandering stars, and what kind of figures they have with each other and the whole, from these we shall harmonize the rest with each prediction of events.

---

[1] That is, Books I-II on general astrology, mundane techniques, and nativities.
[2] *Proairesis*. This is the equivalent of the Lat. *electio*, "choice."
[3] **EG:** That is, independently from human choice and direct control. **BD:** "Fortune" has to do with how indefinitely many causes in the world come together in a matrix of events, to create some set of events. So, Hephaistion is saying that inception charts will show us both what will come about as a result of direct choices, as well as what else (apart from our choices) will happen once events are put into motion.

\<Chapter III.1:\> On fitting signs,
and the observation of the Moon for the inception

1 The[4] signs that rise straight on their rising (those from Cancer through Sagittarius),[5] if they chance to be unharmed, bring about their dealings without impediment. The crooked[6] ones (those from Capricorn through Gemini), without the testimony of benefic stars, indicate what is hard to come about and takes a long time.[7] And the tropical signs, when on the east, quickly change the affairs.

2 In diurnal activities one must watch for Aries, Leo, Sagittarius and Cancer, to see whether any of them is on the east, and the Moon passes through any of them. In nocturnal ones, must pay attention the same way to the diameters of the diurnal signs.[8]

3 When the Moon is eclipsed, it hinders, and especially [if it is] in the natal sign,[9] or those in a triangle to it; also at [the] assembly.[10]

4 *But [the Moon] being in such condition,*
is stronger for evil-doing than the eclipse;
she will also work treacherous things for him who schemes in his mind,
and she manages secret affairs and such things that need silence.[11]

---

[4] For this paragraph see also *Frag.* V.1, **5** – V.4, **1**, sentences **5-8**; and *Excerpt* LIII.

[5] These are the "straight" signs, or signs of "long ascension" in the northern hemisphere; the others (Capricorn through Gemini) are the "crooked" signs or signs of "short ascension." In the southern hemisphere, these roles are reversed.

[6] *Loxos.*

[7] *Poluchronia.*

[8] I confess I do not understand what Hephaistion means here, and I believe there is an error in the text. For one thing, the diameters of diurnal signs are also diurnal signs, so there is nothing nocturnal about taking their opposites at night. Also, is Cancer included during the day because it is also ruled by a light (the Moon)—because if so, does it mean we should also look at Leo in the night for the same reason? Do both diurnal triplicities count during the day, or does Hephaistion prefer the fiery one because the Sun is the diurnal leader of it—in which case, at night should we prefer the triplicity that has the Moon as its triplicity ruler by night (Taurus-Virgo-Capricorn)?

[9] That is, in the sign of the natal Moon.

[10] *Sunodō.* Hephaistion seems to mean that a New Moon (meeting, assembly) in any of these places will act like an eclipse of the Moon.

[11] This is because at the New Moon, she is under the rays.

5 One must also watch for the twelfth-part of the Moon, so that it does not fall where Mars or Saturn is.[12]

6 The[13] Moon must not be full either:

for in that case, it is necessary to be prepared for quarrel and dissension.

7 Nor should she be on the eclipse points, nor subtracting her numbers both in longitude or latitude, nor in the southern limit,[14] nor in the last degrees of each signs (for they are malefic).[15]

♈	♃ 0°-5°59'	♀ 6°-11°59'	☿ 12°-19°59'	♂ 20°-24°59'	♄ 25°-29°59'
♉	♀ 0°-7°59'	☿ 8°-13°59'	♃ 14°-21°59'	♄ 22°-26°59'	♂ 27°-29°59'
♊	☿ 0°-5°59'	♃ 6°-11°59'	♀ 12°-16°59'	♂ 17°-23°59'	♄ 24°-29°59'
♋	♂ 0°-6°59'	♀ 7°-12°59'	☿ 13°-18°59'	♃ 19°-25°59'	♄ 26°-29°59'
♌	♃ 0°-5°59'	♀ 6°-10°59'	♄ 11°-17°59'	☿ 18°-23°59'	♂ 24°-29°59'
♍	☿ 0°-6°59'	♀ 7°-16°59'	♃ 17°-20°59'	♂ 21°-27°59'	♄ 28°-29°59'
♎	♄ 0°-5°59'	☿ 6°-13°59'	♃ 14°-20°59'	♀ 21°-27°59'	♂ 28°-29°59'
♏	♂ 0°-6°59'	♀ 7°-10°59'	☿ 11°-18°59'	♃ 19°-23°59'	♄ 24°-29°59'
♐	♃ 0°-11°59'	♀ 12°-16°59'	☿ 17°-20°59'	♄ 21°-25°59'	♂ 26°-29°59'
♑	☿ 0°-6°59'	♃ 7°-13°59'	♀ 14°-21°59'	♄ 22°-25°59'	♂ 26°-29°59'
♒	☿ 0°-6°59'	♀ 7°-12°59'	♃ 13°-19°59'	♂ 20°-24°59'	♄ 25°-29°59'
♓	♀ 0°-11°59'	♃ 12°-15°59'	☿ 16°-18°59'	♂ 19°-27°59'	♄ 28°-29°59'

Figure 7: Table of Egyptian bounds

---

[12] That is, the twelfth-part of her degree should not indicate a sign where a malefic is. See the table of twelfth-parts in Ch. III.4. For example, if the degree of the Moon falls between 5°-7.5° of Leo, it corresponds to Sagittarius: we would not want a malefic to then be in Sagittarius.

[13] See also *Excerpt* LIV.

[14] *Perati.* This seems to mean her most extreme southern latitude.

[15] This is true in both the Egyptian and Ptolemaic system (see figures). Chris Brennan points out that while this is how the comment about the last degrees are usuall read, they may be malefic for other reasons, too.

♈	♃ 0°-5°59'	♀ 6°-13°59'	☿ 14°-20°59'	♂ 21°-25°59'	♄ 26°-29°59'
♉	♀ 0°-7°59'	☿ 8°-14°59'	♃ 15°-21°59'	♄ 22°-25°59'	♂ 26°-29°59'
♊	☿ 0°-6°59'	♃ 7°-12°59'	♀ 13°-19°59'	♂ 20°-25°59'	♄ 26°-29°59'
♋	♂ 0°-5°59'	♃ 6°-12°59'	☿ 13°-19°59'	♀ 20°-26°59'	♄ 27°-29°59'
♌	♄ 0°-5°59'	☿ 6°-12°59'	♀ 13°-18°59'	♃ 19°-24°59'	♂ 25°-29°59'
♍	☿ 0°-6°59'	♀ 7°-12°59'	♃ 13°-17°59'	♄ 18°-23°59'	♂ 24°-29°59'
♎	♄ 0°-5°59'	♀ 6°-10°59'	♃ 11°-18°59'	☿ 19°-23°59'	♂ 24°-29°59'
♏	♂ 0°-5°59'	♃ 6°-13°59'	♀ 14°-20°59'	☿ 21°-26°59'	♄ 27°-29°59'
♐	♃ 0°-7°59'	♀ 8°-13°59'	☿ 14°-18°59'	♄ 19°-24°59'	♂ 25°-29°59'
♑	♀ 0°-5°59'	☿ 6°-11°59'	♃ 12°-18°59'	♂ 19°-24°59'	♄ 25°-29°59'
♒	♄ 0°-5°59'	☿ 6°-11°59'	♀ 12°-19°59'	♃ 20°-24°59'	♂ 25°-29°59'
♓	♀ 0°-7°59'	♃ 8°-13°59'	☿ 14°-19°59'	♂ 20°-25°59'	♄ 26°-29°59'

Figure 8: Table of Ptolemaic bounds

<Chapter III.2:> Necessary ways to examine general inceptions

1 In every inception, one must watch that the lord of the Hour-marker does not fall in the eighth place (called "deadly"), nor in its diameter (the second place, called "livelihood");[16] and [that it] is neither being with the master of the eighth place, nor overcoming the Moon by a square or diameter. Besides, [that] the master of the post-ascension of the Hour-marker (that is to say, of the second place) should not fall in the second nor eighth, nor should they be with nor oppose each other, nor post-ascend the Moon. Moreover, the rulers of the lunar sign and of the Lot of Fortune should not be in the second or eighth place. **2** These are in a better condition if they become pivotal with respect to the Hour-marker, for thus they work remarkable things.

3 Before anything, in every action it is necessary to seek the Hour-marker and the Moon, [as to] whether they are in good places, or they are present with benefics either by [bodily] connection or by figure, and whether the Lot of Fortune harmonizes with either the Sun or the Moon or the Hour-marker. Besides, the lord of the clime[17] should not oppose the clime in which the inception is located, nor [should it oppose] the Moon; and the stars should

---

[16] *Bios*, biological life itself would normally be *zōē*, but older Greek also referred to property and livelihood using this word.

[17] Climes are normally lines or bands of latitude ruled by various planets or signs (see my *Astrology of the World I*, Part IV), but they can also mean planets which govern a particular country.

not be in diameters with their own houses and exaltations,[18] nor in a weak [condition].[19]

4 Having so examined these things in every inception, it is now necessary that every matter be skillfully approached with happiness.[20] **5** For if anyone urges on to start with any action, he should not necessarily agree with all that has been said,[21] but he would rather use the greatest number of the indications [deemed] powerful according to the occasion.

6 In[22] this way also, observe carefully what sort of end each affair will have. **7** Look[23] attentively to the lights[24] of the Moon, the master of the house she is in, and even the Hour-marker of the inception and its Midheaven. **8** If[25] the Moon happened to be passing through any of the pivots, and her host were in the declines, the beginning of the action will be bright, but the conclusion of it dark and unprofitable;[26] on the other hand, if the Moon were in the declines, and the lord of her house in the pivots, the things at the beginning will be worthless and unprofitable, and its endings bright:

For the beginnings belong to changeable Selēnē
herself, but the accomplishment to the powerful god of the house.

9 If both of them are on the pivots, both the things at the beginning and at the end will be good; but if both are found on the declines, the beginning and the end will likewise be worthless.

10 Also examine carefully the Sun and its ruler in the same way as the Moon, especially in diurnal inceptions. **11** One must also observe the Lot of Fortune in every inception, and place the benefics with it or overseeing[27] it.

12 The following must not escape notice either: as a whole, the Moon in the inceptions will deliver her effects, sometimes immediately, sometimes

---

[18] This would put them in their detriment and fall, respectively.

[19] Lit., "in weakness" (*adraneia*).

[20] *Eudaimonia*, lit. "with a good spirit" (**EG**).

[21] That is, he should not be overly worried about fulfilling every single requirement mentioned above, or perhaps even the requirements of each chapter below.

[22] Until **9**, see also *Frag.* V.5, **16-17**.

[23] This passage about the Moon and her lord comes ultimately from Petosiris, as summarized by Julian of Laodicaea (see Schmidt 1995, p. 19).

[24] *Phōta*. That is, whether she is waxing or waning, *etc.* (**EG**).

[25] For this sentence, see *Excerpt* LVI.

[26] Note the association between the pivots and light, and the declines and darkness.

[27] *Epopteuō*. This may be a synonym for "overcoming" (**EG**).

after a while, once she has come to the sign of the inception,[28] or its diameter or square.

<Chapter III.3:> How one must understand the nativities and inceptions of irrational people[29]

1 As regards the nativities of irrational [people], know them in the same way as we already spoke in the second Book, in the chapter on the irrational and monsters,[30] though I shall speak about it here in a simpler way.

2 When the lord of the Lot of Fortune is found unconnected to[31] the Hour[-marker], or to the master of the Hour and the luminaries (and particularly the Moon), declare that inception to be of someone irrational.

3 Whenever the luminaries become estranged[32] both from each other and from the Hour as regards their figure, and a connection with malefics takes place while the pivots and post-ascensions are occupied by malefics, without the beholding of the benefic stars, it is compelling to declare this a nativity of someone irrational, or of a monster, or of an irrational beast (according to the nature of the signs which cause the events), or an inception with respect to irrational animals; [but] if the benefics are configured, then [the events] produced will be of a civilized nature, and regulated by aid of men.

---

[28] This probably means to its Ascendant.

[29] *Alogos.* Or, "without speech." **EG:** This term normally includes unreasoning or irrational beings such as animals. But it could indicate some kind of irrational person: in those days, such people might have been considered sacred. **BD:** Ptolemy's treatment of monsters in *Tet.* III.9 (which Hephaistion cribs in his own II.9) actually suggests that one can distinguish the nativities of animals as well as those with birth defects. The question is, what is the astrologer really trying to find out here, and why? I suggest that the astrologer is identifying a client whose mind or proposed action is irrational, uncivilized, erratic, or dangerous: thus, any talk of beasts and so on is metaphorical, referring to how the client's mind works.

[30] Heph. II.9, which is virtually identical to Ptolemy's text in *Tet.* III.9.

[31] That is, "in aversion to."

[32] I.e., "in aversion to."

<Chapter III.4:> How someone can know beforehand[33] the inquiries[34] of those wishing to investigate [a matter], from the inception[35]

1 Let any of those who comes forward and wishes to make predictions from the inception, know the events yet to happen in an universal and comprehensive shape, proceeding with the analysis [of the inception chart] very much in a similar way as with the nativity.

2 This is to be aimed at also according to the following: having accurately established the Hour and the pivots of the inception, one must first examine the pivot of the Midheaven and what chances to be on it, and from it determine the matters and activities. **3** One must also observe what is on each of the other two places (that is, the decline and post-ascension of the Midheaven),[36] and consider the stars on those [places], those on the decline showing the past, those on the post-ascensional [place] what is about to happen, those on the Midheaven what is happening under the present circumstances. **4** Should no star be found on the said places, one must take those that look on,[37] and are strengthened with respect to them:[38] in the way these are considered, of such kind will the end and the operation of the matter sought be brought about.

[The effects of the Sun's rays and sect]

5 A[39] star going from sinking [under the Sun's rays] to rising [out of them] means the bright, timely and powerful accomplishment of the issues undertaken; one must especially observe Mercury when he goes from rising towards sinking, as this reveals the relaxation, extinction, and idleness of the issues undertaken before or those planned. **6** If a star in its rising is standing away from the Sun by 12°, it begins to have activity, and is fully operational when it stands at 15° from the Sun. In its setting, at 15° to 7° from the Sun it begins to lessen its power; when it is closer than 7° up to the very degree of

---

[33] *Prognoiē.* This is like making a medical "prognosis" (**EG**).

[34] *Peuseis.* Or, "questions."

[35] See the Introduction §4 for a discussion of this chapter.

[36] That is, the ninth and eleventh, respectively.

[37] *Epitheōreō.*

[38] *Endunamōmenous pros autous.* I take "them" to mean "the places," but I am not quite sure what exactly Hephaistion means by it.

[39] This paragraph may seem to be out of place, but Chris Brennan suggests that it may be an example of how to interpret the flow of events in the action as described above.

the Sun, it becomes very weak. The morning phases by night, and the evening ones by day, are more sluggish.

[The pivots of the inception chart]

7 Other things must be added to this section. **8** As regards the pivots, it is necessary to examine the Hour-marker as signifying the nature of the inquiry, the Midheaven the activity, the setting the end, the underground [pivot] what is hidden or secret. And the Hour-marker points to the dawn, the Midheaven to midday, the setting point to dusk, the underground [pivot] the north.[40]

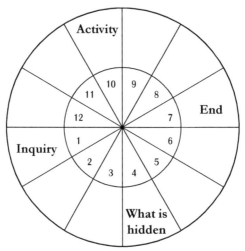

Figure 9: Angles for analyzing inquiries (Heph. III.4, 8)

[Indications of the signs]

9 The tropical signs foster changes easily (for better or for worse), the fixed ones make the matter that is sought unalterable, the bicorporeal ones make the result of the matter sought bipartite.

10 The watery signs mean watery places, the activities through or in water; the amphibious ones combine what is of earth with what is of water; those of dry land [signify] plains[41] and mountains; the fertile and prolific ones crowds and people;[42] the barren ones, deserts and inaction.

---

[40] *Arkton.* Lit., "the Bear," the constellation Ursa Major (**EG**).
[41] *Èpeirous.* This can simply mean dry land in general as opposed to the sea (**EG**).
[42] *Dēmous.* Probably the "common people."

[Nodes, the Moon's connections and flowings-away]

11 The Nodes of the Moon's circle show incomplete and defective matters, and lead towards change into the opposite condition; the connections
and flowings-away of the Moon show results according to the nature of the
stars she has dealings with.[43]

12 The people of Saturn [are] elderly, stout, wrathful, wicked, lurking, and
evil, they have business on earth and sea; it also [means] imprisonment and
detention. Those of Jupiter: refined, honorable, docile, those at their prime,
cheerful, beneficent. Those of Mars: young, bold, passionate, unpleasant,
adulterous, knavish, piratical, fit for command, kingly, and rulers. Venus:
cheerful, refined, graceful, musical, commercial, of luxurious living, effeminate. The Sun: royal, ready to be a leader, men at their prime, masculine. **13**
These are the peculiar traits of each [type]; but should some of them be with
others, one must adapt [one's judgment] according to the combined type.

[Foreknowing through the Lot of Fortune]

14 There is another way we can foreknow [things] once the inception
[chart] is established. **15** When the Lot of Fortune falls in the third sign from
the Hour-marker and the lord of the sign opposes it, one must see that hatred and disagreement with friends is thereby indicated; if the sign turns out
to be bicorporeal, [the enmity] has existed before, and it will show up again
in the future. **16** The star that is the lord of the Lot will show how the people
are made clear beforehand. **17** When the Lot falls in what pertains to friends
(that is, the third), its lord being in the Bad Spirit with the benefics or [with]
the lord of the Hour, the master of the Bad Spirit being on the Hour-marker,
the Moon remaining unharmed, the inception will be found to give indications about the honor and power[44] of freed captives and free men. **18** On the
other hand, if the Lot were found in the place of death together with its own
lord, overcome by a maltreated Moon, the inception will be found utterly
useless.[45]

---

[43] *Koinōnei.* Or, "takes part with, has a partnership with."
[44] Or, "authority" (*archēs*).
[45] *Asuntelēs.* The *–telēs* suggests that it will be incomplete (**EG**).

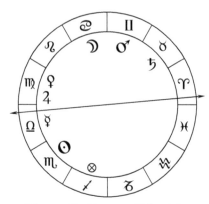
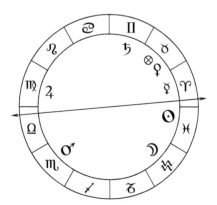

Figure 10: Fortune 10ᵗʰ with benefics and unharmed Moon (Heph. III.4, 17)

Figure 11: Fortune in 8ᵗʰ, overcome by harmed Moon (Heph. III.4, 18)

[Foreknowing using twelfth-parts]

19 For having foreknowledge, the ancients paid attention to the quantity of degrees of the Hour-marker, where its twelfth-part will be. **20** Counting off the quantity of degrees of the Hour-marker, by two <and-a-half> degrees in an orderly sequence, that sign on which it leaves off will be its twelfth-part: and according to it <and> from it is to be known the type[46] concerning every matter, and proceeding from the inquiry.[47] **21** For it is not only necessary to look at the signs themselves, to see whether they are tropical, fixed, or bicorporeal, but especially <whether> the twelfth-part of each sign [falls] in tropical, fixed or bicorporeal ones. It is especially fitting, for the releasing[48] of the inceptions, that a tropical twelfth-part corresponds with a fixed [sign], or a bicorporeal one becomes pivotal,[49] and changes the nature of the sign in the degree-based division of the power pertaining to place.[50]

---

[46] *Eidos.* Or, "nature, category, form," *etc.* (**EG**).

[47] *Pros tēs peseōs.* This could also mean, "on the part of" the inquiry. At any rate, the point is that the twelfth-part reveals the topic of the inquiry (**EG**).

[48] *Lusin.* This seems to refer to how the energy and impetus of the potential inception is actually put into action.

[49] This seems to mean that we want to improve the indications of a less appropriate sign, by making sure the twelfth-part of a key degree or planet corresponds to a more appropriate sign. So, since it is often better to have lasting results (as with a fixed sign), then if for various reasons the Ascendant must be in a movable sign, the twelfth-part of its degree should correspond to a fixed one.

[50] *Tē tēs topikēs dunameōs moirikē diakrisei.* **EG/BD:** Or, "place-related power." Translated this way, it suggests that the regions following the axial degrees provide a kind of power

	0°-2.5°	2.5°-5°	5°-7.5°	7.5°-10°	10°-12.5°	12.5°-15°	15°-17.5°	17.5°-20°	20°-22.5°	22.5°-25°	25°-27.5°	27.5°-30°
♈	♈	♉	♊	♋	♌	♍	♎	♏	♐	♑	♒	♓
♉	♉	♊	♋	♌	♍	♎	♏	♐	♑	♒	♓	♈
♊	♊	♋	♌	♍	♎	♏	♐	♑	♒	♓	♈	♉
♋	♋	♌	♍	♎	♏	♐	♑	♒	♓	♈	♉	♊
♌	♌	♍	♎	♏	♐	♑	♒	♓	♈	♉	♊	♋
♍	♍	♎	♏	♐	♑	♒	♓	♈	♉	♊	♋	♌
♎	♎	♏	♐	♑	♒	♓	♈	♉	♊	♋	♌	♍
♏	♏	♐	♑	♒	♓	♈	♉	♊	♋	♌	♍	♎
♐	♐	♑	♒	♓	♈	♉	♊	♋	♌	♍	♎	♏
♑	♑	♒	♓	♈	♉	♊	♋	♌	♍	♎	♏	♐
♒	♒	♓	♈	♉	♊	♋	♌	♍	♎	♏	♐	♑
♓	♓	♈	♉	♊	♋	♌	♍	♎	♏	♐	♑	♒

Figure 12: Table of twelfth-parts

22 We shall be able to foretell the quality[51] of the inquiry, that is to say, of the matter,[52] when we accurately take the degree of the Hour-marker from a hydrostatic instrument or from an astrolabe or some other instrument to mark the Hour, and know the twelfth-part. For this purpose, we work in the following way:

23 If you find the first twelfth-part of Aries (that is to say, 2.5°) rising on the places adjacent to the Hour, it gives indications[53] for freedom or authority;[54] the second on the manner of living, or home, or animals, or a field, or a woman or refined people or the like; the third <on> trickery[55] or robbery[56]

---

or strength to what falls in them: that is, the quadrant-based angles are strong. But the word for "division" here might also mean "judgment," as in the faculty of judging by distinguishing one thing from another. It could also simply refer to twelfth-parts, since they are gotten by dividing the sign into twelve parts.

[51] *Poiotēta.* Or, its character, its nature.

[52] Note that Hephaistion is not trying to predict its outcome (which would be the normal procedure for a question chart), but determine what the inquiry (*peusis*) or action or matter (*pragma*) is about: this is typical of thought-interpretation or consultation charts.

[53] *Sēmainei.* Note that Hephaistion (or his source material) is now expressing a "signification" view of astrology that is typical of a more divinatory approach—not that astrology itself is purely divinatory, but even if the stars do cause some events, obviously the twelfth-part of the Ascendant did not *cause* the matter for which the client came. Rather, it *indicates* something which was already existing (such as a concern about money, or marriage, and so on).

[54] *Archēs*, here and below.

[55] *Enedra.*

[56] *Klemma.*

or a fugitive; the fourth <on> the theft[57] of silver, or robbery; the fifth on property or authority and the like; the sixth on household management, feminine ornamentation; the seventh on enemies and battle, or demands <or> courts of judgment; the eighth on clandestine and hidden affairs; the ninth on journeys and moving, or sailing; the tenth on hopes or union or harmony; the eleventh on loss or fraud[58] or some punishment; the last one (the twelfth, Pisces) turns out to be about women or going through with matters pertaining to women, or feminine affairs.

24 The first twelfth-part of Taurus having been portioned out, it gives indications for living and eating; and the second (that of Gemini) about shameful affairs or sexual pleasures and the like; the third <about> fraud, or some work, or household management; the fourth, on enemies and robberies;[59] the fifth, <on> agreement[60] and freedom from care, friendship and nobleness of character; the sixth, on the inquirer having fallen into ambiguity and doubt; the seventh (which happens to be of Scorpio), signifies trouble, care, and military campaigns; the eighth, on journeys and sailing and such things; the ninth, about dealings with women, and even something similar to these; the tenth, about sales to various purchasers,[61] and loss and toil; the eleventh, on sexual pleasures; and the last one, which turns out to belong to Aries, is has indications for foreigners and living abroad, or farming.

25 The first twelfth-part of Gemini gives indications for associations and political affairs and things with a similar name; the second, <on> the loss of gold or silver, or movable property of that kind; the third, on loss and bad luck; the fourth, on loaning, loss, and punishment; the fifth, on action and business; the sixth, about the plundering[62] of what has come out of the fire;[63] the seventh, about the chasing of runaways, or journeys, or things similar to these; the eighth, on useful crafts and some cheerful matter; the ninth, on reckoning[64] and actions;[65] the tenth, on battles and enemies, and things with similar meaning; the eleventh, <about> some loss, or fear, or regret[66] or res-

---

[57] *Klopē*.

[58] *Klemma*.

[59] *Harpagē*.

[60] *Symphōnia*. Or: harmony, concord (**EG**).

[61] *Diaprasis*. Or perhaps, "farming [things] out" (**EG**).

[62] *Klopē*.

[63] Possibly the meaning here is the theft of those things manufactured with fire (**EG**).

[64] *Logos*, which can also refer to public accounts, speech, *etc.* (**EG**).

[65] *Pragmatōn*. Or perhaps, "business."

[66] *Metanoia*, lit. "change of mind" (**EG**).

olution [of a problem]; the twelfth and last one, which chances to belong to Taurus, is about farming, living abroad, and things that appear similar to these.

26 The first twelfth-part of Cancer gives indications for authority, high-priesthood and religious service; the second, on a greatest matter,[67] and dignity, and priesthood; the third, on fear because of a certain affair accomplished along with a woman; the fourth, on faith, or loss, or demand; the fifth, on secretly hoarding, or treasure, or deposits entrusted to one's care; the sixth, on journeys, or sailing, or foreign people; the seventh, on a battle because of female persons and jealousy; the eighth, on loss, theft, penalty or denial;[68] the ninth, on association by marriage, and on account of good matters; the tenth, on authority and reputation and priesthood, and if any [other topic, then it is one] close to these; the eleventh, on theft, some runaway, or denial of entrusted valuables; the twelfth, on associations and harmonious affairs and those joined together.

27 The first twelfth-part of Leo would give hints on reputation, the desire of things belonging to another, and greediness; the second, on a great matter, and punishment, and injury; the third, on battle and greediness and being attacked on both sides; the fourth, on the completion of a great work; the fifth, on matters not small but [rather] kingly, or on founding [something];[69] the sixth, on some labor or foreign trade or public revenue;[70] the seventh, on enemies and the like; the eighth, on a matter belonging to another, or care for another; the ninth, on fear and uncertainty; the tenth, on a lounging place or country house or living abroad; the eleventh, on battle and things unexpected; the last one, <on> sacred matters or things of such kind.

28 The first twelfth-part of Virgo gives indications for women's ornaments and for the sake of profit;[71] the second, <on> income or costly ornaments or clothing; the third, on the devising of a clandestine matter; the fourth one, on a change in setting out,[72] or some shared kindness;[73] the fifth,

---

[67] *Megiston pragma*, which can also mean "a man of consequence" (**EG**).

[68] Possibly, of entrusted valuables or property (**EG**).

[69] *Ktisis.*

[70] *Prosodos.* **EG**: This can also mean income, a solemn procession, or even sexual intercourse. **BD**: Revenues and returns or yields from labor and crops is most likely.

[71] *Karpou charin.*

[72] *Aphormōn allagēs. Aphormē* generally refers to a starting point or setting out, especially with respect to war; but it can also refer to one's base of operations (**EG**).

[73] *Koinou tinos charin.*

on farming, a building, or any matter of the kind; the sixth, on a person, or hopes, and business and toil; the seventh (that of Pisces), is about female hatred[74] and the skirmishing of friends; the eighth, on crafts, or sacred activities or an oracular response;[75] the ninth, on the sale of wares or wearisome living abroad; the tenth, Gemini, on some spiteful treatment, or foreign person, or a rustic cause; the eleventh, on theft, or clandestine affair, or treasure; the last one (belonging to Leo), on wounds, illnesses, and the like.

29 The first twelfth-part of Libra throws out hints on income, or judgment, or giving or receiving; the second, on theft and appropriating; the third (belonging to Sagittarius), on commerce or agriculture in foreign lands; the fourth, on clandestine and crooked affairs; the fifth, on business, or ill-doing, or expectations of hope; the sixth, on a matter belonging to another, or commands from a woman; the seventh, on ill-timed unpleasantness, and anger, and battle, or someone's silence;[76] the eighth (belonging to Taurus, on sickness, or wounds, or a royal concern; the ninth, on an association, or reckoning or compacts; the tenth, on income, or dignity, or honor, or prosperity; the eleventh, on some ignorance, or unforeseen outrage;[77] the twelfth, on slaves,[78] or a political burden.[79]

30 The first twelfth-part of Scorpio gives indications on military campaigns or a foreign matter, or the arising of unforeseen sexual intercourse;[80] the second, on sailing, or moving or things like that; the third, on the crowd, or battle and dangerous unpleasantness; the fourth, on deliverance from ill-doing; the fifth, on unanimity, or sailing, or a public affair;[81] the sixth, on imposition of taxes, and dominion, and unexpected violence; the seventh, on someone who has come into foreign lands, or among foreign people; the eighth, on a journey; the ninth, on thefts, [abuse of] authority, or plunder against powerful people;[82] the tenth, on living abroad, or some art, or digni-

---

[74] That is, hatred or emnity *from* a woman (**EG**).

[75] *Chrēmatismos.* Also, legal instruments or a negotiation (**EG**).

[76] *Hēsuchia.* Or, "rest."

[77] *Hubris.*

[78] Lit., "bodies" (*sōmata*).

[79] *Phortiou politikou.* But it seems to me this could also be "public freight," as *phortion* generally refers to a burden or load in the sense of freight and lading (see the first twelfth-part of Sagittarius below). However, I am unsure what concrete things this could mean.

[80] *Mixis.* But this also refers generally to mingling and having *social* relations with others; so it could be some type of social interaction suddenly arising.

[81] *Koinōn pragma.*

[82] *Tōn pros ischurotera prosōpa diapherontōn.* Or perhaps, "transferring [wealth] to powerful people" (**EG**).

ty;[83] the eleventh, on theft because of a woman; the twelfth, on income, or danger, or greedy profit.

31 The first twelfth-part of Sagittarius shows hints for wares[84] in foreign lands; the second, on military campaigns, or living abroad, or the army; the third, on matters and transactions related to the sea; the fourth, on sailing and similar matters; the fifth, on wares; the sixth, on four-footed [animals]; the seventh, on unpleasantness or a runaway; the eighth, on theft and loss; the ninth, on traveling or ambush;[85] the tenth, on erotic love and the like; the eleventh, on income in foreign lands or due to foreigners; the twelfth, on theft.

32 The first twelfth-part of Capricorn is about unclean or insolent matters; the second, on a runaway or loss; the third, on erotic love or sailing; the fourth, on sheep, a building or clothing; the fifth, on agriculture or household management; the sixth, on matters belonging to others;[86] the seventh, on theft and unpleasantness; the eighth, on fear or military campaigns; the ninth, on an art or feminine ornamentation; the tenth, on income[87] or unpleasantness; the eleventh, on affairs turned clandestine; the twelfth, on some affair that presented itself, or sailing.

33 The first twelfth-part of Aquarius throws out hints on slaves;[88] the second, because of maritime affairs or merchandise; the third, about some gossip; the fourth, on one's own suffering; the fifth, on an association, or watery activities; the sixth (which belongs to Cancer), is about theft or unexpected unpleasantness; the seventh, on an art or association; the eighth, on things belonging to the public square or any assembly; the ninth, on income or on adornment, and some just matter, or about being abroad; the tenth (which belongs to Scorpio), on fraud[89] or treasure; the eleventh, on sailing and affairs connected with the water; the last one, which happens to be that of Capricorn, is about matters belonging to others, or on women's faithfulness.[90]

---

[83] Or, "reputation."

[84] *Phortion.*

[85] *Enedra.*

[86] *Allois diapherontōn.* Or, perhaps, "matters of disagreement with others" (**EG**).

[87] *Prosodos.* See footnote above.

[88] *Sōmata*, as above.

[89] *Klopē.* Or perhaps, "theft."

[90] *Pisteōn.* Or perhaps, feminine assurances or oaths (**EG**).

34 The first twelfth-part of Pisces reveals damaged maritime goods;[91] the second one is about order or being yoked together;[92] the third, on making an attempt to undertake some secret task, or on female matters; the fourth, on toil or an association or a foreign matter; the fifth, on wares or a wedding; the sixth one, on some wares belonging to someone else; the seventh, on a feminine craft and similar things pertaining to women; the eighth, on the matters of others; the ninth, on revenues and a fine matter; the tenth, on sailing or some pleasant living abroad; the eleventh, on a female matter or something belonging to a woman;[93] the twelfth-part at the end gives hints on loss, or a runaway, and the like.

<Chapter III.5:> On universal inceptions and observations[94]

1 The Sun and the Moon take upon themselves the royal rank and leading strength of the whole: through the configurations to one another and their significant phases, everything is brought to fulfillment; and receiving the con-figuration of the planets to them, [they contribute] to the growth and intensification of the effects produced. **2** In accordance with the monthly assembly of the luminaries, everything—on land and sea—propagates and changes.

3 It is therefore necessary to examine in every inception the previous as-sembly and Full Moon, just as in every nativity. First, [one must see] whether the Moon[95] is doing business[96] upon the pivots or their post-ascensions, in a sign or degrees or co-presence[97] or figure of a benefic star (similarly with a malefic), and whether after the assembly or Full Moon she connects with a benefic or the opposite. One can thus make an inference about the matter according to the relation of the union [of the luminaries] to the pivots and wandering stars. **4** For if the union comes to be pivotal with benefics, or moves towards benefics, this will reveal great and happiest farings until the

---

[91] Or perhaps, any spoiled matters or actions connected with the seas (**EG**).

[92] *Kosmou ē suzeuxeōs.* **EG**: Possibly of wedded union. **BD**: To me this is more likely "adornment or a wedding union."

[93] Or perhaps a disagreement with a woman (*gunaiki diapherontos*).

[94] That is, general rules for any inception.

[95] That is, at the New or Full Moon preceding the inception.

[96] *Chrēmatizousa.* Or, "busy, transacting business, having dealings."

[97] *Parousia.* That is, being in the same sign.

end—in nativities it produces[98] kings, and fortunate and wealthy natives. **5** When the Moon, being assembled with benefics, is taken towards malefics, it will make natives of noble birth, but as soon as it has the authority of the times, it will make those who fall from better to worse in life; but should the Moon be found in the opposite condition, it will show the begotten [child] to be of ill fortune at the beginning, but of good fortune in the end. **6** If she is taken from malefics towards malefics, it will then lead from abject, toilsome, unfortunate, and ill-fated conditions towards similar things. **7** If she is surrounded[99] by malefics, the assembly will make those without a living, beggars, and unfortunate people.

8 When the ruler of the assembly is eastern,[100] and occupies its own place or is in a triangle to the place, it will produce those who succeed in everything, and those effective in acquisition. However, this will not be the case when found to be in aversion or oppositional.[101] **9** When the union or its lord comes to be in post-ascensions, it will bring out its effects, but after some time; and when in declines, it will render idle and incomplete effects.

10 One must in fact also consider all the effects in an inception in the same way as one would do in a nativity: by examining the previous assembly and Full Moon. **11** One must also diligently look into the Moon's phases: I say, those in which the Moon looks upon the Sun (or is looked upon [by him]) after[102] the unconnected configurations: by diametrical, triangular, or square hurling of rays and testimonies.

12 Should someone inquire about the truth of some report, rumor, or simply the movement of any matter within the city, land, or men taken individually, or about documents, orders, prophecies, or bad dreams, they will all be found to be accurate when the Moon is making a phase, especially if Mercury is also co-present or testifying to her. **13** And should the malefics be absent, they will show that the matter will have a good result; contrariwise, [it

---

[98] *Apoteleō.*

[99] *Perischetheisa.* That is, besieged; in the definitions of Antiochus, this is by sign and not by degrees.

[100] *Anatolas echē.* It is unclear to me whether this means it is in the east, or arising out of the rays so as to precede the Sun.

[101] This probably means, "in aversion to its sign or in opposition to it," the latter indicating its detriment.

[102] *Meta* + accusative. Hephaistion seems to mean the *major* configurations: thus after being in aversion to the Sun (and then passing through the hexagon), she comes to the square and triangle; then she is in aversion again, then comes to the opposition, then in aversion, *etc.*

is] not good. If they happen to be combined, then the judgment will be mixed accordingly. **14** When the star of Mercury, together with that of Mars, look upon[103] the Moon, without [her] making a phase, they will indicate that the matters and events announced will be deceitful, crafty, wicked, and treacherous, particularly when the inception is in the signs of these stars.

15 Besides what has been said, it is also necessary to turn our attention to the nature of the signs. **16** For example, in spite of being close to each other, there is a great difference between Scorpio and Libra: for the former is inclined towards what is just and good, whereas Scorpio tends towards the opposite and what is harmful. **17** When the Moon makes a phase in Libra, the runaway slave will return easily; one who starts a lawsuit, being guilty, will be defeated by the one having justice on his side; what has been lost will be found, and there will be profit in receiving, giving and forming partnerships; lending and borrowing, praying or asking for compensation or favors, is unsuitable; and stealing, overpowering, swearing, cheating or acting in a completely unjust way will not end up well. **18** When the Moon is in Scorpio, the opposite things: to undertake unrighteous and forcible actions will pay, and unsuitable marriages will be consummated.

19 The Moon [being] well placed with Mercury in signs of human shape is good for oracular responses, divination by dreams or prediction; if in the enigmatic and mute signs, especially with Saturn, it shows apparitions of the departed ones, and of wild animals or captives in chains. With Jupiter seeing her, [this will take place] through foretellers, kings, sacred animals, notable[104] men or those who speak the truth. Should Mars [see her], through weapons or soldiers of the houses, sacrificial victims, seizures, and fear of the gods. If Venus, through precious stones and female characters and ornaments.

20 If the Moon is in the watery signs, and Saturn and Mercury are testifying, [it is good for] the building of aqueducts and the digging up of wells. If Mars with Venus [are testifying], something must be received[105] on occasion of taking a bath, and [it is also good] to lay down keels for building ships, or draw ships into the sea, and purchase chariots fit for seafaring.

21 If the Moon is in Sagittarius, Capricorn, Aquarius, Pisces, or Cancer, and Venus and Mercury are co-present[106] or looking on,[107] the malefics being

---

[103] *Epidōsi (ephoraô)*.

[104] *Episēmos*.

[105] *Paralēpteon*. Or, "one must take to oneself," or "one must receive." This could be a medical remedy (**EG**).

[106] Pingree removed "or culminating" from the text, without explanation.

absent,[108] it will be suitable for buying land, and planting in Taurus and Virgo, gardens and vineyards in Cancer, Pisces, and Aquarius, especially if the god[109] is in the east,[110] and Mercury and Venus are observing.[111] **22** If the Moon is in the signs of human shape with the benefics and Mercury, and the malefics are absent, [it is useful] to buy and sell slaves in the marketplace. **23** In the bestial signs (Aries, Taurus, Leo and Sagittarius) it is fine to establish[112] flocks and herd-animals, and herds of horses when in Aries or in Capricorn. **24** In Gemini, it is best for breeding horses; in Cancer and Taurus, oxen.

25 When the god is in Libra, it is suitable to consort with a woman, for they become kindly, affectionate, and attached. **26** The opposite in Scorpio, Sagittarius, and Leo, for they quickly part asunder. **27** In Capricorn, Aquarius, and Pisces, [it is good] to be joined to foreign and strange[113] women, for [their] mixing [together] remains unharmed, especially in Scorpio.[114]

28 In Sagittarius, it is unsuitable to depart to different places. **29** But it is good to make a departure when the Moon is in the dry signs, to take a ship to the sea when she is in watery signs; but should she be in amphibious signs (that is to say, Capricorn and Aquarius), it will be useful for both things. **30** When the Moon is in signs of human shape, the malefics being away, starting a journey by road or sailing will not be hindered.

31 With her being placed in dry and fixed [signs], one must dig into whatever is related to the earth: metals, foundations, treasures, especially in Scorpio (for it lurks in holes); and to build a house in those same signs, except those belonging to the tropics. **32** Being configured with Saturn and Mercury, it is necessary to build memorials and tombs.

33 With her being in tropical signs, [it is useful] to return prayers to the gods, and with her being in[115] a good phase they will be very much listened

---

[107] *Epitheōreō.*

[108] I.e., in aversion.

[109] This must be the Moon, despite the masculine *theou* here (as below).

[110] *Anatolē.* That is, the Ascendant.

[111] *Ephorōntōn.*

[112] *Kathistēmi.* **EG:** Or, "bring down" to a place. **BD:** This might include transporting such animals, or establishing them in certain pastures.

[113] *Allotria.* Or, "belonging to another."

[114] This seems to contradict the previous sentence, but Hephaistion seems to mean that because it is only an affair with a foreigner (or someone else's wife or slave), it can be broken off easily. See **18**, which says unjust associations will work in Scorpio.

[115] *Epi* + genitive, which technically means "upon."

to.

34 Taking deposits of money or property entrusted, when she is in Aquarius, is unsuitable and a source of ingratitude.

35 [It is suitable] to breed cattle in Taurus, horses in Leo, and dogs and asses in Scorpio.

36 To be involved in teaching or the wrestling-school, [with her] in Gemini and Aquarius and Virgo; also for every kind of divination.

37 To go hunting [after wild beasts] with the help of dogs, [the Moon should be] in the bestial signs; after birds, in the winged signs; to go fishing, in the wet signs.

38 Depositing riches under the earth[116] will be useful in Scorpio, Leo, and Virgo; and opening up a workshop,[117] and gathering the means of living, and that which makes use of scales and measures, is better with the god being in Libra according to the second rank,[118] in Cancer according to the third.

39 In Capricorn, purchasing linen and cotton for re-sale, [and] even better in Aries. **40** To do business in the marketplace [with] everything that lives in water, in Pisces and Aquarius.

41 Emigrating and changing from one place to another in signs of human shape, and even better in Cancer (on account of it being her house). **42** Making associations with friends, in signs of human shape.

43 Doing business in slaves in the market in the fixed ones, indicates a stable character but stubborn; in those of human shape, moderate and obedient; in the tropical ones, fit for re-sale.

44 In Virgo, Libra, Sagittarius, to purchase a bedfellow, that is, a young maiden. **45** In Leo, Virgo, Libra, Aquarius, and Taurus, to write down wedding contracts, for then the companionships will be lasting; contrariwise in Sagittarius, Pisces, and Aries. **46** Separation becomes imminent in Scorpio, and especially when the Moon is passing through its pivot; but if any of the malefics looks on,[119] such thing will occur without delay.

47 Vineyards and gardens, in Pisces, Cancer, Aquarius, and in the last [degrees] of Capricorn; sowing, in Taurus and Virgo; gathering fruits, in the

---

[116] *Kata gēn.*

[117] *Ergastērion.* This can include a manufactuary, a barber shop, a perfumery, *etc.* (**EG**).

[118] *Kata taxin. Taxis* is roughly equivalent to the Latin *ordo*, and can indicate a position, rank, arrangement, or class. But its meaning here and in the next clause is unclear to me. It may refer to a decan, reading with Cancer in the next clause.

[119] *Epeidon.*

watery signs, with Venus, Mars, and Mercury looking.[120]

48 In the foundations[121] (and in the other inceptions) it is necessary to carefully observe whether the Moon is void in course and[122] diminishing her light.

49 During breastfeeding of new-born babes, it is necessary to be attentive to Aries, as it will be a cause of sicknesses and a lack of milk. **50** If at the time of giving birth the Moon were found to be brought towards the malefics, without the benefics,[123] the begotten one would perish badly[124] within seven days.

51 In the crises of diseases,[125] if she is found to be with Saturn, waning, one must suppose death (the kind of death being known in advance according to the nativity). **52** Should the Moon be increasing [in light], from this one must make predictions for the sick ones. **53** When someone appearing to spend his days well, falls sick on a good day, let him not be released on the day of crisis, but have a delay, since you should know that such [a condition] is conducive to dangerous ends, especially when the arising[126] of the ruler, or of the sign, is completed. Similarly whenever the Moon is also [related] to the benefics, or their degrees, in the eighth or in the sixth place (which is the deadly place, [and] that of injury), she is not good. **54** It has been observed that many times, among those who have been sick for a long time, or among those who choose to die, instead of living through some overpowering evil of sicknesses and sufferings, or even other misfortunes, when she is connected with the benefics, or also when the benefics are well configured in the transit[127] with respect to the nativity, such [configurations] produce a release from life.

55 When the star indicating the injury is found on the setting pivot, or in the eighth (which is the deadly place), one must determine that there will be an end to that suffering;[128] when the star meaning such injury and sufferings

---

[120] *Horaō.*

[121] *Ktisis.* This may refer to the nativity (**EG**).

[122] This should probably be read as "or."

[123] That is, with the benefics in aversion.

[124] *Kakōs.* That is, the baby will die a bad death.

[125] For more on illness and critical days, see Ch. III.31.

[126] *Anaphora.* This probably refers to the ascensional time of the signs, and the lesser years of the planets (see **Planetary years**) in the main Glossary.

[127] *Parodos.*

[128] That is, by death.

is not contemplated by benefics, then the suffering will also meet its end. **56** There is another thing to watch for: in prominent and fortunate nativities, the evil becomes moderate, just as the good most emphatically does in unfortunate ones.

57 In inceptions, as in nativities, one must also pay attention to the ingresses[129] of the stars.

[Natural significators]

58 In an inception one should observe the givers[130] of each kind and matter, and the lords:[131] each of the effects will turn out according to how harmoniously and thoroughly configured they are with the Moon. **59** For when we seek with respect to land or management or inheritance, we undertake an affair with Saturn in a good position; for issues about kings and leadership, we clearly watch Jupiter; in matters of war, Mars; in erotic affairs, Venus; and about friends, or businesses, [we seek] an unharmed Mercury. **60** It must be noted that when Mercury is together with the Sun, affairs worked secretly are rendered visible.

[The sign of the Moon]

61 In their writings, the ancients also treated the single subject of the Moon's ingresses in great detail, the same things that we shall also explain here:

62 With her being in Aries, above the earth, within[132] [the first] nine degrees, it is fitting to go abroad, and to make elegant[133] purchases, to cultivate the fields, shear four-footed [animals], begin to lay foundations, make treaties, loans, and weaving; it also fits well with what has been said on destruction.[134] In the second fifteenth-part, it is auspicious for those who succeed to an office and receive power [from another] around eastern regions, to perform an unfit wedding, and harmful to receive [by succession]

---

[129] *Epembasis.*

[130] *Dotēr.* Hephaistion seems to mean the natural significators of them, as he describes below.

[131] It is unclear to me whether these are different from the "givers," or not.

[132] *Meta* + acc. This can also mean "after."

[133] *Euschēmon.* Or, "decent" (**EG**).

[134] *Phtherein.* **EG:** Or perhaps, "perishing, corrupting, loss." **BD:** I am unsure what Hephaistion is referring to.

property inherited from the father.

63 In Taurus, around the first fifteenth-part, it is auspicious to walk, till the land, sow, plant; to buy slaves, four-footed animals, buildings, and to make [artificial] wells. It is also good to establish altars and sacred places, and receive power and authority around the southern climes. In the other fifteenth-part, it is suitable to attempt to procure an abortion, [but] unreliable to get married and grow children (for the begotten will be wandering in distress); and letting something out for hire[135] causes loss.

64 In the first half of Gemini, one must turn away from getting started on any matter; and through the other half, it will be profitable to follow through [on it], to marry and raise children, also to purchase houses and fields; to make promises and oaths, to build on ancient sites and foundations, to till the land and plant; to hand over the arts to disciples, bury treasures under earth, appoint governors, receive power in succession and carry out commands; it is also dangerous to attempt to procure an abortion, make enemies, be at sea, or withdraw from places or persons.

65 In the first half of Cancer, it will be auspicious to marry, raise children, to buy up [in bulk],[136] and especially—because it is one of the wet signs—it is safe to be at sea, though with slowness. In the other half, to bring enemies on oneself, be treacherous, fish, practice gardening, plant, sow, dig up mines, rivers, wells, and cisterns, to give entrusted valuables to the earth, give and receive due payment, closely watch the associated business away from dry lands,[137] buy male slaves, flee from enemies and strife (for they will be irreconcilable).

66 In Leo, from the tenth degree, to buy up all kinds of four-footed [animals], especially those of the best quality; to administer the house honorably, apply oneself[138] to authorities and powers, have [money] lent to oneself; though it will be harmful to start a journey by road or sailing, watch closely the house slaves, set upon enemies (the destroyed [enemies] will be hard to carry),[139] and it is not auspicious to marry nor, for women, to attempt to pro-

---

[135] That is, contracting to have someone else work one's property (and similar things).

[136] *Sunōneisthai.*

[137] *Tas apo kserōn ergasias synistamenas.* Probably the docks, or where the ships are left aground. It could also mean "public baths" (**EG**).

[138] *Epiballesthai.* Or perhaps, "throw upon oneself" (**EG**).

[139] *Dusanakomista.* Meaning somewhat unclear; the term could also refer to returning or bringing back, or even to "carry upwards." It probably means that it is hard for the enemies to recover *from the attack*, not that (say) their bodies will be hard to recover.

cure abortion.

67 In Virgo, it is best to purchase grain, gold, silver, garments, slaves, and as many things as are necessary for decoration.[140] Also, to make buildings of any type, use new garments and vessels, to start [working on] mines, plant, sow, till the land (except vineyards), marry widows (for maidens are unsuitable), emigrate, let out for hire, have something lent to one, procure an abortion, take inheritance from the father, start a voyage by sea. Unsuitable to provide with wine and olive oil, but it is suitable to work on weaving and giving birth.

68 In Libra, to buy and sell everything that is lawful, or anything by measure or rule, collect debts, travel, receive power and authority, especially towards northern places, establish foundations of the house without the roof, split rivers, dig up wells, work on weaving, marry, partake of friendliness and rejoicing. But on the other hand, [it is not suitable] to purchase, to hire houses or rooms, nor migrate to another country (and that which [is] from dry lands is well-known to be unfitting);[141] to attempt to procure abortion is dangerous for the patients, even if this happens by accident.

69 In Scorpio, it is useful to travel by land and sea, to plot against someone in purchases and legal documents, make an attempt against enemies, set doors [in place], establish altars and temples, to build on ancient [settlements], to till uncultivated land, dig up wells, transplant vineyards,[142] place entrusted goods under the earth, divide places, to make use of new instruments, to lead [the course of] waters and rivers. **70** All these things are suitable in the first fifteenth-part, but are unprofitable in the second one: if a wedding occurs, the maiden will have intercourse with slaves; it also unsuitable to make associations, and to bring a physician to the sick one; to attempt an abortion is dangerous.

71 In Sagittarius, it is fitting to sail towards home, and also helpful for stud-stables, herds of cattle, and cattle-stalls; to lend and borrow things belonging to others, and bring to the household property from outside. It is effective to oppose enemies, to receive from the father and from other people, build a house and settle foundations, buy dogs, fish, and weave; but it is harmful to be entrusted with something,[143] borrow and lend, go abroad, start

---

[140] *Kosmos.*

[141] *Hosa te apo xērōn sunestēken anarmoston.* We are unclear on what this means.

[142] *Metampeleuein*, not in the lexicon. This is a a combination of *meta* and *ampelos* (vine, vineyard) (**EG**).

[143] *Pisteuō.* This could also indicate being trusted with something generally speaking (**EG**).

a journey [by road] (for it will last long). It is not fitting to go to a physician, nor take medicines, purges, nor attempt an abortion.

72 In Capricorn, it is fitting to buy together nursling,[144] export for sale, travel for business, sail, buy birds, [hunted] animals, dig up wells, break open blocked passages, raise [enclosing] walls; it is good to start something concerning the household, to share with a friend, to return home from being abroad by land and sea, to teach skills and arts presided over by the Muses, to have sexual intercourse, and to weave. It is dangerous to attempt to procure abortion, and it is unsafe to start a journey [by road].

73 In Aquarius, <to start> a journey by sail or road, and buy up things by means of water and by measures, build a house and embellish the household, break open what has been barred, have <sexual> intercourse, till the land, plant, sow, dig up wells, rivers, cisterns, and anything that is laid down in earth, and to weave. It is not dangerous to practice abortion; to swear or be busy with something unrighteous is not fitting, and there is no hindrance in making oaths, and going for everything that is legal.

74 The Moon being in Pisces, [it is suitable] to start a journey by sail or road, to purchase, go out by land and sea, and to procure for oneself anything that comes from water, and particularly from the equipment[145] for the sea for each member of the crew;[146] also to make oneself ready for hunting and fishing, as well as for the army. Also to make an attempt to attack, fight, catch by bird-line, and start any association and friendship; also marrying, and as many things as are suitable for equality, but it is necessary to watch out whether the married woman is someone abusive, lecherous and adulterous. [It is] also [fitting] to build a house.

75 All the words said above become more effective for advantage or suffering, in accordance with the partnership of the other stars: for it is not only necessary to interpret the Moon position by place, but also [to consider] the testimonies of the Sun and the other five stars.

---

[144] That is, an animal that is reared and tended.
[145] *Paraskeuē.* Possibly the equipment and elements required for the sea (**EG**).
[146] *Paidos.*

<Chapter III.6:> On ineffective and effective days,
[and reading entrails]

1 By "effective"[147] days are meant those in which the Moon [is] in the sign of the nativity[148] or in a triangle of this with benefics, or in any sign together with the benefics, the stars that cause destruction being absent (except for the Full Moon and assembly);[149] effective hours are those in which the sign of the nativity marks the Hour, or is in a triangular figure, or when [it is brought] to rise together with the Hour-marker, while the Moon is not configured with any of the malefics.

2 "Ineffective" and evil days, when the Moon is in square to the sign of the nativity, or in the one opposite, with the destroyers, or during the Full Moon, assembly, or else when any of the malefics marks the Hour or looks upon the Full Moon or the assembly, while the benefics are absent. Mercury, being common, mixes with those to which it is associated.

3 In addition, one must carefully attend to the Moon, the Hour-marker, the Lot of Fortune, and the other pivots, inasmuch as they are allotted the authority and the accuracy of the inquiry on the matter, also observing whether the Moon, from the assembly through [her] fullness, is found in places suitable for doing business,[150] or whether she rules the Lot, or chances to be on it; or else whether the star allotted the mastership over her, is together with [the star] having the lordship of the Lot, or if they exchange signs. **4** For, [this not][151] being so, purchases and marriages become irreconcilable and unconsidered, the changes are abrupt, and the judgments and situations un-hoped for. **5** Running from the Full Moon (that is, when she is subtracting [in light]),[152] she indicates delay in what comes to pass, and [a] length of time.

---

147 *Empraktos.*

148 This is probably the natal Ascendant, but perhaps the natal sign of the Moon.

149 That is, the New and Full Moon are not effective; see **2** below.

150 *Chrēmatistikois.* Two versions of the advantageous or busy or profitable houses were handed down in antiquity. The version according to Timaeus has seven: the Ascendant and every sign configured to it except for the third (the Ascendant, Midheaven, seventh, fourth, fifth, ninth, and eleventh). The version according to Nechepso had eight: all four angles and their succeedents. For more, see my *Introductions to Traditional Astrology* (2010, III.3-4).

151 I have added a "not," because it contrasts with the positive indication in the previous sentence, and continues the account of what makes an inception ineffective.

152 Normally this verb is used for being subtractive in numbers, but Valens *Anth.* II.38, **56** and IV.18, **8** do indeed use it to indicate a waning Moon (i.e., subtracting in light) (**EG**).

6 One must also pay attention to her other phases, and the other stars, observing that the benefics do not always produce good things, nor on the other hand do the malefics [always signify bad things, namely] when placed in their own houses, or bounds, triangles, or exaltations, or else appearing as spearbearers according to their own sect (that is, on their morning rising with respect to the Sun, and the evening rising of the night with respect to the Moon); for when they appear unfamiliarly[153] or estranged from their own sect, or post-ascending [a pivot], they become causes of a lack of progress and of evils.

[Reading entrails]

7 One[154] must see that generally, the nature of every art and science is to know, having been transmitted an inception according to each operation, such as in the examination of entrails. **8** As the Moon is the closest to the earth (of all other [stars] in the heavenly realms), when she is in a phase with Mercury at the time of the opening of an animal, she quickly produces changes in the conditions here. **9** She shapes the insides of the entrails, sometimes in one way, sometimes in another, in relation to the co-mixed natures of the stars and hers. **10** She inclines towards good complexion and good health, when she is additive in numbers and light, and is with benefics; to lividity, pallor, a watery state, and a lack of the possibility to foretell, when, waning, she chances to be with Saturn; if Mars is with her (she being full), it makes signals of varied tinges of yellow through the blood, and similarly, it makes all the entrails lukewarm. If, being full, she connects with Saturn; or, waning with Mars, above the earth, [one can expect things] of a fine, auspicious, prophetic nature, and omens clear to be read; contrariwise when under earth, especially with the malefics.

11 The[155] arranged inception thus displays each matter before the opening of the animal victim: and the Hour-marker reveals the sacrificer, the setting [pivot] the sacrificed one or the victim for the offering, the Midheaven the god or gods, and the underground pivot the blame of the household, the way

---

[153] *Anoikeiōs*. This seems to be a general term, meaning positions and conditions incongruous with their natures (e.g., being peregrine, *etc.*).

[154] In this paragraph, Hephaistio is not saying that a good election will yield a *positive* augury, but that it makes the entrails *readable*.

[155] This suggests that the opening of the animal is the inception that also allows an *astrological* reading of the entrails—making the entrails themselves less important.

out of the present state of affairs, and the reason for the sacrifice. One must also consider in which places the stars are placed, their arrangement, phase, and the four Lots: Fortune, Spirit, Necessity and Love.[156]

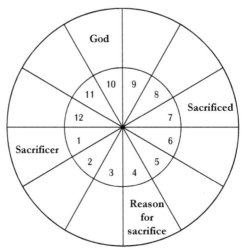

Figure 13: Angles for a sacrifice

12 The[157] right section of the entrails is like the hemisphere above earth, the left part like the one under the earth; and the morning planets indicate the right side, the evening ones the left. The Moon in the northern hemisphere[158] means the right, moving up north until she begins her descent; returning towards the south until she begins her ascent, the left. **13** Besides, when you find <some> of the stars running on the same wind[159] and connecting with the Moon, you will foretell by likening the quality and strength of [the Moon] with that portion of the entrails.

---

[156] I imagine that the Lots of Necessity and Love (*Erōs*) are those according to Valens: from Spirit to Fortune and projected from the Ascendant, reversed at night (Necessity); and from Fortune to Spirit and projected from the Ascendant, reversed at night (Love/*Erōs*). See *Excerpt* XVI, **6**, which suggests that Dorotheus also used these. Necessity and Love according to the so-called Hermetic Lots (Paul of Alexandria, Ch. 23) are as follows: from Mercury to Fortune and projected from the Ascendant, reversed at night (Necessity); and from Spirit to Venus and projected from the Ascendant, reversed at night (Love/*Erōs*).

[157] This suggests that each portion of the entrails has its own meaning in auguries all on its own, which can then be layered onto the chart, *independently* of the angles mentioned above.

[158] This must mean being in northern ecliptical latitudes.

[159] **EG**: Direction. **BD**: But see the footnote to Ch. III.47, **55**.

14 You will distribute the portions of the liver to the stars and the zodiacal circle the following way. **15** You will give the Sun the [portions] of the heart; the sections from the heart through the breast, the right shoulder, right receptacle, hollows or double organs; to the Moon, the garment of the heart, left shoulder and left receptacle (if the Moon is found [to be] full or diminishing, the receptacle and the spleen are found in this manner). To Saturn is assigned the blood-vessels of the thighs, which are around the base, wrapping the left table[160] and the left opposite portion (the same portion of the liver, which belongs to the heart). To Jupiter [is given] the place of the bladder and the left portion of the head. To Mars the ophryoma,[161] the right sickle, which are also called fence and knife; also, of the gates, the right one and the left parts. To Venus, the head, the edges of the liver, and the lungs. To Mercury, the ears, both [parts] of the heart, the hands, the mouth of the liver, and both of the common spaces of the so-called paths of the beings near the gates.

16 Beginning with the zodiac, the parts from the mouth of the heart through the left head, one must assign to Aries; to Taurus, the table and what lies in the midst of it; the right shoulder to Gemini; from the place of the god through the hearth, to Cancer; to Leo, the sharp knife, leg and foot; to Virgo, the bile and what lies on both sides; to Libra, the right gate; <to Scorpio...>;[162] to Sagittarius, the left foot and leg; to Capricorn, the left table, and the hollow of the table through the thigh and the cup;[163] to Aquarius, the left shoulder; to Pisces, the head by the left side, and the bladder.

17 Such things about the liver were expounded among the ancients; let anyone who pays attention, discover even more from what has been said.

---

160 *Trapeza.*

161 *Ophruōma.* **EG:** Unknown, but *ophrus* means an eyebrow. **BD:** Note that it is also called a "fence," as befits a thin ridge or brow.

162 Missing in the text.

163 *Kotulēs.* This indicates anything hollow, a small vessel, cup, or even the hollow of the hand (**EG**).

\<Chapter III.7:\> About foundations and buildings
and foundation festivals[164]

1 When anyone wishes to found a fortunate and enduring city[165] (likewise with the laying down of foundations for the building of ships, houses and walls), watch for the Moon transiting in the royal triangle[166] at the time, and [at] the inception of the circumscription (that is to say, of the foundations);[167] let her also be favorably testified to by all the stars: for if it so happens to be, then disclose that the construction will be cared for and given heed by great kings and rulers, and be the dwelling place of monarchs, and beloved by the gods, remarkable, held in esteem, and long-lasting. **2** Should any of the stars chance to be deprived of suitable testimony, it will be seen that there will be need around the city at that time: for when Mars chances to be declining or in aversion in the inception, there will be want of arms, and [the city] will be weak in matters of war. In the same way, when Venus happens to be unconnected, [the city] will be excluded from favors,[168] luxurious living and politeness, and from being loved as well. If the inception[169] is not beheld by Jupiter, [the city] will be exposed to harm, and will not partake in having attention and solicitude by anybody. When Mercury is unconfigured, there will be no practical wisdom and no exercise of reason[170] in the city.

3 If[171] it comes to pass that the star of Mars, or that of Jupiter, opposes

---

[164] *Kathidrusis*, a festival for the consecration or hallowing of statues or sacred images (**EG**).

[165] *Polis*.

[166] That is, Aries-Leo-Sagittarius (the fiery triplicity).

[167] This refers especially to the inscribing of the foundation-stone.

[168] *Charis*. Or, "grace."

[169] This undoubtedly refers to the Ascendant of the inception chart.

[170] *Logos*. In this context, Hephaistion probably means there will not be deliberate arguments and reasoning used in governing the city, but rather emotion and irrationality.

[171] Hephaistion's instructions here are related to the idea that when the natal longevity releaser is directed to its own square, the native will die or at least suffer a threat to life (see *Tet.* III.11, p. 39, Schmidt translation). But sentences **3-4** are a bit ambiguous as to what is being directed to what. The obvious scenario is the direction of the Moon—who is being opposed by Mars—to the square of that same Mars. But this could happen in two ways: (1) Direct the Moon by ascensions to the *zodiacal* square of Mars; (2) direct the Moon to the *equatorial/ascensional* square of Mars. The diagrams illustrate both possibilities, in a chart with the latitude of Minneapolis, at 45° N (I use the ascensional times as given in the Delphic Oracle software program). Let the Moon be at 15° Gemini, and Mars opposing her at 15° Sagittarius. Counting by ascensions from 0° Aries, the Moon's position corresponds to 50.275 ascensional times (AT), and Mars to 277.545 AT. (1) His zodiacal square to 15° Virgo corresponds to 160.185 AT. The distance in AT from the Moon to

the luminaries (that is to say, the Sun and Moon), the city will make an at-tempt on war, and especially when the Moon comes near the square according to the time of its interval with respect to rising[172] (that is to say, 90° of the zodiac)—but it comes to pass[173] that not all the inhabitants will be exposed to death, or carrying off booty, or slavery: therefore[174] the prepara-tions of the city, and its founding, do not all take their inception at one single critical moment of time. **4** As in nativities, the side of the square imposes the end of life: only then it is accustomed [to consider] that the times are com-pleted, and the equipped city is utterly destroyed, at which point of time the malefic stars altogether bring their rays more forcibly upon the square of the Moon. For it so happens that the concurrence of the misfortune thus in-creases in two ways: from the maltreatment of the square, and the fixing of the position of the Moon.[175] **5** The same things would be fulfilled once the rising of 180° is completed, or else up to the other square, or once the whole circle is filled up.[176] Moreover, if the squares chance to be unharmed by the transit of the malefics and the second and third circle,[177] then the lingering occurrence of evils will only follow partially.

---

this square is 109.91, or 109.91 years. To find (2) his ascensional/equatorial square, we subtract 90 from his times, and get 187.545 AT: this corresponds to 5° 42' Libra. The distance in AT from the Moon to this square is 137.27, or 137.27 years. This is supposed to yield the time at which the city will suffer some destruction. Note that these are *not* the results we would get by using Ptolemy's own semi-proportional arc method of primary directions.

[172] *Anaphora.* This refers to ascensional times.

[173] Or perhaps, "may" come to pass?

[174] *Tôi.* It seems to me that perhaps this should read as "since" or "because"; nevertheless I do not fully understand what Hephaistion means.

[175] This seems to mean the position of the Moon at the inception: in **3** it was assumed that the Moon's place was opposed by Mars or Jupiter. In my diagram, it would mean her position at 15° Gemini.

[176] In other words, if war does not come at the direction to the square, it may come at 180° (the position of the malefic itself), or at the time of the other square.

[177] This could also be translated as, "by the transit of the malefics and [by their] second and third circle" (or "by the transit, and second and third circle of, the malefics"). In ei-ther event I am not sure what this means.

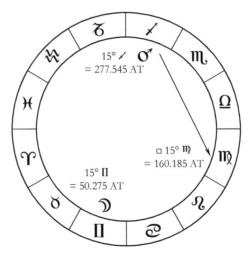

**Figure 14: Direction of the Moon to Mars's zodiacal square
(Heph. III.7, 3-4)**

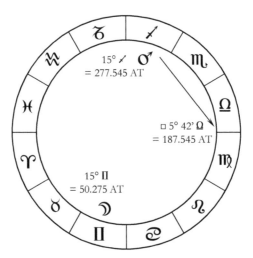

**Figure 15: Direction of the Moon to Mars's ascensional square
(Heph. III.7, 3-4)**

6 Another kind of maltreatment is when the Moon happens to make a subterraneous eclipse, and the inception and the preparation are in the midst of the upcoming assembly,[178] and the Moon at this time <is configured with

---

[178] That is, the New Moon or conjunction of the Sun and Moon (**EG**).

the malefics, or else at the time of> the Full Moon.[179] **7** For it comes to pass that, according to such an inception, there is utter destruction by earthquakes, and very unremitting damage to the cities thus born: in the triplicity of Aries, as it is fiery, [the destruction will come] from fire; in <that of> Taurus, being earth-like, one must suppose harm or aid from earth and agriculture, according to the boundaries[180] of the configurations; in the triplicity of Gemini, as it is airy by nature, [one must expect] aid or harm from the air; in the [triplicity] of Cancer, as it is watery, aid or harm from waters. **8** The builders, and those who have taken upon themselves the care for the preparation, will partake of the dignity and character, according to the nature of the rulers.

9 Dorotheus, in his verses, exhorts thus about building:

10 *On the other hand, whenever you would bring foundations, buildings, and works*
  to perfection,
additive in her phase, and to [her] numbers according to longitude,
let the Horned One be for you, advancing in latitude
towards the northern block of the belt,
while either Zeus or the Paphian are testifying by figure
or by being together;[181] *while the Shining One restrains the intent*[182]
[when] looking on, the Impetuous One stirs the flames around.

[Tearing down buildings]

11 One must pull down walls when <the Moon> has descended from the northern heights;[183] one must remove[184] a stone from foundations when [the

---

[179] This sentence appears to be describing two different thoughts, but I think what Hephaistion means is this: if the inception happens while (a) the Sun is being eclipsed in the fourth, or (b) the Moon is being eclipsed, and *she* is in the fourth, while either of these eclipses is being harmed by the malefics. According to this reading, the Moon will be in the fourth in either case.

[180] *Horous.* This seems to mean that the planetary lord of the bound in which the eclipse happens, will further specify what kinds of beings will be affected.

[181] That is, a bodily conjunction. But this might also simply include being in the same sign as the Moon.

[182] I take this to mean that when Saturn slows down the process and keeps it from moving forward.

[183] Here and below, "northern" and "southern" must refer to ecliptical latitude, just as with Dorotheus in the verses above.

[184] *Anenekteon*, from *anapherō*: bring up, raise up, lead up, carry back, restore (**EG**).

Moon] is in the parts closest to the ground, namely, in the southern end. **12**
<In all these cases, let the malefics be away, and the benefics ones give tes-
timony.>[185]

[Consecrating statues]

13 Within[186] the shrine [of the temples],[187] one must consecrate the statues prepared with the suitable image, also equally of wood,[188] when the
Moon is full in phase,[189] just as the wise Egyptians and the remaining ancients have handed down;[190] the powers [of the images][191] thus perfected,
very godlike[192] and infused with life, are brought to fulfillment from the
cosmic[193] motion.[194] **14** Build and dedicate each of the sacred objects and
statues when the Moon is suitably posited in the triangle of Jupiter, and when
this star is in harmony with her, that is to say, in the same triangle; and let
also the Sun be configured similarly, and let Saturn chance to be posited alike
in the same triangle.[195] **15** With regard to the remaining stars, the statues and
sacred images are to be built this way: it is auspicious to prepare them when
they are still in their own exaltations and houses, and none of the malefic
stars is opposed.

---

[185] Added by Pingree from two of the Epitomes.

[186] For consecrating statues, my feeling is that Hephaistion's source is using constellations
and not the tropical signs. For more on this, see Jiménez 2007.

[187] *Naos*, or the innermost and most sacred sanctuary of the temples, where the statues
and images of the gods are kept (**EG**).

[188] A rehearsal copy in wood (**EG**)?

[189] Or, full in "appearance" (*phasis*): that is, a Full Moon.

[190] See for example the references to consecrating statues in the Latin *Asclepius* (Copenhaver, p. 81).

[191] *Autōn*. If this referred to the Egyptians, one would read: "The powers of those thus
initiated into the Mysteries" (another meaning for *telesthentōn*) (**EG**).

[192] A tentative translation of *theōdesterai*, a comparative adjective (**EG**).

[193] *Kosmikēs*.

[194] The last part of this sentence sounds rather poetic and may be based on Dorotheus or
some other poetic source—perhaps an Egyptian one?

[195] Based on the next sentence, Hephaistion seems to be speaking here of consecrating
statues to the Sun and Moon themselves. In that case, he seems to mean that for the
Moon, both she and Jupiter should be in the fiery triplicity; but for the Sun, he and Saturn
should both be in the fiery triplicity. I say "the fiery triplicity," because Hephaistion
speaks both of the Moon being in the triangle of Jupiter, and that he should be in the
same triangle as her—which suggests that they should both be in fiery signs, since that is
the very triplicity which Jupiter rules. Both Saturn and Jupiter (who are trining the luminaries here) rule the fiery triplicity, a fitting one for consecrating statues to the luminaries.

16 It[196] is necessary to hallow [the Goddess] Fortune when the Moon is in her own triangle and that of Venus,[197] and well posited in Capricorn or in Cancer;

The Mother of the gods[198] in Leo, Taurus, and Capricorn;

Demeter, Korē,[199] and Pluto, in Virgo and Taurus;

Osiris in Pisces, Aquarius, and Taurus;

Victory in Virgo and Cancer;

Serapis in Taurus, Leo, and Sagittarius;

Asclepios and Hygeia in Sagittarius and Pisces;

Dionysos, in Virgo and Capricorn;

Heracles, in Gemini and Leo;

Eros and the Graces in the signs or exaltations of Venus;

Nemesis, in those of Saturn.

17 Similarly with respect to the remaining gods, one ought to make the statues, or images, or figures in relief on seals, finish each of them off, and suitably renew them, when the Moon is in the aforementioned signs.

[Ritual petitions]

18 The approaches and vows[200] are known in the following way: the Hour-marker is the petitioner; the setting, the sacrifice offered; the Midheaven, the god; the underground pivot indicates whether the prayers would be given ears to, and the matter that the prayer or inquiry[201] is about.

---

[196] Because this is a complicated list, I have put each of the gods and goddesses on their own line, for easier comprehension. Please note that these are *not* (so far as I know) versus of Dorotheus.

[197] This must be the earthy triplicity.

[198] Perhaps the goddess Magna Mater?

[199] Persephone (**EG**).

[200] Or, "prayers" (*euchai*): see the next chapter (**EG**).

[201] *Punthanetai*, referring to the *ritual* request for knowledge, for which the client wants an inception chart to be cast.

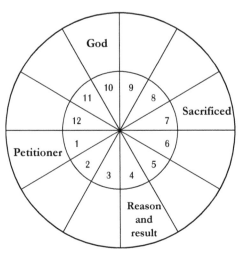

Figure 16: Angles for a ritual petition (Heph. III.7, 18)

<Chapter III.8:> The manner it is required to make an oath[202]

1 The witnesses of an oath[203] pursue the perjurers when someone swears falsely with the Moon in Scorpio, and Mars is with her or seeing from the opposite side;[204] also with the Sun setting in Libra, especially when the oath is about what is lawful.[205] **2** When the Sun, fittingly placed, sets in the remaining signs, make the oath: for then those swearing falsely are not pursued like an avenging fury.[206]

---

[202] Chapter 8 might have been placed here because it immediately follows the previous topic (ritual prayers and petitions).

[203] *Horkoi.* I take this to mean the gods themselves, or the power on/by which one swears the oath.

[204] *Hupenantion.*

[205] *Dikaios.* Or, "just, fair."

[206] *Poinēlatountai.* Or perhaps, actually pursued by the Furies.

<Chapter III.9:> On marriage

1 Concerning marriage, one must investigate in the following manner:

The man, by Helios and the rising Marker of the Hour,
The maiden herself, lovely in spirit, by the setting seventh[207] sign
and by Kythereia of lovely hair,[208] would be indicated.
From the Midheaven, which has turned far from the earth,
[see] how they will both complete life with each other.
For the sake of the dowry, the midmost of the earth will be made known.
2 *Some assign lucky things, some evil ones, to the onlooker:[209]*
Helios disabled by the evil ones, and the Foam-born One [having]
Zeus rushing on hostile or else coming close by her side,
Brings misery to the man, though great delight to the woman.
On the contrary, when the Plague of Mortals, or the Shining One (ice-cold)
sees the Paphian, this is a deadly sign for the wife:
there will be shame, and they will not stay [together] for a long time;
and if also Mēnē prevails over a hateful sign,[210]
this inception would for both ill-omened be.
3 *Moreover, the fortunate ones beholding the swift-begotten of Maia,[211]*
hold a true token of children. **4** *Yet in a tropical*
being,[212] let not Kypris nor Selēnē ever be:
Kypris makes most lustful and filthy wives,
and will lay the pleasing woman on stolen beds;[213]
[while] Selēnē would grant no lasting marriage-bed.
5 *For this reason, when she is in the Ram, refuse marriage*
altogether: for indeed it would quickly be dissolved.

---

[207] Reading for Pingree's "ninth," with the rest of the tradition (including the Arabic *Carmen*) and Hephaistion MS **P**. According to Pingree, **P** has "*7th*" written in the margin. At any rate, the adjective *duomenoio* ("setting") clearly points to the seventh sign (**EG**).

[208] "Lovely-haired" (*eukomos*) is a common epithet for Aphrodite (**EG**).

[209] That is, an aspecting planet.

[210] *Stugeron peri sēma genētai.* **EG:** This literally means that the Moon "remains above" or "prevails over" a hateful "sign/omen" or "constellation." **BD:** It probably means simply that she is in a bad house or otherwise has malefic indications.

[211] That is, Mercury (**EG**).

[212] *Zōiōi.* That is, one of the signs (*signs*), which are normally living animals or beings (**EG**).

[213] That is, illicit beds: she will sleep with many men (**EG**).

6 The[214] first and third decan of Taurus refuses [marriage], the second one is fitting for marrying. **7** In Gemini, the degrees from the first through the fifteenth do not bring about [marriage], but the remaining degrees are well-disposed. **8** Cancer as a whole is inauspicious. **9** Leo is not bad, though it makes the man badly lavish. **10** In Virgo, it is auspicious to marry a widow, but not a maid. **11** In Libra, it is unfitting to marry, but auspicious for being courted. **12** In the first section of Scorpio, auspicious; in the second one not quite, as they will not last long. **13** In Sagittarius, it is necessary to keep watch because of a scarcity of children, and similarly in Capricorn, except when one wishes to get married [with the Moon] in the second and the third [decans] (for in this case one must not turn away), but [with the Moon in the first decan][215] roving people and liars will be found. **14** In Aquarius, it is unfitting [to marry]. **15** In Pisces it is fine to marry, but it makes the woman warlike and a silly talker.

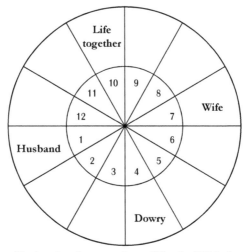

Figure 17: Angles for marriage (Heph. III.9, 1 and 38)

---

[214] Some of the positions in this paragraph seem to be fifteenth-parts (see Introduction), while others are faces or decans; but I cannot see a consistent rationale for recommending or prohibiting marriage in them.
[215] Adding based on the Arabic *Carmen* (**EG**)

[Instruction on Venus]

16 Above all in these inquiries, one must observe that Venus should not be with the malefics nor in their testimonies, but rather in the bounds or in the sign of an effective[216] one. **17** For when Venus happens to be in the bounds or the signs of a benefic, and decimates[217] the Moon, being in turn decimated by Jupiter (that is to say, [with Venus occupying] the tenth from the Moon, and the fourth from Jupiter), it foretells the happiest, heart-pleasing, and child-begetting marriage, especially when one of the benefics chances to be in signs abounding in seed: for thus it will produce the quickest pregnancy. **18** The same also will be brought about by a triangular figure, when the signs are abounding in seed; and the malefics in a triangular figure from signs abounding in seed, testified to by benefics, also show childbearing.

19 Besides, one ought to examine the charts of both marriage partners, to see whether the benefics altogether are in, or are configured with, the benefic places (that is to say, doubly) at the time of the wedding.[218] **20** But if the Midheaven were arranged[219] both according to the nativity and according to transit,[220] and the place of the benefics in the chart of the woman fell on the man's Midheaven, one must know that there would be child-begetting within the same year, and the companionship will be prolonged and well-pleasing, and especially when the important[221] places of the nativities (which are the Moon, the Sun, the Lot [of Fortune], and the Hour-marker) are truly harmonious.[222] **21** If the sign at the peak[223] is also abounding in seed, the

---

[216] *Euergeos.* **EG**: Lit. "working well," but also "well-wrought, easy, effective." **BD**: This must be a benefic: see the next sentence.

[217] *Epidekateuō.* That is, making a superior square from the tenth sign from it (**EG**).

[218] This seems to mean, "in or configured with good places *in both nativities* at the time of the wedding": for instance, if Jupiter were in or aspecting the eleventh house of both natal charts. Chris Brennan suggests that it might rather mean the places in which benefics were *located.*

[219] *Kosmoumenos.*

[220] This is ambiguous. Gramaglia suggests that it means that the Midheaven of the inception is on the Midheaven of the nativity. But it seems more likely to me that Dorotheus means that the nativities and the inception, and the relation between them, is suitably adorned and arranged (*kosmoumenos*) as in the previous sentence. 'Umar's *Carmen* (V.16, **25**) combines **19-20** together, saying that one of the benefics is in the Midheaven of both (which does not make sense).

[221] *Epikairos.* This can also mean "fitting, opportune, advantageous."

[222] *Huparchōsin.* Among other things, this verb means "to exist really, truly"; perhaps it could be understand as being harmonious "by nature" (**EG**).

conception will safely occur the first time they come together. **22** And if a benefic chanced to be on the place at the peak, being [in addition] under the rays at the time of the wedding, it means that the pregnancy and child-begetting will be obscure,[224] particularly for those women who have such a chart as [their] lot; even when Venus is under the rays with Mars, they secret-ly lead a maiden's life,[225] and if Jupiter is testifying, the forced ones[226] are led toward marriage.[227] **23** However, it similarly happens at the time of the incep-tion also when Venus is setting with respect to the Sun.[228]

24 *If[229] anyone—husband or wife—has Mēnē in the animal*
that occupies the place of the Bad Spirit of the other,
That one will wield the strength over both: the one who has
Selēnē by the twelfth region from the Hour-divider
In the nativity of the other, like a master will be.[230]
25 *Towering over him, once and again, at the fullness of the month,[231] troublesome*
she will be to the husband,

—namely, the time of the Full Moon. **26** Moreover, the Moons of the two nativities, when they oppose each other, are ill-omened, in that they are the cause of discord. **27** On the other hand, the one having the Moon above earth will equally prevail, in the love of victory.[232] **28** Venus in a masculine [sign], and Jupiter in a feminine one—this figure is good for men; the contra-ry [is so] for women:[233] when Venus is in a feminine [sign], and Jupiter in a

---

[223] *Koruphē.* That is, the Midheaven (**EG**).
[224] *Skoteinēn.*
[225] *Lathraiōs partheneuontai.* This seems to mean that while they appear to want children and have a healthy sex life, behind closed doors it is a different story.
[226] This suggests a forced or arranged marriage. Jupiter can show family relations, or per-haps a forced marriage for the sake of social respectability.
[227] Note that Jupiter has more to do with social institutions and respectability, while Ve-nus herself indicates personal, emotional states.
[228] That is, simply going under the rays (**EG**).
[229] See also *Excerpt* XVII, **3**.
[230] Here Dorotheus seems to be repeating himself—or at least, clarifying. The partner whose Moon is in the twelfth of the other person—also known as the house of the Bad Spirit—will be in charge. For similar statements in relation to friendship, see Excerpt XVII, **3**.
[231] *Pammēnos.* **EG:** This the Full Moon, as Hephaistion clarifies below. **BD:** This seems to mean that marriages at Full Moons lead to the dominance (or independence?) of the wife. See also *Excerpt* III.
[232] *Philoneikia.*
[233] That is, "the opposite is *good for women.*"

masculine one.

29 These things Dorotheus expounds in his verses. What follows comes from what the other ancients have made trial of.

[The Lot of Fortune and the previous lunation]

30 Above all, as regards unions and getting together by marriage, one needs to pay attention to the lord of the Lot and of the Hour, and even also to [the lord] of the previous assembly, and to the disposition of figures[234] toward each other, toward the luminaries, and the death-bringing[235] star. **31** For when the Lot or its lord happens to be toward[236] the setting [pivot], or[237] the lord of the setting pivot happens to be on it with the star of the Lot, or on <the> star of the Lot, or similarly <if> it happens to be on the sign of the Lot (obviously with the star of the Lot), with the Moon bearing witness, it indicates marriage and union.

[Separations and breakups]

32 Indeed, one should guard against a morning Venus[238] being retrograde and moving towards Jupiter, for thus the marriages will be unfit and unreliable, as those coming together turn out to be of a light character.[239] **33** And if [Venus][240] chanced to be in a feminine sign, of such quality would the men be deemed to be; on the other hand, should [Venus] be in a masculine sign, of such quality [would be] the women. **34** If a separation should occur with Venus in such condition, the woman will come back again no sooner than [when] Venus has turned additive in numbers.[241] Should Mars be retrograde

---

[234] *Schēmatothesia.*

[235] *Thanatikos.* In context this must be the lord of the seventh (which does sometimes indicates enemies, threats, and death), but here used as indicating marriage.

[236] *Eis.*

[237] The three situations that follow seem to be these: that the lord of the seventh is (1) on the seventh, with the lord of the Lot; (2) either in the seventh and actually conjoined to the lord of the Lot—but perhaps simply conjoined to the lord of the Lot anywhere; (3) on the sign of the Lot, again with the lord of the Lot.

[238] That is, in a position so as to rise before the Sun in the morning, no matter where she happens to be in the chart at the moment.

[239] That is, they take things lightly and are changeable.

[240] The text does not identify which planet this is, but Venus seems more likely than Jupiter.

[241] That is, once she turns direct and moves towards the Sun.

at the inception of the separation, when Mars has turned round and become additive [in numbers], the man will change and go to seek the woman.

35 Should the lord of marriage[242] chance to culminate[243] in the inception, in a feminine sign it will prove the woman very fertile; in a masculine one, the man.

36 But when Jupiter happened to make a square to the marriage-star,[244] it is indicative of dissent in the wedlock; the Moon falling in a masculine sign is also pernicious. **37** When the lord of marriage marks the Hour, it gives a wedding that is blaming; and in particular, Jupiter in a feminine sign, one without a dowry, of feigned wealth, or brought to trial; and in a masculine one, it gives the man such qualities.

[Planets in the pivots]

38 Having said that the Hour-marker is the marrying husband, the setting [pivot] the woman taken as wife, the Midheaven the unanimity and endurance of both, [and] the subterraneous pivot the dowry and the result of the wedding—it is indeed clear that when Saturn marks the Hour, the husband will be older and dirty; Mars, younger and given to anger; Jupiter, rich and noble, middle-aged; Venus, cheerful, cleanly, of pleasant living, lewd towards women; Mercury, well-educated, intelligent, amorous toward children; the Sun and the Moon, well-born and remarkable.[245]

39 When Saturn chances to be on the Midheaven, a breaking up of the marriage will occur due to filth and stinginess; when Mars, due to instability and jealousy (when Venus is also with him, or testifying, due to adultery; when Mercury is with [Mars], due to sexual desires for a child). With Jupiter and Venus [on the Midheaven] there will be concord and child-begetting; the Sun and the Moon [culminating show that] they will be remarkable.

40 Happening to be on the setting [pivot], they show about the woman things of a similar quality as those of the man in the Hour-marker.

41 And if Mars, Saturn, or both, were found under the earth, it will be indicative of the loss of one's own children and of the dowry, and a premature death of the husband; but if Jupiter and Venus were subterraneous, they will spend a long time with each other, and there will be children; and should

---

[242] Again, probably the lord of the seventh.
[243] Lit., "be at mid-heaven" (*mesouranōn*).
[244] Again, probably the lord of the seventh.
[245] *Episēmos.* Or, "significant."

they be in a masculine sign, the man will outlive the wife; if in a feminine one, the woman the husband. Mercury in turn exhibits all qualities in the way that the testimony from the other stars is received.

[Other rules]

42 When the Sun is maltreated, and Venus is testified to by a benefic in the inception, one must indicate that the woman rules the man; contrariwise with the reverse situation. **43** If the Moon is maltreated, it is prejudicial for both, and for the dowry.

44 The Hour-marker and the Midheaven having benefics indicate child-begetting, [and it is] suitable; but if malefics, loss.

45 One should also avoid taking a wife for oneself when the lord of Fortune is maltreated. **46** Also difficult is when the bridal star is in such a condition in the nativity.

47 The Moon being void in course indicates promiscuous [people], but it is good when under the earth in a feminine sign; the Sun being in a masculine one makes her submissive.

<Chapter III.10:> On coming together

1 Let the marrying husband who is about to come together with his wife be merry, and let him not be excessively weighed down by food and strong drinks because of merriness and lack of sorrow. **2** Keep watch over the Sun, the Moon, and the Lot to make sure they are neither in the eighth place nor in its diameter; also observe carefully that the lord of the Hour is unharmed. **3** Let the Lot be in [the place] of friendship, or in that of children, or on the Midheaven, or in [the place] of God (that is to say, the ninth). Besides, let the Moon be unharmed and harmonious to the Hour-marker. **4** Mercury happening to be on the east, testified to by Jupiter and Venus, at the moment of the foundation,[246] makes the progeny fortunate,[247] well-educated, and happy.[248]

---

[246] *Katabolēs.* I take this to be the inception chart.
[247] *Eutyches*, lit. "of good luck" or "of good Fortune" (**EG**).
[248] *Eudaimon*, lit. "blessed with a good Genius or spirit" (**EG**).

5 Those around Petosiris[249] say that the sign in which the Moon is found at the time of the conception, will mark the Hour at childbirth; and where [the Moon] is transiting during childbirth, that [sign] marked the Hour at conception. 6 Let this much be said about marriage and things related to it.

<Chapter III.11:> On separations [of spouses]

1 Their separations and returns are to be examined in the following manner. 2 <In> the inception[250] in which the separation occurs, or else at the time that someone inquires from you,[251] look at Venus and the Sun: accordingly, if you found the Sun on the Midheaven or in the eleventh, and Venus an evening [planet], retrograde,[252] tell him that his woman will return to him in a heart-pleasing way.

3 *Should the bed-partner abandon the man's house*
When Mēnē passes through a diameter of Helios,
Not very easily she will come to the house of the man.
When she turns from her fullness and goes toward Helios,
At this time foretell the returns will take place,

…but with difficulty, at the time of her assembly.[253] 4 If the Sun—in [the time in] which the Moon, having passed over, completes the circle—were found in another, feminine sign, while Venus is with him, the man will marry another woman once the wedlock is dissolved.[254]

5 One must also watch for the Hour-marker and the Moon: if these happen to be in fixed signs in the inception, they produce steady things; if in bicorporeal [signs], things like that;[255] and in tropical signs, unstable things liable to change.

---

[249] What follows is a version of the so-called "Trutine of Hermes." See Appendix C in my *Persian Nativities II*, which explains it in detail.
[250] *Katarchē*. Or simply, "beginning": that is, "at the moment of the separation" (**EG**).
[251] See my Introduction §4 for a discussion of this passage.
[252] That is, in a later sign and degree than the Sun, retrograding toward him.
[253] That is, the conjunction at the New Moon.
[254] That is, he will find another woman, symbolized by Venus.
[255] That is, having two aspects or parts, doubled or repetitive, *etc.*

<Chapter III.12:> On the removal[256] of fetuses

1 When the women have the fetus[257] in the womb, and wish to attempt to procure an abortion[258] when they are incapable of bearing completed[259] offspring, it is fitting [to do it] when the Moon is in straight signs and on the Hour-marker, diminishing in light and southern in latitude. Besides that, observe that both Mars and Venus are with, or looking upon, the Moon, from a square or triangle, and let the Moon fall into a feminine sign. **2** <In these matters, as much as it is necessary to closely watch the Moon, one must as well have the Hour-marker placed in straight signs and under the testimony of Mars and Venus.>[260]

<Chapter III.13:> On those who attempt to procure abortion

1 They say that it is dangerous to attempt an abortion when the Moon or the Hour-marker—especially when Saturn is configured—is found within the following degrees:[261] of Aries, from the 1st through the 11th degree; of Gemini, from the 1st through the 30th; of Cancer, from the 1st through the 15th; of Leo, from the 1st through the 11th; of Virgo, all degrees; in Libra, from the 11th through the 30th; in Scorpio, from the 11th through the 30th; in Sagittarius, from the 1st through the 11th; in Capricorn, from the 1st through the 15th; in Aquarius, from the 20th through the 30th; the remaining degrees are easy and without danger.

---

256 *Diapherō.*

257 *Kuoumenon,* lit. "the one carried or born in the womb" (**EG**).

258 *Ektitrōskō* (here and below), "to bring forth untimely" (**EG**).

259 That is, physically complete in its growth.

260 Added by Pingree from three of the Epitomes.

261 Currently I do not know the rationale for these degrees. They are not exactly the decans or faces because some of them go to 15°; and even the decanic portions are not restricted to those ruled by malefics.

<Chapter III.14:> On farming[262]

1 As regards farming, when the Moon herself[263] is in Aries, it is fitting to till the land, to establish[264] nursling [animals], plant trees, <sow or reclaim wild places; in Taurus>,[265] to sow on fallow ground, but it is unsuitable to farm out land; in Gemini, to till and plant, work fallow ground, and gather fruits; in Cancer it is good to till the land, make gardens, and reclaim dry lands; in Leo it is favorable to sow wheat and barley, and to begin with the tillage; in Virgo it is harmonious to plant (except grapevines), and to sow [on lands] altogether subject to tribute; in Libra it is suitable to plant and till the land; in Scorpio, to plant grapevines, and only partially till the land; in Sagittarius, to establish places for horse-breeding, nursling [animals], and herds of cattle; similarly in Capricorn, mainly nurslings; in Aquarius it is fitting to plant fruit-trees and till the land; in Pisces it is good for tillage and to renew the beginning.[266]

2 When the Moon is together with the benefics or configured with them, and also in harmonious signs, it is best for tillage, especially if she chances to be in subterraneous places.

<Chapter III.15:> On the digging-up of wells and ponds

1 On digging up ponds or making channels for bringing in water, take a close look at the Lot of Fortune and its lord, to make sure they fall into any of the watery signs, and make the rulers of the second and the eighth places pivotal. **2** For it is good that these post-ascend the pivot above the earth[267] and the one underground,[268] because they are of no account when declining, especially when the waters come from afar, or they are transferred from one place to another, or diverted. **3** Besides, it is necessary to closely watch the lord of the Lot, especially when it is underground, to ensure that neither it nor the Lot itself are in the post-descension [of the western pivot], nor in its

---

[262] *Geōrgia*. This can refer to farming generally, or tilling in particular.

[263] *Kath'heautēn*. Or, "in her own right," *etc.* I am not sure why Hephaistion is emphasizing this.

[264] *Kathistanai*. See below, where Hephaistion talks about establishing *places for* animals.

[265] Added by Pingree from Epitome IV.

[266] *Archē*. Unclear, but Gramaglia suggests "cycle."

[267] That is, the eleventh.

[268] That is, the fifth.

diameter (that is to say, the post-ascension of the Hour-marker).[269] These conditions having been observed, the work would be accomplished without harm and assured from danger.

<Chapter III.16:> On purchases of different kinds

1 Examine[270] the inception like this. **2** One must take the Hour-marker to indicate the seller, the setting pivot the buyer, the Midheaven the price, the underground pivot the purchased commodity;[271] from the stars bearing witness to the places, one must make an inference about the result.

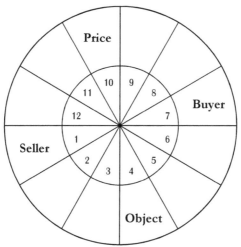

Figure 18: Angles for selling (Heph. III.16, 2)

3 On the subject of purchasing, there is still another way: to assign the Moon to the sold slave, property, or any other commodity; the star from which the Moon is flowing away, to the one who sells; [the star with which the Moon] connects, to the one who buys. Besides all these things, also pay

---

[269] Namely, in the eighth and second, respectively.

[270] For **1-3**, see also *Excerpt* LXII and *Frag.* V.9, **1-7**.

[271] **EG:** The Arabic *Carmen* (V.9, **6**) reverses the Ascendant and seventh here, making the Ascendant indicate the buyer and the seventh the seller. **BD:** But "Dorotheus" in the *Nine Judges* §7.59 agrees with Hephaistion. In practice the difference is probably negligible, since the Ascendant indicates the client who wants to undertake the business, whether he is buying or selling.

attention to the testimonies.

4 From the Moon, one must consider whether the one who sells is harmed or not. **5** Generally, when the Moon herself[272] is in Aries, the purchased household slave[273] is a runaway and a wanderer; in Taurus, strong and enduring; the purchased slaves are beautiful when found [with the Moon] in the third decan of Gemini; in Cancer, sluggish and deceitful; in Leo, highborn, rapacious and greedy, but with a sensitive stomach; in Virgo, it indicates an intelligent slave; in Libra, industrious and civilized;[274] in Scorpio, strong, of deceitful character, and sullen; similarly in Sagittarius; in Capricorn, untrustworthy and a liar; in Aquarius, industrious; in Pisces, evil and abusive.

6 Whenever the Lot of Fortune falls into the place of friendship, and its lord is found in the place of household slaves with the star ruling the Hourmarker, they give indications for the purchase of a household slave. **7** And should the Moon make a connection with the lord of marriage,[275] with Venus being placed on what belongs to marriage,[276] it means coming together or partaking of friendship with the purchased male or female [household slave]; but should Mercury happen to be on the Lot, it makes [him] well-educated. **8** One always ought to make a purchase of household slaves when Mercury is unharmed by the malefics or under the rays.

9 For the purchase of land, let the underground [sign] be the ground; if it is a watery sign, one must conclude that the land is near a river, or sea, or lake; if amphibious, that it combines the mixed and twofold features from mountains and plains. [Let] the setting [sign be] the cattle and store[277] of the property; the Midheaven the trees, plants and farm buildings; the Hourmarker the dwelling-place, what the house contains, and the works carried out;[278] and the one among these found unharmed, or maltreated, gives information on that allotment. **10** The rising of the Hour-marker indicates the extent [of the land]: for as many degrees as it adds up, it reveals so many landmarks[279] and stades[280] [that the parcel of land has].

---

[272] *Kath'heauten*, as with Ch. III.14, **1**.

[273] *Oiketēs*, here and below.

[274] *Dikaios*. Or, "just," "lawful" (**EG**).

[275] This seems to be the lord of the seventh.

[276] *Tou gamikou*. This seems to be the seventh itself. But the next sentence has Mercury on the Lot of Fortune, which suggests that perhaps this means "what belongs to *Fortune*," i.e., the Lot of Fortune.

[277] That is, stored crops and capital.

[278] *Ergazomenous*. Or, "buildings made" (**EG**).

[279] *Sēmeion*, lit. "sign." Here, the boundaries or limits of the parcel of land.

11 When the Moon is full, additive in longitude and latitude, on the ascending Node, the buyer in the market will pay a higher price; but when she is waning, subtractive in numbers, and on the descending Node, the buyer will pay a smaller price. **12** For thus speaks Dorotheus:[281]

13 *When Selēnē passes by the up-leading Node,*[282]
if, full of light, she also increases her course in numbers,
[for] whatever you buy, you will give more than what you need to give.[283]
But going on the down-leading paths, on which she decreases,[284]
going towards less, easy[285] *will the purchase be.*
14 *And they say that if you look upon when Selēnē comes out*
from the assembly, and first enters the four-sided figure[286]
of the fiery-looking Helios, better will it be for fairer [dealings]:
for you will pay money for something worth buying,
and a more agreeable deed is to offer neither too inferior a price
nor a much too superfluous amount. **15** *Until she into the diameter*
moves, it will suit the one who sells or demands payment.
16 *Again, when the quick-glancing one*[287] *goes into the third side of the square,*[288]
then it is good to buy—or steal[289]*—whatever one desires.*
17 *The Goddess being on the fourth side and moving towards the assembly,*[290]
if you give little from much,[291] *better will this be for you.*

---

[280] An ancient stade was 600 Greek feet or 606 3/4 English feet, about 1/8 of a Roman mile. A longer stade, of which there were 7 1/2 in a Roman mile, is implied by Dio Cassius. See Liddell & Scott, p. 1631 (**EG**).

[281] Compare this with the Arabic version, in *Astrology of the World I* (Section II.2).

[282] That is, the north Node.

[283] That is, one must pay more than the object is worth.

[284] That is, decreasing in latitude toward or around the south Node—reading *elēxa* with MS L, which was corrected by Kroll and adopted by Pingree as *elexa*. But this would mean, "the down-leading paths which she chose" (**EG**).

[285] *Elaphrē.* That is, inexpensive.

[286] Between coming out of the rays and the first quarter of the Moon.

[287] The Moon.

[288] Between the Full Moon and her third quarter.

[289] *Diaklepsai.*

[290] Between the third quarter and the New Moon.

[291] *Baion an ek pollou doiēs.* That is, if you give little money for something which should cost much. In other words, the price will be low (**EG**).

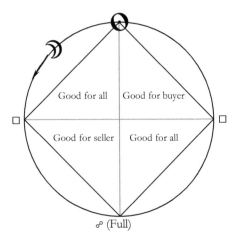

Figure 19: Phases of Moon for buying (Heph. III.16, 14-17)

<Chapter III.17:> On ship-building [and purchasing]

1 With regard to the purchase or building of ships, one must assign the stern to the rising [pivot], the mast <and> the things in the middle to the Midheaven, the prow to the setting [pivot],[292] the keel and things around it to the underground. According to [the pivot] on which the malefics were found (the disposition [of the stars] having been established),[293] in that part one must conclude that the ship would be damaged.

2 It is also necessary to look out for the benefics, to make sure they are on the underground pivot or testifying to that place. Let the underground pivot be in signs which are able to swim: Taurus, Gemini, Cancer, Virgo, Sagittarius, Pisces, and Capricorn, in the extreme[294] degrees (Taurus being the strongest one, with it Pisces, then Gemini). **3** Take also the Sun in a triangle with the Hour, the Moon increasing in light, computation, and latitude, and testified to by benefics; but keep watch [to prevent] the malefics from hurling rays at the Moon or the Sun, or being together with them.

---

[292] This must be because the seventh signifies the destination of a journey (Ch. III.30, **1**; *Excerpt* IX, **1**).
[293] That is, the inception chart.
[294] That is, the last degrees.

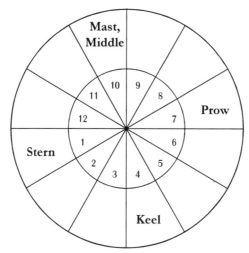

Figure 20: Angles for ships (Heph. III.17, 1)

<Chapter III.18:> On the purchase of horses

1 Regarding the purchase of horses, consider that Aries is the head, Libra the rear parts, and the remaining signs the parts on each side: where you find the malefic stars, there one must consider that the cause[295] and the injury of the horse [are to be found].

<Chapter III.19:> On the purchase of cattle

1 As regards the purchase of previously-tamed animals, it is fine and helpful to buy them when the Moon and the Hour are in Aries and Taurus. As for those animals which lack taming and subjection, let the Moon and the Hour be in Leo and in the last fifteen degrees of Sagittarius.

---

[295] *Aitia.*

\<Chapter III.20:\> On the way one should meet with the ruler or king

1 It is harmonious to meet with rulers when the Moon is in Aries, Taurus, Gemini, Virgo, Libra (especially when you have some legal[296] matter or demand[297] money), in Scorpio, Sagittarius, and Capricorn. Indeed, if the benefics look upon[298] the Moon, and she is unharmed, [it is also harmonious] to raise petitions as long as she is in Leo, Aquarius, and Pisces. **2** Due to the ambiguity[299] of Sagittarius, it will be fitting to make petitions about matters directed toward an accusation, but what pertains to the request for a favor will be of no avail.

3 If you also examine the nativities of those whom you desire to meet with,[300]

and, on turning in a circle from the Hour,[301]

posited in any sign for a year, when in that [sign] he has Selēnē,[302]

whomever you meet with, him you will much regard with affection.

4 *If for both [people] the year equally fell into one harmonious place,*

the same it would be on signs that hear or see,[303]

but let the number[304] *of the eclipse not pass*

through the sign of friendship[305] *at that time.*

---

[296] *Dikaion.*

[297] *Apaiteō.* More specifically, this refers to demanding something *back* (such as things rightfully belonging to one) (**EG**).

[298] *Epiblepō.*

[299] *Amphibolon.* This adjective especially means for something to be thrown around or attacked on both sides. Hephaistion seems to be referring to the double-bodied nature of Sagittarius as being both a horse and a man.

[300] In Excerpt XIX, **1**, this is about making friends, not just meeting with someone.

[301] This refers to the profection of the Ascendant.

[302] That is, if the client's profected Ascendant falls on the other person's natal Moon. See also *Excerpt* XIX, **4**.

[303] This seems to mean, "If both people's profections fell on signs which hear or see each other." See my Introduction for these signs.

[304] *Arithmos.* According to Kroll, this means "degree" (**EG**).

[305] **EG:** Kroll's own edition (*CCAG* VI, p. 107 ll. 19-21) reads differently: that "the number [sc. degree] of the eclipse does not transit the sign of Kronos and the Paphian" (Saturn and Venus). **BD:** Kroll's notes to these lines express his doubts (*dubitans*) about his own changes, and suggest that his Kronos (Saturn) might be *chronō* (referring to the time lord, the lord of the year) and his "sign of the Paphian" might be "Lot of friendship." In that case, we would not want an eclipse to occur in some important relationship to the lord of the year or the two people's Lots of friendship. According to *Excerpt* XVI, **6**, the Lot of friendship is taken from the Moon to Mercury, and projected from the Ascendant; it does not give instructions for reversal by night.

5 *Even*[306] *when you are about to need a start of friendship,*
let first the luminaries be readily combining with each other,
and the good ones be their witnesses, but let the ruinous ones
be turned away: for very evil indeed
Arēs and Helios would be when opposed or in square,
but also when Phainōn the bright-orbed Mēnē
in the same way beholds. **6** *Better when stars become*
dark, having been granted as [their] lot glorious positions,
they rejoice in their sects.[307]

7 You[308] should also make the stars fit with the people: the military kind to Mars, the ruling and kingly kind to Jupiter, the elder kind to Saturn, the feminine to Venus, the thinking to Mercury.

<Chapter III.21:> On the freeing [of slaves]

1 Let the one inquiring about freeing [slaves] assign the Hour-marker to the one who frees,[309] the setting pivot to the freed one, the Midheaven indicates in the presence of whom[310] the liberation would take place, the underground [pivot] will indicate of what sort the obligation to continue in service[311] and gratitude[312] will be.

2 <Someone could examine [this matter] with more certainty in the fol-

---

[306] See *Excerpt* XIX, **1**.

[307] *Ameinon epei ke pelioen asteres orphnaioi thesias lelachontes agauas, <hai> resiessi ganuntai.* This is a difficult sentence. Dorotheus is contrasting this situation of glorious positions, with the previous situation of the luminaries being harmed by planets of the opposite sect. But it is unclear exactly what he is envisioning. It could simply mean that *if* this situation cannot be avoided, the malefics should at least be in some kind of sect-related rejoicing condition: for example, putting Mars below the horizon in a diurnal chart and above it in a nocturnal one; or Saturn above it in a nocturnal chart, and above it in a diurnal one.

[308] See the slightly different lists in *Excerpt* XVI, and XIX, **2-3**.

[309] This and the next version of the angles are based on two different conceptions of what the undertaking is, or perhaps who the client is. The first (**1**) is the election of the master, while the second (**2-3**) is the beginning of the slave's new life.

[310] *Par'ō.* This might simply mean "where the liberation takes place," or "in the house of whom" (**EG**).

[311] In the Hellenistic era, freed slaves were frequently obliged to perform certain services for their former masters.

[312] A slave could be manumitted as a gesture of gratitude: for instance after long years of service (**EG**).

lowing way: by picking out the Hour-marker as the freed slave>;[313] from the lord of the sign <which marks the Hour> and from the configurations to it will be understood of what sort he would chance to be. Should it happen to be arising,[314] he will be sent forth with unconditional freedom, and his liberation will bear fruit; if setting,[315] there will be some foolery and dishonest prosecution.[316] **3** The Midheaven will disclose the place in which he would establish [himself]; the setting [pivot], the one who frees (of what kind he is, from the lord of the sign); the underground, the results of the liberation, clearly according to the observations of the stars. **4** When the lord of the Hour-marker opposes the setting [lord],[317] the one who has freed, and the freed one, will become opponents and enemies.

5 There is also a need to watch the Moon at the beginning, to ensure she is unharmed and connecting to good ones; when she comes to be in the opposite [condition], slavery will be much better than freedom, as Dorotheus says in [his] verses:

Slavery might become better than freedom.

6 And one must see the hemisphere above earth, and the one underground: for the [stars] above earth will indicate what comes after the liberation; the ones under earth the things in [the course of] it. **7** And should any of the benefics be in the hemisphere above the earth, the prognosis on what comes after the freeing and the length of life, are all favorable.

8 *But Mēnē with them on the setting [pivot], having a destructive one,[318]*
would quickly and utterly destroy, having fled the day of slavery,

...that is, the Moon turning out to be thus, destroys straightway what comes after the liberation.

---

[313] Pingree has added this from Epitomes II and IV.

[314] *Anatolikos.* Or, "eastern." This probably refers to being outside the rays, or else in the process of coming out of them.

[315] *Dutikos.* Or, "sinking." This probably refers to sinking under and being hidden by the Sun's rays.

[316] *Sukophantia.* Or, false accusations or blackmail.

[317] That is, "the lord of the seventh" (the setting place).

[318] This seems to mean, "if malefics are also in the setting place." The Arabic *Carmen* (V.13, **7**) does not have the Moon with the benefics as well (as the verse seems to suggest), but only with the malefics—certainly, the Arabic makes more astrological sense to me.

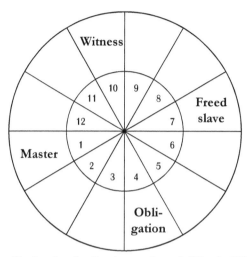

Figure 21: Angles for freeing a slave 1 (Heph. III.21, 1)

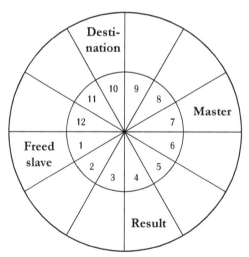

Figure 22: Angles for freeing a slave 2 (Heph. III.21, 2-3)

\<Chapter III.22:\> On games and public spectacles

1 In inceptions of games[319] and public spectacles[320] one must assign the Hour-marker to the stage-building,[321] the Midheaven to the god, hero, or king to whom the games are consecrated, the setting [pivot] to the one celebrating[322] the games or spectacles, the underground to the performers.[323]

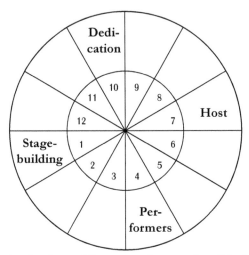

Figure 23: Angles for public games/spectacles (Heph. III.22, 1)

\<Chapter III.23:\> On effective hours and dreams[324]

1 As regards the effective hours for everything put to one's hands, especially that which is prophetic, it is necessary to observe the ruler of the

---

[319] *Agōn.* That is, the assembly of the Greeks for the national games: thus it refers to athletic competitions such as the Olympics (**EG**).

[320] *Theōria.* Also, "contemplation." This must therefore refer to being a spectator at the theater or games, or simply games themselves considered as a spectacle (**EG**).

[321] *Skēnē.* In 465 BC, the playwrights began using a backdrop or scenic wall (*skēnē*, thus the English "scene") behind the orchestra, which also served as an area for costume changes (**EG**).

[322] Or, "the one who orders" the games (**EG**).

[323] *Akroama.* Or lecturer, singer, player; it can also refer to anything heard, recited, played, *etc.* (**EG**).

[324] This inception seems to refer to choosing times for consulting oracles (in the first paragraph) and for getting legal advice (second paragraph). But perhaps the second paragraph also has to do with going to an oracle for advice on property.

God,[325] aiming at not having it fall in the place of the Bad Spirit, nor on the setting [pivot], nor opposing the Moon or her ruler: for when these configurations take place, the prophecies will be contrary, false, and full of fears.

2 For those who inquire about inheritance or property entrusted, one must closely watch the ruler of the God, to make sure it does not chance to be opposed to the lord of the Lot, nor to the Lot itself: for being so, it would show things contrary to this inquiry.

<Chapter III.24:> On which days of the Moon the dreams are true

1 As regards the affairs of those who seek for the future with hope, the end would turn to good fortune when, once the Lot of Fortune is comprehended, the lord is found pivotal, in its own sign, and the luminaries are richly endowed.

2 The ancient Egyptians looked out for the days profitable in dreams: the 1st day from the assembly, the 2nd and 3rd not being fitting (for the things contemplated are [of a] distressing [nature]). In the 4th, 5th, and 6th, the things seen turn out well; in the 7th they turn out well in four days; in the 8th, in course of time; in the 9th, the dreams do not come off; in the 10th and 11th, within four days; similarly in the 12th and 13th, after which[326] it is also auspicious; the 14th day is significant for cheerfulness; the 15th is effective but also harmful; the 16th, 17th, 18th, and 19th fulfill the visions within 10 days; the 20th and 21st are all right;[327] the 22nd immediately fulfills what comes from dreams; the 23rd in 8 days; the 24th in 12 days; the 25th fulfills in 24 days; the 26th is without effect; the 27th will bring on completion; the 28th and 29th, in three days; the 30th is fruitless.

---

[325] That is, the ninth.

[326] *"Meta tou,"* "in the midst of," or also, "after which." So it could also mean: "after which [period of four days spoken of above] it is also auspicious" (**EG**).

[327] *Koinai.* This word is normally "common," which in this case seems to be of a neutral-to-good indication.

\<Chapter III.25:\> On a request for favors[328]

1 For those who ask for favors it is needful to watch the Moon to ensure she is on the Hour-marker or in its triangle (even better if she happens to be in her own house), increasing in light and numbers, and configured with Mercury, Jupiter, Venus, and with those [stars] that are well-posited. Let her as well be kept away from the testimony of the malefics. **2** With this figure, it is favorable for women and men to have intercourse.[329]

\<Chapter III.26:\> On proposals[330] and treaties

1 If someone wills to address a proposal about any kind of business,

assign that [person] to the Hour-divider, yourself to the setting [pivot],[331]

...the matter [itself] to the Midheaven, the end of it to the underground.

2 Consider also whether the rising signs are straight or crooked, because from these you figure out the intention[332] of the one that approaches [you]. **3** Do not fear cunning if a benefic star is on the Hour-marker. **4** Should any malefic happen to be on the Midheaven, the matter to which the proposal is addressed is not favorable, and will bring about disgust. **5** Similarly with a disowned[333] malefic on the setting or underground [pivots]. **6** Besides, examine how the Moon is placed, so that you, from all these things, may learn the truth beforehand.

---

[328] *Charis.* Or, "gratifications, delights," *etc.* This word can also have a sexual meaning, as in **2** (**EG**).

[329] *Enteuxis.* This word can also refer simply to meeting and conversing: i.e., "social" intercourse (**EG**).

[330] *Hairesis.* This term is usually translated as "sect," but it more broadly refers to taking sides and making choices and commitments to one thing versus another; hence it also refers to embassies, proposed courses of actions, and so on.

[331] This is an unusual case, because it seems that the client is making a proposal to the astrologer—or rather, it is a general scheme for any person (the seventh) who is approached by someone with a proposal (Ascendant). In any event, the proposer is initiating the action (Ascendant), and the seventh should be assigned to the one responding to it: I have labeled the diagram with this in mind. Thanks to Chris Brennan for suggesting the proper interpretation of this passage.

[332] *Nous.* Or, "mind, resolve," *etc.* (**EG**). See Ch. III.1, **1**.

[333] *Apanainou.* This seems to mean "peregrine."

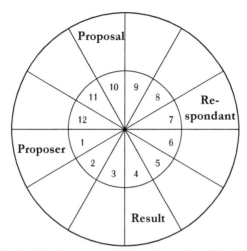

Figure 24: Angles for proposals and treaties (Heph. III.26, 1)

\<Chapter III.27:\> On letters

1 For sending letters, watch for the Moon to ensure she is with Mercury, or looking upon \<him\> without the gaze[334] of the bad ones; let \<Mercury\> be free from the rays of the Sun, and add\<itive\> in numbers: for in this way, should you send a message, it will not fail to reach [its] goal.[335]

2 When a letter is said to have been brought, and Sagittarius marks the Hour, we shall know that it is false; and if Capricorn, Gemini, Taurus, and Libra [mark the Hour], it has been delivered by some person of middling [wealth],[336] a household slave, or in favor of someone poor. **3** Besides, it is necessary to keep watch on the Moon when in these signs, and the destructive [stars]: for if they are configured, they become the cause of deceit. **4** If [the letter] is brought in Aries, Cancer, Leo, Virgo, Scorpio and Aquarius, it will reveal certain and true things, especially when the benefics are observing.[337] **5** Let these things be expounded just as was written among the ancients, and consider in the same way with respect to rumors and messages.

---

[334] *Theōrias.*

[335] *Skopou.* Or, its "mark." I take this to mean that it reaches the intended recipient; but the use of "mark" suggests that the letter will have its intended *effect upon* the recipient.

[336] *Metrios. Metrios* really means "moderate, middling, just sufficient, not too great," but later it came to mean "poor." It can also refer to someone's character (**EG**).

[337] *Ephoraō.*

<Chapter III.28:> On loans

1 Following those of former times, let the one who lends money be the Hour-marker; the one who borrows, the setting pivot; the money given, the Midheaven; and the pivot underground will reveal the fulfillment of the obligation. **2** The flowing away of the Moon will be understood in relation to the person who lends; the connection [to another planet], to the one who borrows. **3a** The foretellings will follow according to the stars which help or hinder.

3b Some focus on the Sun and the Moon, assigning the Moon to the one who lends, and the Sun to the debtor; though if the Moon is decreasing in light, contrariwise.

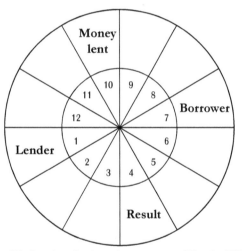

Figure 25: Angles for loaning money (Heph. III.28, 1)

4 The Moon becomes bad when on the Nodes or in her southern latitude. **5** For lending, attentively avoid the standing[338] of Mercury with Saturn, and even that of the Moon at the beginning of Leo, Gemini, and Sagittarius, and when the beginnings of these signs...

---

[338] *Stasis.* Normally this word means a "station," but since the rest of the sentence speaks of the *stasis* of the Moon (who is never retrograde), it must simply mean the planets' "position" in general, where they "stand."

...rise up above the earth.

6 *If you are willing yourself to contract a debt, let the following*
be best for you: in the Water-bearer, the Scorpion, and the Lion
let heavenly Selēnē be; also around the Fish
or in the Archer, and let her be wanting in light
as likewise in number,

...and let also Venus, Jupiter, and Mercury bear witness to the Moon. [It is] much better yet if [they] also [testify to] the Hour-divider.[339]

<Chapter III.29:> On sureties[340]

1 If you do not wish someone to make a pledge that [would] embarrass you, watch out for[341] the Moon [being] with Saturn and Mars, or with them marking the Hour. Having so observed, then meet with the one who [would] embarrass you, and then the things of the pledge will have no fulfillment.[342] **2** You should get away from the annoyance by means of the same figures [as those] of the money-lender.[343]

---

[339] This probably refers to the actual degree of the Ascendant.

[340] *Egguēs.* This chapter has generally to do with taking responsibility for someone else's deed, such as paying a debt or appearing in court. This can happen in many ways (as in different scenarios for getting a bail bondsman), and can even apply to promises to get married. So the key point here is that the client wants to elect a good time to make the agreement so that the other party will pay bail, show up at court, pay a debt, fulfill a promise, *etc.*

[341] *Epitērei.* That is, make sure the Moon is *not* with Saturn and Mars, *etc.*

[342] It seems that Hephaistion is adding irony to this reversed election. Normally, he tells us what we *should* do, and then warns what will happen if we do not. Here, he tells us what *not* to do, and then advises that (if perhaps we don't believe him) we should take the risk anyway and watch our own failure! Only afterwards does he make oblique references to the proper procedure in Ch. III.28.

[343] **EG:** This sentence could also be translated as: "You should get away from the annoyance of the money-lender by means of the same figures." **BD:** If we go with the translation above, then Hephaistion is referring back to Ch. 28. If we follow the alternative here, then Hephaistion is simply saying that we should avoid having the Moon with the malefics, *etc.*, when making loans. I think it makes more literary sense to go with the text as we have it.

<Chapter III.30:> On being abroad[344]

1 *Should[345] someone now go away from the father's towards foreign lands,*
him the Hour-divider will well show; the country towards which he departs,
the setting pivot; his business, the midmost height; and finally, what end there will
*   be, will be*
clearly and thoroughly judged from the animal underground.

2 They say, look for the benefic stars to know what kind of position[346] and figures they have, for it is generally favorable to live abroad when none of the stars stands still[347] or is configured with the Moon. However, it is most suitable to go abroad when the Moon is increasing her light and is additive in latitude and longitude numbers.

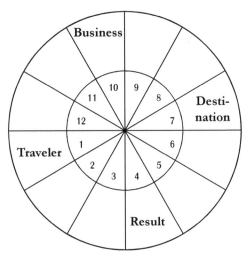

Figure 26: Angles for travel (Heph. III.30, 1)

3 It is necessary to watch the pivots as well. **4** Should benefics chance to be on the Hour-marker or testifying to it, the journey by road or land will be most pleasant. If Mercury is with them, at a morning rising,[348] the person will

---

[344] See also Ch. III.47, **85ff**; and *Excerpt* XXII.
[345] See also *Excerpt* IX.
[346] Or perhaps, "station" (*stasis*).
[347] Here Hephaistion seems to be using *stasis* and the verb *sterizō*, with the meaning of a bodily conjunction and not as a solar phase (**EG**).
[348] *Heōias anatolēs*. This seems to mean being in an earlier degree than the Sun, and out of the rays, so as to rise in the morning before the Sun.

quickly and cheerfully manage the affairs due to which he travels abroad. With Mercury happening to be on the setting [pivot], testified to by Jupiter and Venus, those affairs will be better, profitable, and even remarkable. **5** Generally, as regards living abroad, it is needful to observe Mercury, so that he does not subtract,[349] nor is under the rays, nor damaged by malefics in whatever figure, and when you are about to enter a city, or disembark, pay attention to this. **6** For they carefully observed that when Mars and Saturn are on the setting [pivot], or seeing it, bodily weaknesses, damages, and stoppages[350] will occur. **7** From the stars that look upon the Midheaven or are on it will be known the matter for the sake of which living abroad takes place; the end, from the underground. The confirmation of everything is effected from the configurations, especially of the Moon—which one must keep from being in the place of the Bad Spirit or in that of Bad Fortune for the departure: for then not only is she a cause of ill success, but also conducive to misery.

8 On these things Dorotheus instructs in his verses, as follows:[351]

A fortunate one being on the Hour-divider is best in everything,[352]
a fortunate one being on the setting [pivot] tells of that advantageous land
to which someone departs, even if he sets out to that
on account of good repute. But should there stand fiery-bright
Arēs or the chilling Phainōn, sometimes heavy diseases,
sometimes renewed battles, at another time dreadful violence [are to be expected].
9 *Do not set on the task of going abroad*[353] *with Selēnē being*
in the [place of the] Bad Spirit, or [Bad] Fortune (precisely that which lies
sixth from the Hour-divider), for this produces either misery or
sluggishness, or else some outrage in the means of living.
10 *Assign the lords of Mēnē and the Hour-divider*
to the ship, and let them not be either hidden anywhere

---

[349] This probably means being retrograde, but might even mean that he is slowing down and approaching retrogradation (i.e., descending in his epicycle), so that he is moving much more slowly than usual.

[350] *Epochai.* That is, some kind of delay or halt in one's progress (**EG**).

[351] See also *Excerpt IX.*

[352] *En pasin.* But this could mean, "for everyone," referring to the one undertaking the journey.

[353] *Xenia.* This mainly indicates the hospitality shown to a guest, and state of being an alien as opposed to that of a citizen; it can also mean a friendly relation between two states (**EG**).

under the gleaming splendor of Helios, nor divided.[354]
Should any from the two ruling ones[355] *stand still,*
the man will with slowness complete his journey and business.

11 Generally, from observation, when she is on the setting pivot or in its decline,[356] she makes the staying abroad long; and for those who go home from foreign lands, the same figure shows the return to be quick. **12** However, they say, one must take a look at the ruler of the Moon and of the Hour-marker, to ensure that they are not under the rays or stationary: for then they work delays and want of action. **13** It is also necessary to closely watch the malefics in square to or opposing her; if the benefics are mixed up with them, then one must suppose the return home to be [of an] uneven [nature].

14 Having examined the pivots, it is necessary to look upon the stars that are about to leave the signs in which [it][357] is, for in this way the departures and journeys abroad will be revealed. On the other hand, the returns [are known] from observing whether the moving over is from another's [house] into its own house or exaltation, or the other way round. From this, therefore, the things related to going abroad, and the return, will become evident. **15** Besides, the stations show delays and turning back, in the same way as the settings[358] [show] deaths or inaction in all ways; the risings[359] make staying abroad brief, obviously when the configurations of the Moon and the pivots of the inception hold the testimony and word for the aforesaid.

[Sailing]

16 One must especially watch the Moon in diameter to the watery signs or [being] in them, while the malefics are beholding[360] her according to strong figures (that is to say, diameters and squares): for then these inceptions are most difficult for ships and those who sail. **17** When the Moon has been mal-treated, but the watery signs are testified to by the benefics, the ship[361] will

---

[354] *Dedasmenoi.* This seems to mean that they should not be in aversion to each other.
[355] That is, the lord of the Moon and the lord of the Ascendant.
[356] That is, the 6th.
[357] It is unclear whether this refers to the Moon, or each pivot individually.
[358] *Duseis.*
[359] *Anatolai.*
[360] *Theōreō.*
[361] *Skaphos.* This is more precisely the hull of the ship, but is here taken (as it frequently is in poetry) as denoting the whole ship (**EG**).

not be destroyed together with all the men: some will be able to be saved, even the majority. Once the ship is broken up, each one will return home at the appointed times according to the interpretation of [the inception chart cast at the time of] stepping upon the ship. **18** The [inception of] setting sail gives hints on the things related to the sea and sailing; the [moment of] stepping upon the ship [gives indications on] the things about each [person], changing the matters at the speed of the change of the pivots.[362] Similarly, as regards those who travel, one should keep in mind the dry and four-footed signs. **19** Exceedingly long-lasting will be the evil things for many, when the malefics go stationary in those signs, within which[363] they make the experience of going back or [suffering] illnesses.

20 The Hour-marker and the Moon are rightly partners for those who sail, as distinct from the five wanderers.[364] [The Moon] happens to be suitable as follows: **21** In Gemini she will be suitable (even when the things related to sailing will be slow), also in Cancer, Capricorn, Aquarius, and Pisces. **22** But she is not suitable in Aries, for not only is it unpleasant to begin to sail, but also to start any business ([although] Dorotheus does not accept this); those who go abroad from their own country must beware to do so [with the Moon] in Taurus and Leo. **23** Let the Moon not be waning nor in an assembly with Saturn, or at the Full Moon with Mars.[365]

[Land travel]

24 To[366] make journeys [by land] with the Moon in Aries is suitable (for the returns become quick), and it will also be suitable to return home from abroad. **25** In Taurus it is fine to start a journey [by land] and return home. **26** In Gemini, the lingering abroad will be long. **27** To start the way back

---

[362] *Ta kata hena hekaston.* This seems to mean that, since stepping on the ship and setting sail are different inceptions, the meaning of the pivots will change between one action and the other, with the inception for stepping on the ship meaning something different for each person who steps aboard (**EG**).

[363] *Meta tou.*

[364] That is, the planets apart from the Sun and Moon.

[365] These refer to her phases with the Sun. The Greek here makes it seem as though she should not be waning *but also not* in an assembly with Saturn, which is not quite the traditional doctrine. Rather, the two must be combined: she should not be waxing (and up to the opposition at the Full Moon) *while being* connected with Mars, nor waning (and up to the conjunction at the New Moon) *while being* connected with Saturn.

[366] For this paragraph, cf. **39-50** below.

from abroad will be suitable [with the Moon] in Cancer, as well as in Gemini.[367] **28** Beware of travelling abroad [with the Moon] <in> Leo within [the first] 15 degrees: from the 15th through the 30th degree, there is lesser evil. **29** In Virgo it is fine to return home. **30** In Libra it is fine after the 10th degree. **31** In Scorpio it is suitable both to travel and return to one's own country. **32** But it is not fitting to do so in Sagittarius (as one will be roaming about aimlessly), though it is good to return home, and similarly in Capricorn and Aquarius. **33** In Pisces it is suitable to go to war. **34** It is also necessary to reconcile what has been said (in connection with the sign suitable for being abroad), with the testimony of the benefics to it and to the pivots, and in this way make an inception.

[Distance and other general rules]

35 The <...>[368] observed in detail the things related to journeys by sea or land, and discovered the following: bringing together the landmarks of the road or sailing route as stades, and dividing into six portions, so that to each sign, from its rising till its setting, is given one portion, they assigned the first one to the Hour-marker, which indicates <the first 1/6 of the extension of the road>,[369] and the second one to the 12th and so on in a regular manner, so that the last one falls to the setting pivot, which reveals the lodging of the trip. **36** Next they distinguished the association of the stars with each sign, obviously revealing that the testifying benefics produce good things and a good journey, and similarly that of the malefics the opposite; the stations showing delays, going backwards, and annoyances in the corresponding places of the sailing route or road from the division of the signs, in which the 1/6 proportionally falls: Mars happening to be a cause of wreckage, especially when the place on the top[370] gets damaged with his presence. **37** And such things [say], on one hand, Nicaeus Protagoras, [and] on the other Dorotheus, in their verses on putting a ship to sea:

---

367 In Cancer she is already in her home (symbolizing the client's home), while in Gemini she is about to enter it.
368 There is a lacuna here, with a plural noun (probably, "ancients") (**EG**).
369 Added by Pingree from several of the Epitomes.
370 That is, the Midheaven.

38 *To those who crave sailing, these unerring words you would say:*[371]
39 *When to Selēnē no evil, nor good [star]*
testifies, and she is brought underground
passing from the first degrees of the Ram
towards the tenth, it would thus be judged good for sailing.
40 *In the Bull, a great storm, but do not let any evil one see her,*
because it always works a baneful end of the matter for those [men].
41 *In the Twins, when someone sets sail from the eighth,*
then a long journey that will be, though delightful.
42 *On the other hand, the Crab would grieve with much stillness of waters,*
but he would also arrive at where he wants, without having been harmed at all.
43 *If she chanced to fall into the hairy Lion,*
some danger there will be above the salt[372] *for this man*
some destroyer testifying will place grief upon grief.
44 *The Virgin bearer of corn ears is in no wise fast for the ship:*
but she will bring sailing tides for the harmed men. **45** *Around the Scales,*
from the tenth degree, she does not find fault with neither the moist
road nor any other, even if the man goes home.
46 *Going around the Scorpion, she will place those upon the sea*
secure from danger, though here she is accustomed to trouble the soul.
47 *The Archer draws storm and other fears upon the man.*
48 *When the Goat-horned One, good for sailing, passes through nine degrees,*
in the same way she carries some upheaval to the spirit.
49 *Sluggish Water-pourer, for you the end is not blaming.*
50 *In the Fish, it indicates renewed danger, illness on those,*
especially with the Impetuous One looking on
in mournful testimony. And keep an eye on the ship's mast!

51 He[373] next adds: let the Moon not be connecting with, nor in a square to, stationary Saturn. **52** For he says that if she were in a triangle they would be thus saved, with toil and pain, by throwing away the goods; and when stationary Mercury is arranged with them, then there will be more evils and worse (though if a benefic is seeing them, the evils will be light to bear).

---

[371] For the following, cf. **24-33** above.
[372] "Salt" is a poetic synonym for "the sea" in Greek and Latin poetry and literature (**EG**).
[373] That is, Dorotheus. Cf. *Carmen* V.25, **16**.

53 *Similar to these behaves Kronos, as he divides the Hour*
and [remains] apart from[374] *quick-glancing Mēnē. But if he*
were in the sign in which he was before,
when the man was expelled from his mother's [womb],[375]
or even in a triangle or in a square to it,
[the evils] would then outright become greatest.
54 *If such a disposition of Phainōn already referred to,*
Ares has with Mēnē…

…gone into the upper hemisphere (that is, having moved towards the tenth from herself), it mainly means evil things, hate, seditions in the ship itself, even till bloodshed. **55** <If also Mercury were co-injured, even worse things will come about; and if the benefics are looking on, the evil things are made less.>[376]

56 *When Pyroeis and Phainōn all together, and third Hermēs,*
each one from a different place, or even from the same place,
look upon Selēnē in such condition, [there will be] abominable and inevitable ruin;
the same things when the destructive Arēs has mixed with Stilbōn.
57 *If Kronos and Arēs, the one sees Hēlios, the other looks on at*
Selēnē, for them it discloses shameful and baneful things.
58 *When four-sided Zeus*[377] *sees the beautiful-horned Mēnē,*
going up above earth, the sailing will then be favorable,
and the affairs and hopes that are in their hearts
will follow them, very much[378] *when lovely Kythērē*
gazes from the same place at the Aegis-bearing One, and even if she sees
from another place, then she will grant whichever favors that are chosen.[379]
59 *When she alone sees swift Selēnē, queen Kypris will give*
beautiful things and some quick profits,
quiet sailing, and the fond words of a woman…

---

[374] *Chōris;* or, "severed from." This must mean, "in aversion to."
[375] **EG:** The Arabic has it as though Saturn is *both* in the Ascendant, *and* that this is the same sign he was in (or configured to it, etc.) at the nativity. **BD:** But it is not clear to me that the Greek Dorotheus connects both conditions together.
[376] Added by Pingree from several Epitomes.
[377] This is a traditional epithet for Zeus, and not a reference to an astrological square.
[378] *Mala.*
[379] This phrase can also mean, "favors already spoken of" (**EG**).

…<though without Jupiter she helps less, [and] with Jupiter, much more help she does give. **60** Venus being under the rays, under the earth, with the Moon,

affords fair weather and stillness of the air,

and those who set sail, continue in their voyage.>[380]

61 *When the fortunate ones who distribute to both luminaries,*
Helios and Mēnē, become witnesses along with Hermes,
there will not be any better beginning of sailing than this.[381]
62 *When the cunning stars*[382] *appear on the Hour-divider,*
and the benefactors associate with the swift Selēnē,
or contrariwise,[383] *they make the sea mischievous.*

63 <The Moon, when un-testified to[384] by any star, and void in course, and the Hour-marker having some sign of those fitting for sailing (which are: Taurus, Gemini, Pisces, Capricorn, Cancer, Virgo, and Sagittarius) with any of the benefics, it is favorable for those who depart into the high sea. If the Moon and the Hour-marker, both void in course[385] and un-testified to by any other star, occupy one of the aforesaid signs which are fitting for sailing, it will not be bad for those who have set sail. **64** It is particularly necessary to look at the Moon, so that she is not harmed by being in any of the places [mentioned] in the second chapter of this book.[386] **65** Then reckon the inception of the sailing [in general] when the seamen draw the anchor from the

---

[380] This prose-poetic insertion by Pingree was taken from several of the Epitomes.

[381] See Carmen V.25, **33**, which reads as follows (my translation from the Arabic): "And if Jupiter and Venus together were looking at the Sun and the Moon, and the Moon was with Mercury, then it indicates that the inception in that hour of rowing the ship in the water or on the sea is like the more excellent of inceptions which there is, and the inception is more excellent than that."

[382] That is, the malefics (**EG**).

[383] Above (**20**) it was said that both the Ascendant and the Moon were indicators of the journey—thus if the malefics are harming one, but the benefics are benefiting the other, it will make the experience very mixed.

[384] *Amarturētos.*

[385] The Ascendant cannot be void in course, but perhaps Hephaistion means something like the medieval "wildness," in which a planet (or here, sign) is in aversion to all other planets. See my *Introductions to Traditional Astrology*, III.10.

[386] Ch. III.2 above.

sand; and the inception for each one [in particular] among the many who sail, when he lays his foot inside the ship.>[387]

66 If you wish to learn whether there will be delays in foreign lands or not, when the man travels from that city towards that place towards which he is bound, take a look at the second place from the Hour-marker of the entrance into the city, and its lord: and if this is retrograde he will quickly go out empty and unavailing; if it is stationary, thus again, aside from being una-vailing, he will also waste time in the city. **67** These things being so, if the same ruler happens to be setting,[388] it will become the cause of illnesses and unpleasantness for him who travels; if it happens to be on the underground pivot, look about carefully to ensure it does not become cause of death. Should it be found additive in numbers, and on the Hour-marker or on the Midheaven, he will quickly go out well-accomplished.

68 <Also take a look at the Sun of the exit [from the city], and its square and diameter. If the benefics were in [one of] these [signs], the return will be happy and fast; consider also whether the malefics change places, and the benefics enter instead of them:[389] for then the return must be expected either when the Sun is re-established,[390] or when he comes to his own square and diameter. Also examine the Moon in the same way as the Sun. **69** It is also necessary to closely watch the following: when someone goes to a city, exam-ine the four pivots, by which stars they are seen, and toward which stars the Moon is taken. **70** Cancer is not considered good when marking the Hour at the time of the entrance into the city, for those who meet such conditions will be miserly, and with no gain; and if he wishes to make a payment, he will give more than what it is due.>[391]

71 <In general>, also know that Mars, seeing the Moon in an evil figure from Sagittarius, brings on blows on the way, or other crises.

---

[387] This insertion by Pingree was taken from several of the Epitomes. That is, calculate the separate inceptions for boarding the ship, as described in **17-18**.

[388] This probably means "on the Descendant."

[389] *Ei de kakopoioi skopei pote allaxousi tous topous kai ant' autōn agathopoioi eiseleusontai.* This seems to mean that the malefics are in these positions instead of the benefics—in which case, they would delay the return until the Sun had made the transits described here.

[390] That is, when he returns to where he was at the departure. The Arabic (*Carmen* V.22, **3**) says to use the beginning of the (entire) journey, but perhaps—depending on the length of the journey—it could mean the departure to return home.

[391] This sentence added by Pingree from two of the Epitomes.

<Chapter III.31:> On being sick[392]

1 One must see that those who begin to be sick when the Moon is brought towards the benefics, in the first square (that is to say, in 7 days), once the illness has been judged,[393] it will heal, especially when [the Moon], having come to the square, favorably connects to the benefics again. **2** Brought towards the malefics, she produces a discharge of evil till her diameter; and if a benefic were found together with a malefic, there would be a mixture of relaxing and an increase in intensity. **3** The illnesses that arise from the Full Moon [till the New Moon] are lighter compared to those from the assembly [till the Full Moon], for the waning Moon relieves the suffering. **4** If it happens that there is no critical day within the whole month, it will be a common fate for the disease to extend until the square of the course of the Sun.[394]

5 As regards those who are judged and then rise from bed in a few days, the Moon is found [to be] going from her fullness along the first and second quarters,[395] so that she joins the assembly or assembling sign, leaving more or less six, or 5, or 4, or at the least 3 days of her path remaining, in which the health is restored. **6** The same things come to pass from the first quarter till the Full Moon, for such a number of days is gathered at the time: being released from the first interval, the Moon turns toward the second[396] temperateness of figure.

7 One must be watchful when taking to one's bed occurs: for if the Moon is one sign apart from the assembly, the one taken to bed will not cease to be sick, but once the Moon starts to shine and increase in light, the illness brings an increase in intensity. **8** Such illnesses are fatal or at least hard to cure, and

---

[392] This chapter has to do with "decumbiture" charts, taken when someone is so ill as to take to bed (Lat. *decumbo*, Gr. *kataklinō*). The special days on which one judges the prognosis are commonly called "critical" days, from the Greek *krinō*, "to judge, decide." Galen himself wrote a work on illnesses called *De Diebus Decretoriis*, which likewise means "On Decisive Days."

[393] *Kritheisēs tēs nosou.* Or, "once the illness has been brought to a crisis." However, here it seems to be alluding to the "days favorable for judgment," which we also find in *Carmen* V.41, **28** (**EG**).

[394] That is, until the Sun himself moves into the square of his own position at the beginning of the illness. Thus if the lunar month ends without a resolution, we consider the Sun instead.

[395] Or rather, along the third and fourth sides of the whole square which is imagined as forming the four quarters of the Moon.

[396] Lit., "the other" (*heteran*).

there are symptoms and remissions according to the figurations of the Moon: for they alone are judged every three days when the Moon has changed place from sign to sign. Those [figurations] of the fourth day [are judged] according to the hexagon, on the ninth day the triangle, on the fourteenth day, the diameter. When the Moon has come to the first and twentieth [day] in the right square, as she passes under such a configuration, judgment[397] takes place. **9** Increase in the intensity of evil is to be expected with the contemplation[398] of the malefics, a relaxing with that of the benefics.

10 On the seventh day,[399] it occurs that the Moon is either brought ahead of time towards the seventh, or, with delay, to the eighth (in the first case when she moves with her minimum speed, in the second with her greatest): whence it strictly follows that one must not consult any of the physicians without paying attention to the movement of the Moon.

11 It is also necessary to know which part of the human body is ruled by each sign: the head by Aries, the neck by Taurus, the shoulders and the arms by Gemini, the ribs and the breast by Cancer, the chest by Leo, the belly and inward parts by Virgo, the buttocks by Libra, the private parts and the seat by Scorpio, the thighs by Sagittarius, the knees by Capricorn, the lower leg[400] by Aquarius, and the topmost feet by Pisces. **12** Observe then which of the 12 signs, according to the fixing of the nativity, has been spoiled by any of the malefic stars. **13** And if the beginning of the disease happens with the Moon in a sign harmed from the beginning,[401] and the times cast out from the Hour-marker[402] will arrive at such a sign in which Saturn or Mars were (according to the [natal] disposition), or the releasings[403] cast from any of the luminaries, or the pivots, or Lots, fall into the destructive rays of the malefic stars, the disease will come to be most dangerous. **14** But if they flow away from Mars or Saturn, there will be humours and suffering from the nerves.

---

[397] *Krisis.*

[398] *Epitheōreō.*

[399] *Tēn hebdomaian.* As it is, this sentence does not make much sense to me, since in no way can the Moon reach anywhere near her own opposition within seven days. But this sentence is very close to two others (which disagree amongst themselves). First, *Carmen* V.41, **57** says to watch out for the Moon transiting in the sixth or eighth or fourth from the *Ascendant* of the decumbiture. Second, *Frag.* V.41, **35-68** (**11**) has her in the fourth, sixth, or eighth of the *nativity*, or even in her own natal place.

[400] *Knēma:* the portion between the knee and ankle, the shin and calf. (**EG**).

[401] *Ex archēs.* That is, at birth (**EG**).

[402] *Ekballō.* This sounds like the profection of the natal Ascendant to the year in which the illness occurs.

[403] *Apheseis.* That is, a primary direction.

15 If the malefics in the nativity are in bicorporeal signs (especially in Gemini and Pisces, due to the parting off of these two signs from each other), and if, with such a condition, the malefics, as it was said, from the beginning, surround the Moon[404] (which lies in the midst of them) in Gemini, they bring gout in the hands; in Pisces, in the feet.

<Chapter III.32:> On surgery

1 One[405] ought to perform surgery of the limbs with the Moon waning, and brought toward the benefics or assembling with them. **2** One must pay attention when she is in Taurus, Virgo, Capricorn, and Pisces, for these signs become a cause of spasms.[406] **3** One must also beware when she is in the tropical [signs] and in an assembly with the Sun and on the ecliptical Nodes. **4** And it is that part [of the body] where the operation is needed which by nature is familiarly related[407] to that sign where the Moon is; above we have made known that each of the parts of the human body is familiarized to one of the 12 signs.[408]

5 One ought to treat medically or operate on the eyes when the Moon is full in light and numbers, connected with benefics, and away from the testimony of the malefics.

6 In his [verses] on surgery, Dorotheus says the same things, and to that he adds: **7** It is necessary to make sure that not only the Moon, but also the Hour-marker, is unharmed; moreover, if a malefic, being pivotal, is retrograde, one must reject this as unfitting. **8** If the Moon is in a tropical or bicorporeal sign, he says, and a benefic connects to her, it is fitting to do surgery; but without the benefic it is not: for [with the Moon] in those signs without the benefics, a relapse in illness occurs, and surgery [will be required] again for a second time.

---

[404] *Periechōsi.* That is, "besiege." Like *obsideo* (the standard, equivalent Latin term in astrological texts), *periechō* can have the military sense of besieging, blockading, *etc.*

[405] From this point until Ch. III.33, **1**, added by Pingree from Epitome 2.

[406] Or, "convulsions" (*spasmōn*).

[407] *Oikeiutai.*

[408] See Ch. III.31, **11**.

<Chapter III.33:> On diseases[409]

1 ....>[410] *having hidden, he introduced*
some medicinal solutions. **2** *However, neither the glittering Crab*
nor the Lion is sufficient for those. **3** *Now the Maiden*
is favorable, and equally the Scales. **4** *But the Scorpion,*
which scratches the earth with its feet, is not so any more.
5 *For the Arrow-bearer, and also the Goat-horned One,*
it avails. **6** *With Mēnē or the Hour in the Water-bearer*
you will do everything in vain.[411]
7 *In the Fish, it is possible for you therefore to pursue baneful [procedures].*[412]
8 *Zeus and the Foam-born One, being beside Mēnē and <the Hour>,*
or gazing [at them], will forthwith dispel misery.

<Chapter III.34:> On vomiting and purgation[413]

1 It will be fitting to cause vomiting and purgation when the Moon is waning, and is configured with or connecting to the benefics. **2** One should make sure that one does not undertake any of such things when she has her position[414] either in Aries or in Taurus, for then it harmfully draws up these things.[415] **3** It is fitting to cause vomiting when the Moon is on the ascending Node, and cleansing the cavity[416] on the descending Node.

---

[409] Unfortunately, it is hard to know what this chapter is even about, despite its medical context.

[410] Here ends the addition by Pingree from Epitome 2; the text is still missing the first few lines of these Dorotheus verses, which must have included statements about Aries, Taurus, and Gemini.

[411] Lit., "windy," a metaphor for something vain or useless. Thus, it is useless or vain to attempt a cure with the Moon or Ascendant in Aquarius (**EG**).

[412] *Lugra.*

[413] See also *Frag.* V.38, **1-2**.

[414] *Stasis.*

[415] That is, by vomiting.

[416] That is, laxatives or enemas.

<Chapter III.35:> On the use of new implements

1 One must use implements or garments for the first time with the Moon in Aries, Taurus, Cancer, Virgo, Scorpio, and Pisces, increasing in light, brought toward the benefics, or when they are marking the Hour, without the association[417] or assembly of the destructive ones.

<Chapter III.36:> On dinners[418]

1 Some have already set forth the manner by which it is fitting to know about dinners, and how they will turn out, in this way. **2** Having fixed the pivots, it is necessary to assign the beginning[419] of the dinner to the Hour-marker, and the dinner-preparer and the attendants[420] to the Midheaven. **3** Make your inference regarding the rest of the signs, in such a way that the third sign[421] is assigned to the vessels;[422] the fourth, the place where the dining-room is; the fifth, the guests;[423] the sixth, the wine; the seventh, the cups; the eighth, the Hall Masters;[424] the ninth, the cooks; the tenth is to be applied to the one in charge of buying fish and other dainties;[425] the eleventh, <to the preparation;[426] the twelfth,> to the mistress of the household. **4** Having

---

[417] *Koinōnias.* This probably means, "configured."

[418] *Deipnou.* This should be understood in terms of formal meals, banquets, *etc.*

[419] This undoubtedly refers to the reason for the banquet, as with Sahl (see below).

[420] *Hupēretas.* These are servants who assist the meal-preparer (**EG**).

[421] Below I have provided two diagrams. The first is the apparent order of houses with which Hephaistion is working, so that the "third sign" mentioned here is the third house. But this order puts the elements of the banquet in many strange places, such as the wine (a pleasurable thing) in the sixth; it also leaves the second sign empty. The second diagram shows the more compelling proposal by Jiménez (2002, p. 250-53), that the order of signs given here applies to a certain order of *importance*: pivots or angles, post-ascensions or succeedents, declines or cadents. Thus the "third sign" here is not the third *house*, but the third sign in the order of the angles, viz. the *seventh* house. Jiménez compares his arrangement to many similar ones in Greek literature as well as the Latin Sahl, whose account of the same topic (*On Quest.* 13.17), undoubtedly from the same source, is the same as or close to Jiménez. As an example, Jiménez's ordering puts the vessels (the third listed) in the seventh house, while the Latin Sahl puts the butlers there—but the butlers are precisely those who bear the vessels of food.

[422] Or, "instruments" (*skeuesin*).

[423] Lit., "the summoned ones (*keklēmenoi*).

[424] *Apantōntes*, those in charge of welcoming the guests.

[425] *Opsōnountos.* Or more simply, the one buying the victuals.

[426] *Paraskeuē.* This may also imply a wedding, and the preparation for it (**EG**).

fixed these, one must as well consider the signs: their condition, and how each one is figured in relation to the other stars, and which of them is in its own place.[427] **5** From the observation and commixture of each type, it is possible to understand which meal is well-pleasing and lavish, and which moderate: for one does not fail if the examination of the places has been carefully and closely attended to.

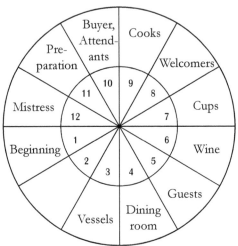

Figure 27: Given houses for banquets (Heph. III.36, 1-2)

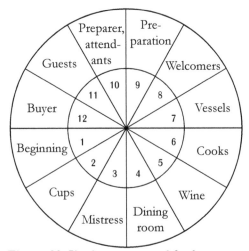

Figure 28: Jiménez proposal for banquets

---

[427] *Idiotopoien.*

\<Chapter III.37:\> On [courts of] judgment, the judge, victory, and defeat[428]

1 One must consider the courts of judgment and the bringing of charges [against someone] this way: by distributing the Hour-marker to the accuser, the Midheaven to the judge, the setting to the accused, the underground to the judgment and the result of the matter.

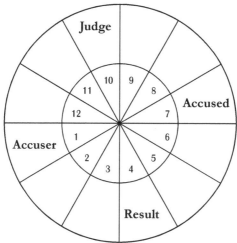

Figure 29: Angles for legal accusations (Heph. III.37, 1)

2 And if a tropical sign marks the Hour, the matter will not come to an end; if a bicorporeal sign, the one accusing will change his mind; if a solid sign, there will be delays, and the one pursuing the case will be implacable. **3** When it is also seen by Mars, bold, insolent, and relentless; if the place were testified to by Saturn, it would show a crafty and toilsome old age; in an assembly with Mercury, it means payment \<in\> silver coins to introduce the accusation, and even forgery; similarly also the star of Mercury with Mars. **4** Jupiter would show someone held in esteem, and Venus, of noble birth; Mars, daring and well-born; Mercury, spirited[429] and busy about many

---

[428] Both this chapter and the next seem to be about event charts rather than elections, since normally the feuding parties do not have a choice of court dates. On the other hand, they could refer to the chosen moment when someone makes the accusation or files charges/the lawsuit. If the client were the accused, then the time of the chart would be the event chart for that filing or accusation.

[429] *Gorgon*: vigorous, spirited, vehement, fierce, grim, terrible.

things.[430]

5 These things one must suppose about the judges, in proportion to the signs and stars which lie on the Midheaven: for if there are benefics in that place, the judge will handle the matter with justice; if malefics, wrongly. **6** In the same way, if the sign is tropical it will be successful for the one selected to arbitrate to pronounce the judgment anew;[431] and if the Sun and the Moon are there, they will make everything manifest, along with the judge being held in honor and well-born.

7 When the benefics happen to be on the setting [pivot], one must forecast victory to the accused.

8 The place which is underground anticipates the result: when the malefics are under the earth, the sentence will be unjustly given against the accused; when the benefics are there, justly.

<Chapter III.38:> Another manner of inquiry [about court cases]

1 Apart from that of the four pivots, there is yet another way to understand the subject of the courts of judgment, [and it is] as follows. **2** The Moon increasing [in light] is taken for the pursuer, the Sun for the accused and indebted; on the other hand, when the Moon is decreasing she is the indebted, the Sun taking up the rank of pursuer. **3** In fact, having observed which one is best placed (as regards place, bound, testimony from benefics, and the hemisphere above earth), in this way, from the reckoning and weighing of the greatest, we deliberately choose the one who will prevail, the full Moon being understood as great sedition, strife and destruction.

4 There is another way of considering the same things, and it is as follows. **5** He who denounces the matter must by needs be the flowing away of the Moon; the matter, the Moon herself; the connection, the accused; and from the bounds and the stars are revealed the things surrounding the matter.

6 The same line of thought and manner as those about journeys and emigration will be useful here.

7 We would more manifestly and unfailingly learn about the courts of judgment, and of what sort the accuser and the accused are, and even the judgment and the result of the matter, from the four pivots, as has been said

---

[430] *Polupragmōn.*
[431] This sounds as though the arbitrator or judge will not be consistent.

before, always taking Mercury, who, being under the rays, is useful for those against whom the proceedings are taken, and for those who manage clandestine affairs; but when eastern,[432] it will be useful for those who bring charges against someone, and for those who intend to do something manifestly.[433]

8 One ought to keep an eye on the Moon on the critical day,[434] and if she happens to be in Libra (especially if she is setting), it is prejudicial for him who brings in unrighteous things (for he will be defeated), but who justly brings a charge against someone, will succeed.

9 Let Dorotheus' words about these matters be expounded, for the sake of beauty of language and remembrance:

> **10** *Verily, thus you will proclaim to them,*
> *who urge to a successful judgment, and crave for the truth:*
> **11** *Take the accuser from the sign which divides the Hour.*
> *Should it be solid, keep watch on the disposition*[435] *it has;*
> *from those which are called bicorporeal, out of repentance*
> *they will turn from one way, and come to another one;*
> *but in tropical signs, his efforts will be incomplete.*

[More on the angles]

12 <Should[436] Mars harm the Hour-marker, he who brings the case into court will be dishonored; if Mercury marks the Hour with some benefic, the pursuer will keep silent after having accepted money [in return]; if Saturn harms the Hour-marker, the accuser will be fined.

13 Let the Midheaven be the judge: if the Midheaven gets harmed by a malefic, then the judges will differ without coming into agreement amongst themselves, the judgment being put off: but even if the judges reach agreement, their judgment will equally be unreliable, and the agreement will be entirely upset.

14 Saturn culminating is a cause of unjust judgment; the benefics culmi-

---

[432] That is, out of the rays so as to be visible.

[433] I.e., "openly."

[434] This must refer to the day on which the legal judgment is handed down, not the day of the legal proceedings themselves.

[435] *Gnōmē.* This also means a token, sign, inclination, or disposition (**EG**).

[436] This whole insertion through **32**, was added by Pingree from a combination of Epitomes.

nating[437] produce righteous judgment.

15 Let the setting be the one presented charges against, and from what has been said about the figurations of the stars to the Hour-marker, in an analogous way, search with respect to the setting and the accused. **16** If Mercury harms the setting together with any of the malefic stars, the pursued will be under false accusation, or else some witness will come up to give testimony against him.

17 The end of the trial will be taken from the underground.

[Lords of the Ascendant and the seventh]

18 It is also necessary to study the rulers of both the Hour-marker and the setting, and determine which of them is under the rays while the other is eastern:[438] for evil things are signified for the one in familiarity with it.[439] **19** If both are under the rays, there will be an interruption of the trial for some time, and the judgment will be passed on again at a later time. When both of them are eastern, the adversaries will reconcile to one another. **20** Those of the benefics which have familiar ties allow a fair victory; but the malefic ones of the stars, if they are out of the rays and in alien or incongruous[440] places, become a cause of defeat. **21** The malefics occupying their own place, pivotal, and eastern, grant an unjust victory for the person familiarly related to them.

[Support and allies]

22 One ought to observe as well the second and eighth places, and the testimonies of the stars to them, so that we learn [about] the ones who aid on each side: the second from the pursuer reveals the assistants,[441] and the second from the eighth, those of the prosecuted one. **23** The benefics will more excellently set free those which they post-ascend; the malefics, worse. **24** It should also be observed with whom the master of the Midheaven has familiar ties (that is, either with the person of the pursuer or of the prosecuted):

---

437 That is, on the Midheaven (*mesourantountes*).
438 That is, out of the rays so as to be visible, here and in **19**.
439 That is, evil things are expected for the person signified by the planet which is *under* the rays of the Sun (**EG**).
440 *Anoikeiois.* Or, "unfitting, foreign," *etc.*: a synonym for being alien or peregrine.
441 *Symmachos.* Or, "those leagued or allied with him."

for when it is testified to by it, or exchanges places with it, or is ruled by only one star,[442] or is in its places, this more than the other brings about a state of confidence.

[*The Moon*]

25 Not only from the four pivots should one aim at learning about these things, but it is also necessary to look at the Moon to see how she is placed, and her flowings-away and connections as well. **26** If the Moon is harmed by being observed[443] by malefics, this is an evil sign for the pursuer: for not only will he be defeated, but also treated outrageously and hurt. **27** When the Moon is assembled under the rays of the Sun, then the stronger will vanquish the more abased one.

[*Suing for money*]

28 If the trial is about money, one should proceed like this. **29** Let the waxing Moon be the money-lender; the Sun, the debtor. Should the Moon be waning, then the other way around: the Sun is the money-lender, the Moon the debtor. **30** Of the two, the one which is placed in a stronger place, and placed by house[444] more strongly than the other, and rejoices greatly, that makes the person in familiarity[445] stronger than the other.

[*Fortune*]

31 It is necessary as well to examine the Lot of Fortune and the ruler of the Lot: for if it approaches the Hour-marker, the pursuer will be stronger; if the setting [pivot], the prosecuted. **32** If the Lot makes a square to both the Hour-marker and the setting [pivot], being underground, the adversaries will come to each other on friendly terms; if it culminates, the judges will do [so].>

---

[442] That is, both the Midheaven and the person are ruled by the same planet (**EG**).

[443] *Ephoraō.*

[444] *Oikeiotopeō* (possibly equivalent to *oikodespoteō*, "to rule" or "to be the master of the house"). **EG**: This seems to mean that it has better dignities where it is.

[445] That is, the person ruled by this planet.

[More on the lords of the Ascendant and seventh]

33 *When both of them,*
the kings of the Hour and of the setting,[446] *are in one sign,*
coming to their familiar faces,[447]
declare them adversaries at law. **34** *And being both in the sign of*
Hermes, [the strife will be] because of a child, or someone in the position
of a child. If in the Paphian's [sign], it will be against[448] *women*
or sisters, or daughters, or kindred ones,
or a female, who has obtained a public marriage.[449]
If then the houses of the Warlike One...

<the struggle [will be] either of brothers against themselves, or of cousins, or
of such>,[450]

When, on the other hand, the place is that of the Aegis-bearing One,
it [will be] because of the contending older brothers
or uncles. If you find [them in the houses] of Kronos,
[it will be because of] the fathers or grandfathers,
or those in their position from long ago,
and from the clan; the same also [when] in the territory[451] *of Helios.*
In [the house] of Selēnē, [because of] the mother or stepmother.

---

[446] That is, the lords of the Ascendant and Descendant.

[447] *Prosōpos.* The meaning of this is unclear. A "face" can indicate a decan, but each sign
has only three decans, with no guarantee that it will belong to either planet.

[448] *Katenanta.* But perhaps this should be understood as "because of" or "in relation to."

[449] This line was difficult to render. First, the verb *lagchanō* normally means "to obtain by
lot," and the word we translate as "public" (*ksunos*) normally means "common." This
would yield something like a woman who has obtained a common bed by lot—which
suggests perhaps prostitution or promiscuity, but does not really make much sense
(**EG/BD**).

[450] Added by Pingree from several Epitomes.

[451] That is, the sign or domicile.

<Chapter III.39:> On those who are banished or flee from the country, and on child exposure[452]

1 We shall draw the knowledge regarding ones who are banished and al-ienated from the native land, from the stars to which the pivots belong, according to their rulership: if these were found in their depressions, and looked upon[453] by malefics, they would make someone who is banished be-yond the frontiers. **2** According to the fixing of the nativity, as soon as they have the times, or the ascensions of the signs,[454] in the same time they would chance to be fulfilled. **3** The same, when the [planetary] ruler comes to be the cause of the exposure of the child: if the star is eastern,[455] the exposed will live; if setting,[456] he dies. **4** In particular, the stars being in their own depres-sions [and] on the setting pivot or the one underground, they are sent beyond the frontiers, and are liable to voluntary exile. **5** When malefics are found in their own depressions in the Hour-marker or on the Midheaven, they bring about bonds and oppression; while with the benefics harmonious-ly looking upon[457] them, they re-establish them to their familiar places. **6** And if at the hour of the judgment the benefics see the Hour-marker and the Moon, they indicate the return.

<Chapter III.40:> On the imprisoned

1 To consider this subject, one should inquire in which sign the Moon by herself[458] happens to be at the hour of the imprisonment. **2** If she happens to be in Aries,

do announce a quick release.
3 *In the Bull, he will stay for a long time; but if he suffered punishment*

---

[452] This chapter seems to be a combination of natal considerations and event charts.
[453] *Epitheōreō.* My sense is that this should be considered equivalent to overcoming.
[454] That is, "having the times" by being time lords, or else having the ascensional times of their signs expire.
[455] *Anatolikos.* This should probably be understood as, "pertaining to arising," i.e., emerg-ing from the Sun's rays, as it is paired with "setting" or "sinking" in the next clause.
[456] *Dutikos.* See footnote above.
[457] *Epiblepō.*
[458] *Kath' heautēn.* Hephaistion or Dorotheus does not mean that only the Moon is here, only that we should pay attention to the sign she is in.

on account of property he will lose it,
though later he will flee from jail and pains.
4 *In the Brothers,*[459] *if he does not obtain freedom within*
the first three days, he will linger for a long time in chains.
5 *The Crab will too long keep him in distress.*
6 *When [Selēnē] is carried over the roaring Lion,*
on account of a mighty and powerful man
pains will follow, and be with him for a time not short, but long.
7 *Around the Maiden, much will the scales turn on either side,*
but you should judge that what comes as a benefit will be more abundant.[460]
8 *In the Scales, there is escape.* **9** *If Selēnē goes into the eight-footed*
Scorpion, he will be kept in chains
and there he will stay for not a short time, but long;
yet all the same he is released at the end.
10 *The Centaur will put the man in great pains.*
11 *The Goat-horned One will grant release, and not bondage.*
12 *However, in the Water-bearer and the Fish they remain*
oppressed, suffering in a difficult and evil plight.
13 *These things with the Moon alone being in those signs I mentioned before, though*
the dispositions of the stars will change it,

…that is to say, when the benefics are with or see them, they cause a quick release; but not the malefics. **14** <Mercury with Jupiter, he being configured with her, quickly provides favorable things, and the release from evils. **15** Mars maltreating the Moon becomes a cause of scourges, bloodshed, and ill-treatment. **16** Saturn working this way makes the evils long-lasting and hard to undo.>[461]

17 *If the Son of Maiā, Phainōn, and Arēs are together,*[462]
the men-destroying fate[463] *reaches him there in prison.*
18 *Observe which stars bear witness to the Hour*
(that one, which begot and guided the man into the day).[464]

---

[459] That is, Gemini.
[460] That is, there will be a mixture of good and bad, but the good will be more abundant (**EG**).
[461] This addition by Pingree based on Epitome IV.
[462] *Homou.* "together, in the same place."
[463] That is, death (**EG**).

19 *Better it will be for them with Selēnē diminishing;*
increasing, meaner works she accomplishes.
20 *And Queen Mēnē, when about to loosen her bond;*[465]
judge this sign as an escape from evils.
21 *Even if she chanced to be under the rays of Helios,*
and made a connection with Kypris, having the mortal suffer dreadful things,
she would then release him from the chains and shameful pains.
22 *Whenever she makes a connection with a setting Hermes*
[who has] become [an] evening [star],[466] *she grants the failure of evils.*
23 *Commingling with Kypris and being with Hermes,*
in the middle of the animal circle,[467] *from the heights of the sky*
till setting,[468] *so that the inclination is southward,*
she saves from bondage. **24** *And if the quick-glancing Queen*
the Aegis-bearing and Kronos see in a triangle,
not without <good reputation[469]

...and honor they would be freed. **25** The Moon being in the same signs, and testified to by Mars, it quickly releases the imprisoned one from the chains, either living or dead.

26 The semicircle from the Midheaven up to the underground pivot, leading and descending, is called "western";[470] the semicircle from the Midheaven till the underground pivot, following and ascending, is called "eastern."[471] **27** The Moon happening to be in the western semicircle, harmed by Mars, means that the prisoner has been unjustly seized, and will remain in chains for a long time; in the eastern semicircle, she announces liberation. **28** The Moon in the western parts, under a triangular figure from Mars, and under a square from Jupiter, indicates the liberation of the bonds. **29** The Moon being assembled[472] with Saturn, and squared by Jupiter from whichever side, frees from bondage as well. **30** Mars in a square to the Moon, Saturn in di-

---

464 That is, the natal Ascendant.
465 That is, leaving the Node (*sundesmos,* lit. "bond, ligature").
466 *Gegaōti hesperiōi.*
467 I.e., on the ecliptic with no or little latitude.
468 This seems to mean, "from the Midheaven to the Descendant."
469 What follows from here up to Ch. III.47, **52**, is added by Pingree from Epitome IV.
470 *Libukos.*
471 *Apēliōtikos,*" lit. "from the *Apēliōtēs,*" or east wind.
472 *Sunodeuousa.*

ameter to her, jointly harassing [her],[473] restrain the prisoner in misery for a long time. **31** If Mars makes a triangle to the Moon, and Saturn a square, either the prisoners will shatter the chains, or dig through the walls of the prison, or else they will come up with any other such innovation with the purpose of escaping. **32** One should especially observe the underground pivot, for the result is shown by it.

<Chapter III.41:> On livelihood and possessions

1 It is needful to observe the second place (that is, the post-ascension of the Hour-marker), and according to the divisions of the times, see in which sign it leaves off.[474] **2** And[475] according to the fixing of the beginning,[476] and the advancement[477] of the times, the malefics being in, or making a diameter, or squaring, each place, both according to the fixing and the advancement, the benefics not helping, neither at the fixing nor by transit,[478] the livelihood and property of that man will suffer loss. If it comes to be contrariwise, that is, if the second place (according to the fixing and to the releasing of the times), either by falling into a co-presence with benefics, or by being squared, or in a diameter with (both according to the fixing and the advancement of the times), is benefited by being testified to by the stars, there will be an increase in the livelihood and property of the man. Should [the natures] be mixed, there will be a mixture (that is, [an alternating] rise and fall of the livelihood).

3 It is also fitting to closely watch the Moon in the inceptions of daily activities. **4** For if she chanced to be passing by those places in which the malefics were placed at the fixing, or to which they made a square or a diam-

---

[473] *Blaptontes.* See Glossary. This seems to be equivalent to besieging.

[474] The "division of times" (diaresis tōn chronōn) is a standard reference to time-lord techniques, and in this case probably refers to profections (see **2** below). Thanks to Chris Brennan for pointing this out.

[475] Hephaistion seems to be saying we should look at the second of the nativity, and at either the profected Ascendant or profected second, and the transits to both.

[476] *Archēs.* That is, the nativity.

[477] *Epembasis*, here and later in the sentence. To me, this sounds like profections (which also means "advancement" in Latin).

[478] *Parodos.* **EG:** This might not be a transit in the modern astrological sense, but as a synonym of the advancement of the times above. **BD:** But taking the transits of the planets at the solar revolution, when profections are made, is a standard procedure in Perso-Arabic astrology.

eter, while none of the benefics is helping (either according to the fixing or transit), and the malefics are hindering by transit, be it bodily or by figure (especially the square and diameter), that inception would then turn very pernicious and climacteric.[479] If contrariwise, that is, if the Moon in the inception chances to be passing by the places of benefics according to the fixing, or in square or diameter to those places, while none of the malefics are hindering, either at the fixing or by transit, and the benefics, either by being together or by figure (especially the square), are beneficial according to transit, that inception becomes most fine[480] and successful. If the above referred to figures to these [places] were a combination of beneficial and hindering [influences], then the inception would show as result a mixture of both good and evil.

5 It is necessary to know that it is impossible that much of good or bad could result from the inceptions about human affairs, unless the position of the Moon chances to be in a place to which either a benefic or a malefic, be it at the nativity or by transit, makes a square figure, since the diametrical figures have rivalry and opposition, the triangular figures are harmonious and sympathetic, though not as strong as the square figures. The hexagons are much weaker, and more vaguely help or hinder.[481]

\<Chapter III.42:\> On the matter of loss, and whether what has been lost will be found

1 Here it is needful to set forth the verses of Dorotheus that paraphrase on these matters, since they are better expounded than the rest.

2 The Sun and the Moon, he says, in a triangle to each other, indicate an easy finding of the lost item. **3** If they were in square to each other, this would show difficulty in finding what has been lost, and the object lost will be carried over from one [place] to another. **4** If the Sun and the Moon make a diameter to each other, this would show that the lost item will not be easily

---

[479] *Klimaktēriōdēs*. This word as such is not found in the dictionary. However, it may suggest that the chart is subjected to periodical or "climacteric" crises that emerge at regular intervals of time, according a distribution of the times (**EG**). For more uses of this word, see *Fragment* V.41, **36-68** (**6-7**).

[480] *Kallistē*. Or, most beautiful, happy, honourable, noble, *etc.*

[481] In other words, apart from conjunctions (which are not aspects or figures), squares are the most dramatic of the aspects.

recovered. **5** If the Moon went void in course (that is to say, when, being within the 120 degrees, she does not connect bodily any of the stars)[482] it would show that the finding will be slow.

6 The Moon assembling with her own ruler indicates finding, and particularly <if the Sun or>[483] Jupiter sees her. **7** When the twelfth-part of the Moon falls into the Hour-marker, or Midheaven, or the Sun, or the Moon's host,[484] or the star making an eastern phase,[485] the lost item will be found very close-by. **8** The Moon in the seventh place or setting [pivot] makes it impossible to find the object, unless the Sun testifies to her. **9** The Moon on the ecliptical Nodes makes the stolen thing[486] hard to find. **10** The Sun and the Moon chancing to be under the earth cause the object to disappear.

11 The Sun being with the Lot of Fortune, or looking upon it, quickly makes the lost item evident. **12** The Moon without the Sun, seeing the Lot of Fortune, indicates that the finding will not be quick. **13** If neither the Sun nor the Moon sees the Lot of Fortune, the stolen object will never be found. **14** The Moon marking the Hour shows a quick finding. **15** The Moon under the rays of the Sun and unlit, makes the stolen thing disappear completely. **16** The Sun and the Moon together marking the Hour not only reveal the thing stolen, but also the thief. **17** The Sun and the Moon making a square to the Hour-marker makes the lost object hard to find, since some fight or delay will ensue. **18** The Sun marking the Hour, unless he is in the triplicity opposite to his own (that is, Libra, Aquarius and Gemini)[487] makes the object easy to find; but if he marks the Hour in one of those signs, the stolen item will prove impossible to find.

19 In relation to these things, we know that the nativities should be aimed at the following way. **20** If the Moon happens to be in a place where a malef-

---

[482] The Hellenistic definition of being void requires that the Moon not complete or perfect a connection with any other planet for the next 30° (see Schmidt 2009, p. 192). By definition, this means that there are 120° of the zodiac in which there cannot be any planet, which are equivalent to the number of degrees in four averted signs: this is part of the "120° group" of configurations I describe in my *Introductions to Traditional Astrology* (III.9, Appendix B), along with wildness, reflection, and besieging. However, especially since Hephaistion refers to the Moon's *bodily* connection and not aspects, we cannot be sure exactly what he means here. Thanks to Chris Brennan for pointing this out.

[483] Added by Pingree from Epitome II.

[484] *Oikodektōr.*

[485] *Anatolikēs.* That is, arising out of the Sun's rays, probably so as to rise before him.

[486] Up to now, the object searched for has been referred to as "the lost thing"; now Hephaistion begins to refer to it as "the *stolen* thing" (**EG**).

[487] The airy signs are opposite the fiery ones (since the Sun is the diurnal lord of the fiery signs, and he rules a fiery sign, Leo).

ic is placed according to the fixing from the beginning, the stolen item will not be found; if according to the fixing the Moon is found in a place of a benefic, then it reveals that the object will be found.

21 If the inception indicates finding, in order to know when the item will be found, one should proceed this way: **22** taking the quantity of signs from the Hour-marker up to the Sun, and—again—the quantity of signs from the Hour-marker up to the Moon, combine the number: and as many as are found from both numbers, say that after such a quantity of days, or months, or years, the object will be found, provided that a benefic testifies; if a malefic, the item is not found.

23 Regarding these matters, one should investigate as follows. **24** Let the Hour-marker be what has been stolen, the Midheaven the seeker, the setting the thief, the underground the place where the thief carried the object. **25** Then, if benefics see or are with the Hour-marker, the lost object will be found. **26** From the setting sign or star, or its ruler, or those stars testifying to it, make your inference about the appearance and character of the thief. **27** Besides, examine the star that culminates: if it is in its own places, then the possession sought is his own, not another's; if in alien[488] places, he does not seek after anything of his own household, but something that belongs to another.

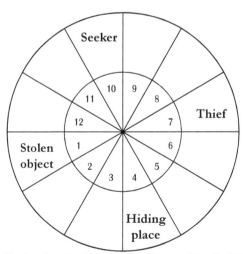

Figure 30: Angles for lost/stolen items (Heph. III.42, 24)

---

[488] That is, "peregrine."

28 If the underground is bicorporeal, know that the stolen object was carried out to brothers, or someone from the family. If it is not bicorporeal [but rather movable],[489] the stolen item has been carried out to only one [man]; if the underground pivot is a masculine sign, the possession is with a man, if feminine, with a woman; and in a like manner with reference to the bicorporeal signs. **29** But one should thus examine the setting as well, and see whether it is masculine, or feminine, bicorporeal or not. **30** The Sun and the Moon testifying to it suggest that the lost item is placed with relatives. **31** If the underground sign is moist, the object is placed outside by a pool, river, or well; if four-footed, the stolen item was placed in a farmstead, or in a shelter of animals; if it is of human form and has the seeing of benefics, it lies in a clean and pure spot. With the malefic stars seeing it, if it is Mars, near a brazen object[490] or kitchen; if it is Saturn, with a slave or in some place dark, humid, filthy, or high.

32 If Jupiter is under the earth, the object lies with a well-born individual; if Mars is under the earth, he who keeps watch on the stolen item is an emancipated slave; if Venus is in the pivot under the earth, if she is up to 20° degrees far from the pivot, know that the object lies with a free and notable woman; and if she is from 20° till 30° from the pivot, with a slave or emancipated slave woman; if Mercury is in the pivot under the earth, if he lies within the first 10° far from the pivot, say that the item is with someone noble and rich; if within the second 10°, with someone free, though poor; if within the third set of 10°, with a slave or hired servant.

33 The Sun seeing the Lot of Fortune reveals easy finding; the Moon alone (without the Sun) seeing the Lot, indicates that the object will be hard to find; if none of the luminaries sees the Lot of Fortune, neither the lost possession nor the slave will be found, since he flees. **34** The Moon being in the extreme degrees of the sign changes the stolen thing from one place into another. **35** The Sun making a square, triangle, or diameter to the Moon makes the thief evident. **36** If, from the clues given by the Sun, it appears that the object will be found, while from the signs[491] from the other stars the item is judged hard to find, then conclude that the object will be eventually found after having taken some delay in time, since the power of the Sun is mightier, and the signs from him afford steadier things. **37** The Sun in a tri-

---

[489] Adding based on *Carmen* V.35, **28** (although *Carmen* has "tropical," which only includes Cancer and Capricorn) (**EG**).

[490] *Chalkeios.* Or, a cauldron.

[491] That is, the indications (not zodiacal signs), here and later in the sentence.

angle, or square, or diameter to the Hour-marker means the same things as his being with the Moon meant (that is to say, square, triangle, diameter). **38** As it is said about thieves, such things we must investigate as well with respect to runaway slaves.

<Chapter III.43:> What is the thing lost [or stolen]?

1 With the Moon in the bounds of Saturn, Saturn being in Libra or on the Midheaven, the lost thing will not be valuable, but old or filthy; if Saturn is towards one of the declining places, or in Aries, [the item] was lost worthless, cheap, filthy, and old. In addition to these, if Saturn himself testifies to the Moon, the stolen thing will be rugged, well-suited for hard work, such as a two-pronged fork, a bag, a rope, or pruning knife.

2 The Moon in the bounds of Jupiter shows that the stolen item is some highly esteemed treasure, very expensive clothing, or anything golden or silver.

3 The Moon in the bounds of Mars indicates that the stolen thing is something that contributes to manufacturing with fire, iron, or anything of the like. If, these things being so, Mars or Mercury is looking, the stolen object will be of fair form, lovely, many-colored and skillfully wrought; but without Mars, if Mercury and Venus see the Moon, the object lost is pleasant, beautiful, and well-colored.

4 When the Moon is in the bounds of Venus, the item lost is gold, silver, precious stones, or it is a many-colored and highly-priced dress, earring, necklace, or arm band, or else simply a female fragrant ornament, perfume, or unguent. If in addition also Venus and the Moon are in feminine signs, the lost possessions belong to a woman; if Mars also testifies to Venus, it shows some beautiful, many-colored crystal works in relief.

5 With the Moon in the bounds of Mercury, documents, books, coins, rolls [of papyrus], or something useful for travelers was stolen.

6 In order that we are able to more accurately make our inference about these matters, it is necessary to consider the natures of the signs the following way. **7** With the Moon in Aries, say that the lost thing is thread, wool, carpets, a headband, clothes; the Moon in Taurus, gold, silver, a garment, headdress, necklace, or else sheep or four-footed herd-animals; with the

Moon in Gemini, coins, tokens,[492] rolls [of papyrus], images, and whatever is useful for feasting; the Moon in Cancer and Capricorn, [something related to] the daily [affairs] of men, such as food, or anything moist, cheap and small; the Moon in Leo and Aquarius, works in gold or silver or copper; the Moon in Virgo, the things lost are ornaments or coins; with the Moon in Libra, aromatic herbs, unguents, perfumes, or as many things as can be purchased by measure, and also what has been put together or molded by the hands, like earrings, incense, or any work in relief; with the Moon in Scorpio, the lost thing is gold, silver, copper, precious stones, and the like; the Moon in Sagittarius and in Pisces, things of many colors and shapes, of good size and well made.

8 The Moon increasing in light and additive in numbers shows things new or recently made; if the Moon is waning, and subtracting in numbers, she shows the lost items to be old things. **9** If a bicorporeal sign marks the Hour, what has been lost is something double, or yoked together, or they are some two things. **10** But if the Moon is in a bicorporeal sign as well, similar things are foretold. **11** Taking the interval in degrees from the position of the Moon till that of Mercury, if the number signs is even, many objects are lost, not only one; if the number is odd, then only one item is lost.

<Chapter III.44:> Who is the thief?

1 If the Sun and the Moon see the Hour-marker, they forecast that the thief is from the same household; if only one Light sees the Hour-marker, say that the thief comes from outside, not from the house, but it is someone of those who has frequent dealings within the household; and if none of the luminaries see the Hour-marker, say that the thief is foreign or from another place.

2 We shall know the form and appearance of the thief in the first place from the stars, but chiefly from the star that is on the setting pivot. Should none of the stars occupy the setting place, then [the thief will be known] from the star in the 9th place; if no star is found there, then the one in the 12th place will show [the thief]; if no star were there, then the one aiming[493]

---

[492] *Symbolaion.* Or, a mark, covenant, contract.
[493] *Epechō,* "to direct towards, aim at," but also "prevail upon, predominate" (**EG**).

bodily at the Moon, that is to say, connecting to her. If no star adheres to[494] the Moon, examine which one had made a phase or station seven days before the theft, or which changed from one sign to another: from that star know the appearance and shape of the thief.

<Chapter III.45:> On the appearance of the thief

1 If the star of Jupiter shows the thief, he will be of pale complexion, in good bodily condition, large-eyed, with small pupils, not quick-sighted, of good discernment,[495] fleshy, well-fed, thick-bearded.

2 If Saturn, the thief will be unshapely, black, short-sighted, small-eyed, with wrinkles on his mouth, pale,[496] a liar, with a propensity to hide his thoughts, of crooked mind, hairy, gloomy-faced, smelling like a goat.

3 If Mars, he will be blond, with long and straight hair, gorgon-eyed, round-faced, having small ears, fierce, sensible, fickle, with quick impulses,[497] rapidly excited to action.[498]

4 If Venus, the thief will be of fair form, with beautiful eyes, black-eyed, of pale complexion, slightly black-skinned[499] on certain parts, fleshy, and of good knowledge.

5 If Mercury, the thief will be thin, slender, proportionate, of curly hair, well-born, of varied knowledge, greenish-yellow.

6 If the Sun or the Moon are found to signify the thief, according to the nature of the stars they mix with, such will the appearance be that he will be shown to have. **7** But if they do not have a house relationship[500] with any star but are only in their own, then the Sun indicates that the thief is well-fed, solid,[501] and slightly pale; if the Moon alone, tempered, with beautiful eyes, fleshy and round-faced.

8 You will more accurately learn about the same things not only by the observation of the stars, but also of the signs in which the significators are

---

[494] *Kollaō.*
[495] *Agathognōmōn.* Not in the dictionary, but possibly also "of good customs" (**EG**).
[496] *Xlōros.* Or, "greenish," "yellowish."
[497] *Oxuormētos.* Since this is not in the lexicon, we have read it as *oxu + hormē.*
[498] Also, "ready to be sent to war."
[499] Also, "sunburnt."
[500] *Sunoikeiōthōsin.* That is, they are not in the domicile of another planet.
[501] *Puknon.* Also, "shrewd."

found. **9** Aries shows the thieves as hairy and tall, their face bending downward, with curly hair, cowardly,[502] playful, and foul-mouthed. Taurus, flat-nosed, with a hairy body, with a sugar-loaf [shaped] head,[503] with a broad front, having the hair girded up, hiding their thoughts, deceiving in their reply, with feigned reasonableness, with wide nostrils, wide-necked, black-eyed, with thin lips and big brows. Gemini describes the thief as proportionate in measure, with a long nose, delicate,[504] of good judgment, with their shoulders easily taking an impression, some also knowing how to write, and trusted. Cancer shows them as bony, hairy, flat-faced, black-skinned (some with twisted teeth), of proportionate stature, having their lower parts bigger. Leo, bluish green, yellowy-red,[505] fair of form, having the upper parts bigger, thin legs, wild of judgment[506] and face, gluttonous, some also knowing how to wrestle. Virgo, proportionate in stature, with a ductile[507] body, straight in their ideas, of well-ordered customs, faithful through writing, or teaching some art through writing. Libra, of beautiful eyes, white-skinned, useful as a servant, of flexible limbs, well-proportioned,[508] easily changing,[509] prone to women. Scorpio, with girded-up hair, somewhat grey, middle-sized eyes, round-faced, with a prominent throat, big legs, with good feet, of broad chest, rapacious, bold, a sorcerer, daring, fool-hardy. Sagittarius, with big legs, of beautiful ankles, ductile, some also bold-headed, with pointed chin, red-skinned, pot-bellied, swift-footed, divers,[510] sheep-loving, impressionable, lavish, inclined to anger. Capricorn, hairy, thin-shanked, bony, inclined downwards, with a goat's-eye, with pointed chin, doubtful, unreliable, exciting laughter, rather stupid. Aquarius, middle-aged, with a solemn countenance, pointed chin, fond of play, lavish, voluptuary, having one leg thicker than the other, unlucky in their pursuits. Pisces, with flat shoulders, beautiful hair, small head, narrow front, black eyes, unaffected, vacillating, changeable, some handling [things] in thought, others pursuing [them in ac-

---

[502] *Deilós.* Also, "wretched, miserable."

[503] *Prokephalous.* Since the Middle Ages at least, sugar-loaves were shaped like a cone rounded off on top. It is hard to imagine exactly how a head would be shaped like this, so perhaps some other shape is meant.

[504] *Trupheros.* Also, "effeminate."

[505] *Pyrros.* Or, flame-colored, tawny.

[506] *Agriognōmōn.*

[507] That is, flexible and thin.

[508] *Ruthmos.* Also, "orderly, graceful."

[509] *Eutrapelos.* Also, "tricky, deceitful."

[510] *Kolumbētēs.* Also, "one who draws water from wells."

tion].[511]

10 So these are the methods[512] of finding from the stars and the signs. However, one should not consider that all the indications on each issue are found unfailing, but one should go through with what is skillfully[513] accepted, and select the method from the configured stars. **11** If a benefic testifies to the star signifying the thief, this will be a free man; if a malefic, a slave, poor man, or hireling. **12** If Venus signifies the thief, the author of the theft is a woman; if Mercury, a child; if Mars, a man in his prime; if Jupiter, a middle-aged man; if Saturn, an old man.

13 On the other hand, in the case of Saturn, Jupiter and Mars, if the star signifying the thief is an eastern riser, it foretells him a child; if it makes the first station, a man in his prime; if achronical,[514] middle-aged; if it makes the second station, half-grey; if the evening setting, an old man. **14** For instance, let Saturn, as a significator of the thief, be on a morning rising: the thief is neither a child on account of being eastern, nor old because of Saturn, but middle-aged, thus combining the inference from the child and the old man. **15** In the case of Venus and Mercury, if they are evening risers, they show the thieves as young, be it a man or a woman; if after the first station, they make an evening setting, middle-aged; if morning risers, old men. Some say that if Venus and Mercury are morning risers, they indicate that the thief is a young man or woman; if setting, an old man or woman.

16 Now, if the star that signifies the thief is in its own exaltation, this indicates that he is of big body and of good size; if it is in the sign of its depression, then small: according to the distance, proportionally draw your conclusion about the magnitude of his size. **17** For instance, let Mars indicate the thief, occupying the third decan of Aries: we say that the thief is middle-sized (for from the third decan of Capricorn [till the third decan of Aries] the interval is the middle of the semicircle).[515] **18** If it were in Pisces, or in Scorpio, we would say that the size is bigger than middle; if in Taurus, or Virgo, less than the middle. **19** If the star showing the thief happens to fall under the rays of the Sun within seven days after the theft took place, know that the thief has fallen into some trouble; if also Mars testifies to him, he has

---

[511] *Alla men metacheirizomenous en dianoia, alla de diōkontas.*
[512] *Stochasmos.* That is, the power of guessing that comes from practice.
[513] *Entechnos*, lit. "within the range of the art."
[514] That is, in the opposition to the Sun so that he sets when the Sun rises, and *vice versa.*
[515] I do not quite understand what Hephaistion/Dorotheus means here

fallen[516] into wounds, agony and difficult dangers.

20 If the Lot of Fortune is not seen by a malefic, there was no theft, but the object sought has been misplaced and hidden; and if only the Sun sees the Lot, it was not stolen, but hidden.

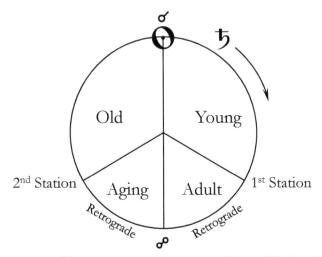

Figure 31: Thief age, superior planets (Heph. III.45, 13)

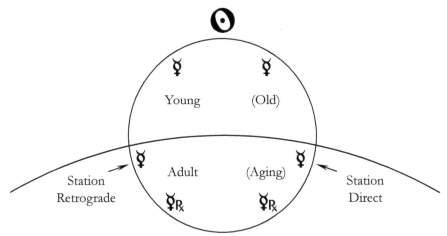

Figure 32: Thief age, inferior planets (Heph. III.45, 15)

---

[516] *Peripetēs.* This gives the idea of a "reversal" of fortunes (**EG**).

<Chapter III.46:> In which way is it lost?

1 If Saturn testifies to the Hour-marker and the Moon, it would show that the theft has been perpetrated through some cunning and treachery; if Jupiter, the thief is shown as someone trusted because of his feigned good disposition, and reasonableness in his reply for having stolen what he stole. If Mars, the theft has been perpetrated by force, violence, housebreaking, substitution of false keys, or removal of the door.[517] If Venus, through falsely alleged friendly pretexts, associations, merriment, and women. If Mercury, through knavery.

<Chapter III.47:> On runaways

1 We shall get information about the runaway from those [stars] which meet with the Moon and the Hour-marker; the master, from those with the Sun and the Midheaven. **2** For if the Moon or the Hour-marker chanced to be in tropical or equinoctial signs, impediments will come in the way of the one who flees, not being able to reach anywhere far, neither by land nor by sea;[518] if in bicorporeal signs, he has not fled alone, but has hardness and perseverance. **3** If a crooked sign marks the Hour, [it is] bad for the one who flees (for he will have much wandering on his way); if straight, he will promptly arrive wherever he would wish. **4** The Moon in a bicorporeal sign till the 15th degree, would show that the runaway fled once, and he will flee again for the second time; and when she is found after the 16th degree, up to the 30th, she would show that he has already run away before, and not only then.

5 The Moon marking the Hour tells that the runaway urges on towards the east; culminating, towards the south; setting, towards sunset; in the underground pivot, towards the north. **6** In the intervals in between, in a proportional way: for example, in the ninth place, towards the south [but] more westerly; if in the eighth, towards setting [but] more southerly; and sim-

---

[517] Taking the noun *metochlēsis* as coming from the verb *metochlizō*, which means to remove by a lever, or to hoist a heavy body out of the way (**EG**).

[518] This does not make astrological sense. It should probably read that *fixed* signs impede movement, and movable signs enhance movement: see *Carmen* V.36, **2**. Thanks to Deb Houlding for pointing this out.

ilarly with the other places.

7 If stationary Mars connects with the Moon, either bodily or by rays, the one who flees will perish, or, having been seized, will be enchained or thrown into prison, especially if also Saturn, beholding [her], harms her: for then he is destroyed [by] having been plotted against, be it secretly or openly. **8** If stationary Saturn sees the Moon, or holds her in a connection, the runaway will die, hanged by his own hands, if no benefic (seeing the Moon) relieves the evil. **9** If Saturn, not stationary, receives[519] the Moon, the runaway will lose whatever he is carrying; faring ill, he will either be led off [as captive] to his own master, or become a prisoner in foreign lands.

10 When the benefics see the Moon or connect with her, or mark the Hour, it is favorable for the runaway: he will be cheered on or finally freed. **11** But between these, Venus is better [both] for the one who flees and for the thief, because—even if they were taken captive alive—nothing evil would fall upon them from their masters on account of Venus, but on the contrary they will become more valuable.

12 With the Moon increasing in light, the runaway will be found with difficulty (for he is hidden [while] not fearing his own master); with the Moon diminishing in light, the runaway will neither be able to go too far, nor hide for a long time (for it is his lot to be caught).

13 When the Sun is setting, and Saturn is post-descending [him] in the 8th place, if some slave runs away, before he is caught his master will have perished. **14** When the malefics are either culminating or with the Sun, if some slave flees away, it is of no profit for the master to seek him, as he will not find him; but even if he found him, he will not be useful, as he will be disabled. **15** When the Moon is setting and Mars post-descends [her], while no benefic testifies to the Moon, it indicates a cruel death for the one who flees. **16** Again, if the Moon is setting, Mercury is post-descending, and Mars is making a right[520] triangle to Mercury from the underground place, it shows a difficult death for the runaway. **17** If the Moon is under the rays of the Sun, seen by Mars, the runaway will perish by fire or iron.

18 If you also want to know of what kind the death will be, and by whom it will take place, search this way: examine the sign that the Moon occupies, as well as the Hour-marker of the inception. **19** If they are of human form, the evils will come at the hands of robbers (and in a word, men); if four-

---

519 *Dechêtai.* This probably means that he receives her aspect, just as with Mars above.
520 This aspect would be to Mercury's right, but actually cast from Mars's left.

footed, through beasts; if mixed (that is, [a combination of] human-shaped and four-footed [signs]), through hostile horsemen;[521] if earthy, by falling off a cliff, or an accident.[522]

20 If, as it is said, Saturn sees the Moon from a watery sign while she is under the rays, and Leo marks the Hour, the evils are shown to be more certain: for neither will the runaway be found (but he will be utterly destroyed), nor will the kind of death [be known]. **21** If Mercury conspires[523] with this maltreatment of the Moon, the runaways will perish by their own hands. **22** When they are looking on,[524] the benefics relieve the aforesaid maltreatments, especially when they are out of the rays.

23 If the Moon is brought to Mars, the latter not being stationary but additive, the runaway will be caught, to experience whipping and torture. **24** When Mars sets, the Moon post-descends [him], and Jupiter is looking upon her,[525] the fleeing one will be put under dangers and fears, but through Jupiter he will keep away from evils. **25** And if the malefics occupy the underground pivot or the Midheaven, or the setting [place], the runaway, being seized prisoner, will die in jail.

26 When the Moon culminates, being surrounded[526] by malefics (Mars from the right, and Saturn from the left), the runaways will be killed by strangling; if Mars surrounds her from the left, and Saturn from the right, the fleeing one will be crucified. **27** The Moon culminating, or setting, or in the underground pivot, being surrounded by the Sun and Mars (from whichever side each chances to be, either on the right or on the left), the runaway will be delivered alive to the fire.

28 When the ruler of the Moon is under the rays, and it does not behold[527] her, it indicates that the master of the runaway will quickly die. **29** When the Moon, her ruler, and the [ruler] of the Hour-marker are in tropical signs, the fleeing one will voluntarily return to his master in repentance. **30** If the Moon is seen by both a benefic and a malefic, the runaway will not escape his master, especially when the malefic makes a square or diameter to

---

[521] *Hippeus.* Or, one who fights from a chariot.
[522] *Symptōma.* Or, "collapse, sinking, demolition."
[523] *Synpneuō.*
[524] *Epitheōreō.*
[525] *Epitheōreō.*
[526] *Perichomenēs.* That is, besieged; see Greek-English glossary, and *ITA* IV.4.2.
[527] *Theōreō.*

the Moon. Roughly in those days in which the Moon, by going around,[528] passes through the degrees of the malefic of the fixed point,[529] the fleeing one will be hunted or will encounter some evil.

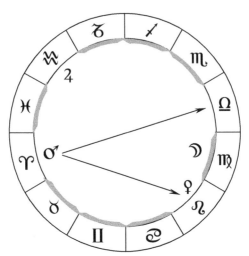

Figure 33: Malefic enclosure/besieging by sign[530]

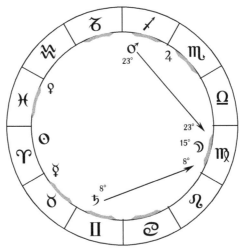

Figure 34: Malefic enclosure/besieging by degree

---

[528] *Peripatos.*

[529] *Epochēs.* This seems to mean, "at the time of the event chart."

[530] For a discussion of besieging, see my *Introductions to Traditional Astrology* IV.4.2.

31 When both the Moon and the Hour-marker are maltreated, and not helped by any of the benefics, the runaway will run risks and be hurt; if both the Moon and the Hour-marker are assisted by benefics, being besides that unharmed by Saturn and Mars, and the benefics being in solid signs, the runaway will never be found; if in bicorporeal or tropical signs, either the fleeing one himself will return in repentance, or else will be involuntarily seized; [but] having supported no evil, his master will be abashed, and will be taken by pity for him.

32 The Sun beholding[531] the Moon and the Hour-marker makes all the hidden things come to light. **33** As regards the inceptions that give indications[532] on finding, Mars shows a quick finding, and Saturn a slow one. **34** With Jupiter setting, the runaway, even if he is seized, will suffer no evil, for the master is appeased. **35** When Venus indicates finding, she shows the escaping one to be in a sacred place.

36 If a star in its own house was also looking at the Hour-marker and the Moon, it would show that there has been no flight; but if who you think has fled does wander somewhere nearby, he has not gone too far away. **37** For every star [which is] retrograde and seeing the Moon and its own house, tells you that the one sought has not escaped, but has just wandered somewhere nearby.

38 The Moon and the Hour-marker, without[533] the testimony of any star, when they are in each sign by themselves, they reveal these things about the preceding chapter, as they are next appended:[534] **39** Aries having the Moon or the Hour-marker brings [the fleeing ones] back quickly; some even return voluntarily; if the Moon is in Aries, while Leo, Sagittarius, or Gemini marks the Hour, the runaway will not be discovered. **40** Taurus having the Moon or the Hour-marker brings the fleeing one back home through some powerful man, but he is found with difficulty. **41** Gemini having the Moon or the Hour-marker, if they are within the first 15°, either the runaway will be found within 2 days, or [if not found], the master will see him or hear some infor-

---

531 *Theōreō.*

532 *Hupophainō.* Or, "bring to light from under," or "show just a little."

533 Or perhaps simply, "apart from"?

534 Or perhaps, "as follows." We can take this sentence in two ways. If we take "chapter" literally (and not as a synonym for "heading"), then Hephaistion is indicating Chapter 46—which does talk about the testimonies of the stars to the Moon and Hour-marker. But if we take it to mean "heading" or "section," it must indicate **31-36** immediately above, which likewise deals with the same topic (**EG**).

mation about him after the third month; if after the first 15°, the fleeing one will quickly be found. **42** Cancer having the Moon or the Hour-marker suggest that the runaway, if not found within 2 days, he will be tardy found hiding in a sacred place. **43** Leo having the Moon or the Hour-marker within the first 15°, brings the fleeing one back; within the next 15° it makes him unseen, and brings him to the household of some rich lord, for which reason he will be difficult to find. **44** Virgo having the Moon or the Hour-marker reveals a difficult finding of the runaway, for the winged feature of this sign gives hints on the runaway being unseen. **45** Libra having the Moon or the Hour-marker brings the fleeing one back, though alleging as an excuse that it was reasonable for him to run away, so pleading his cause before the judge.[535] **46** Scorpio having the Moon or the Hour-marker brings the runaway back into some sacred precinct, and frequently it makes him return of his own accord. **47** Sagittarius having the Moon or the Hour-marker makes the runaway wander towards different places, and causes his discovery to take time. **48** Capricorn having the Moon or the Hour-marker <makes the runaway die, if not found within five days, and his place will not be known>.[536] **49** Aquarius having the Moon or the Hour-marker, within the first 15°, brings the runaway back; in the last [15°] it makes him be unseen. **50** Pisces having the Moon or the Hour-marker, within the first 15° it makes the fleeing one be unseen; along the remaining degrees, makes him evident. **51** These things are disclosed according to the 12 signs themselves, without the testimony of any star. When the observation of the Hour of the inception of the runaway is uncertain, it is necessary to place the Hour-marker [at the time] when the master of the runaway [first] heard the message about the flight.

52 And>[537] Dorotheus [expounded] these things in his verses; let it now be set forth what has been said by others: from a compilation by Nicaeus Protagoras, so he explains: **53** if[538] you find the ruler of the Hour-marker of the flight retrograde, the fleeing one will voluntarily return to his master; if it is found in its own place or bounds, not retrograde, the runaway is within the household, or in the city, or will be found in some place around, more quickly so if it happens to be in the hemisphere above earth, and more slowly if in the lower hemisphere.

---

[535] *Dikaiologoumenon.*
[536] Pingree has filled this lacuna in Epitome IV from the Arabic Dorotheus.
[537] Here ends the long section added by Pingree, which began at III.40, **24**.
[538] See also *Excerpt XXVIII.*

54 If[539] the Moon is in the right square (that is to say, on the Midheaven), the runaway has made his way of escape through the right portions of the building from which he ran away; similarly, in the left square, through the left portions: for the Hour-marker is thought to be over against the gates of the household.

55 The Moon,[540] from the limit of the northern wind, descending north, discloses that the runaway has fled in the direction of midday, and will be found in 25 days. Descending south, in the places of the setting of the Sun, in 42 days, in watery places, wild and stormy. Ascending south, it will be disclosed, in eastern places, with difficulty, in 64 days. Ascending north, in arctic places, the finding will be difficult.

56 It is from the nature of the signs that one must infer the place towards which the runaway fled: for instance, Pisces means some marshy and fenny places; equally Aquarius; Capricorn, territories moist and by the sea; Sagittarius, rugged lands and vineyards; Aries, pastures and plains; Taurus, flat lands, and hardly-worked ground; <Gemini...>;[541] Cancer, lands with an abundance of water, dry and high lands; Leo, steep, jagged and deserted lands; Virgo, lands sown with corn; Libra, plains; Scorpio, rugged [places] and [places of] pirates,[542] having also vineyards; Aquarius, lands marshy and near rivers.

57 Some also divide the pivots this way: [they assign] the setting to the runaway, the Midheaven to the master, the Hour-marker to the things carried [away], the counter-Midheaven to what one encounters.[543]

---

[539] Passages like this must have inspired question texts on finding buried treasures, as we see in al-Kindī's *Forty Chapters* Ch. 35.

[540] It is unclear to me what Hephaistion is referring to by "winds," not to mention how he is deriving these numbers of days. If we take "wind" to mean "declination," then the limit of the northern wind is 0° Cancer, and descends to 0° Libra, where the "wind" becomes southern—and so on throughout the circle. Or, Hephaistion could mean the limit of her northern latitude in the ecliptic. Yet another possibility is found in Valens *Anth.* III.4, in which the most northern part of the "wind" of each planet is the degree of its exaltation: in that case, 3° Taurus is the most northern "wind," 3° Scorpio the most southern, and the squares at 3° Aquarius and 3° Leo are the transition points between winds.

[541] Missing, but typical Gemini locations would be in cupboards or containers, high places, cultivated mountainous places. See for example *Introductions to Traditional Astrology* (I.3); for another list, see Dykes and Gibson 2012, Appendix 1.

[542] *Lēstrikous.*

[543] *Apantēsanti.* It is unclear whether this is a person or thing. I am inclined to take this as the "outcome," which is typical for many of the elections in Hephaistio/Dorotheus. But I also note that "Erasistratos" (Schmidt 1995, p. 37) and the Arabic Dorotheus (*Carmen* V.35, **20**) assign it to the hiding place of the goods (which is also supported in III.42, **24**).

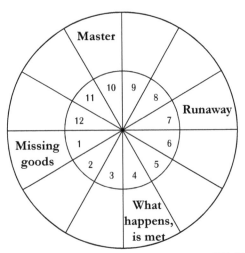

Figure 35: Houses for runaways (Heph. III.47, 57)

58 Some do it differently,[544] and assign [it in] the following way: the Moon and the Hour-marker to the runaway, the Sun and the Midheaven to the lord.

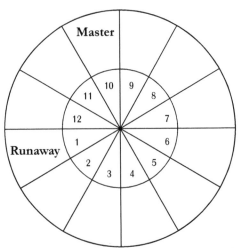

Figure 36: Houses for runaways (Heph. III.47, 1 and 58)

59 It is also necessary to pay careful attention to the Moon, for she reveals everything. **60** First, when she traverses the hemisphere above earth, she makes the finding easy; but under the earth, difficult, just as it is said by

---

[544] See *Carmen* V.36, **1**, and 'Umar al-Ṭabarī in *Judges* 7.73.

<..........>.⁵⁴⁵

61 She being bound in⁵⁴⁶ the Hour-marker or in the signs following it, it uncovers that the flight has taken place towards the east; on the Midheaven, towards the north;⁵⁴⁷ in the setting, towards the setting [Sun]; in the underground pivot, towards midday.⁵⁴⁸ **62a** The pivots also show the exit: through which gates the fleeing ones will withdraw.

62b And the length of the road [is known from] the interval of hours from rising or setting, through the Moon herself. **63** For should she be found in a tropical sign, the way of the flight is short; and when she travels slowly, it means that the way from the place he fled will not be long; and if in dry, or crooked, or bicorporeal signs, [it means] that he will not be taking a straight way, and that he has not escaped alone.

64 According to the rising or setting of the sign, one must know the straightness and crookedness of the path: the beginnings from the risings, and the ends from the settings.⁵⁴⁹ **65** The under-parts⁵⁵⁰ of the signs also pose some danger to the fleeing one, especially when the difficult stars are added: for then the evils are made more evident, especially when Mars comes to be under the earth with [the Moon], and is also stationary. When Saturn distributes,⁵⁵¹ they hang themselves or throw themselves down a precipice. **66** When she connects with the benefics, or when they control the Hour, while the malefics are configured, they return from repentance; but if [the malefics] are turned away,⁵⁵² they will be in freedom close by.⁵⁵³ **67** If Venus, pivotal and in her own place, is present to help, not only will they not be

---

⁵⁴⁵ Pingree does not indicate how big this lacuna is; at any rate, it does not seem to be in *Carmen.*

⁵⁴⁶ *Katalēphtheisa.* That is, being in it.

⁵⁴⁷ *Pros arkton.*

⁵⁴⁸ That is, the south.

⁵⁴⁹ In general, when straighter signs rise in the east, more crooked signs are setting in the west. Thus if a straight sign is rising (such as Libra or Scorpio), it means that while the beginning of his flight is straight and direct, while the end of it is crooked (Aries or Taurus).

⁵⁵⁰ *Ta huptia.* This seems to mean the lower hemisphere under the earth (see the comment about Mars later in the sentence).

⁵⁵¹ *Merizontos.* This seems simply to mean that he is playing the same role with the Moon that Mars was, in the previous clause.

⁵⁵² That is, in aversion.

⁵⁵³ We take this to mean the following: (a) if both benefics and malefics are configured or involved, then he will return due to the malefic indications; but (b) if they are in aversion, he will remain free and not return.

insulted, but they will also be comforted.[554] **68** If the Moon is found in the midst of Mars and Saturn,[555] they will be in chains for a long time, sometimes dying in prison, especially when the benefics are estranged.[556] **69** With [the Moon] connected to Mars, they will be slain.

70 One should also observe the following. **71a** When a star is on the pre-ascension of the Hour-marker,[557] it shows that he has already fled before; in the post-ascension,[558] once caught, he will flee again; and if the Moon is on the Hour-marker he will be from another household, not from that of the one who is looking, and in addition he will be brought back. **71b** If some star sets, he will be found straightaway, and close to the house.

72 It is unsuitable for the runaways when the Moon is increasing in numbers, but suitable when decreasing in numbers.

73 The Sun setting or culminating with any of the malefics, or looked upon by a drastic figure (that is, a square or diameter) means that the master will die before the discovery of the runaway, or that he will undergo much <damage>[559] and harm. **74** The Sun seeing the Moon in the hemisphere above the earth quickly facilitates the information through accomplices; similarly Saturn [being] on the upper pivot with the Moon makes the transmission quick, through foul women or female slaves, and in a similar way if Venus is on the upper pivot with the Moon testifying, the information will come through some free woman <....>[560] **75** If the Hour-marker is in four-footed signs, likewise. **76** It should also be known that, if the Moon by herself is culminating, they are found asleep; Mercury post-descending her, they will be misled by someone in the neighborhood, or who sat together with him. **77** With Venus and Jupiter, or else the Sun, setting, the misleading one [just mentioned] will be well-born, and will appear to be a free man. **78** When Taurus, Gemini, Cancer, Leo, Virgo, Scorpio, and Pisces mark the Hour, while Jupiter and Venus look on,[561] he will appear in a sacred place,

---

[554] Also, "summoned," "invited," or "encouraged" (**EG**).

[555] This must refer to besieging.

[556] *Allotriōthentōn.* We might expect this to mean "peregrine," but in this case I believe it means they are in aversion to the Moon—so that she is only affected by malefic influences.

[557] That is, the twelfth.

[558] That is, the second.

[559] Added by Pingree from several Epitomes.

[560] Lacuna.

[561] *Epitheōreō.*

and will be found appearing clearly beforehand;[562] when Mars is with the Moon, the runaway will have cuts on his face [made] by iron. **79** If Saturn also happens to be marking the Hour together with Jupiter and the Moon, it indicates that the fleeing one carries money with him, and that he will be found; the benefics marking the Hour with the Moon, frees the runaway from cares, and shows besides that he carries sufficient money. **80** Mars and Saturn post-setting with the Moon,[563] within 160 or else 170 days[564] they will return to the master's authority.

81 Mercury with the Moon and Venus, both marking the Hour or culminating, indicates a child, or virgin, or young man, and he will be found when the malefics look upon [them],[565] in around 50 days; if Mercury and Mars, the one sought will be of a mixed type; if Saturn and Mercury and Venus, a man, woman and child; if Saturn, Jupiter, Mercury and the Moon, the fleeing one is a eunuch. **82** When Mars, Venus, and Mercury are on the Hour-marker, he is revealed as a hermaphrodite; Jupiter, Venus, the Sun and the Moon, the runaways are free men; Mars looking upon Jupiter, they are held back under the power and watch of someone. **83** With Mars and Saturn marking the Hour, they hand themselves over to the power of someone. **84** Mars and Venus marking the Hour indicates that much was wasted in sexual pleasures, and because of this the flight was undertaken.

85 It is needful to accurately investigate the figures of the Moon, as well as to know her connections and Nodes, as we have said before, and inquire in which decline from the pivots they would be found: for from all this will be made clear, not only the issues about the runaways, but also about those who make a long way travelling abroad by land and by sea. **86** When the Moon chances to be in the signs around the setting pivot, and constrained[566] by the declines from the Midheaven, she does not cause the migration to be within the boundaries [of the city]; but she does so if on the Hour-marker and on the Midheaven, since for the most part they are found roaming about in the city, and lodged in the house of someone. **87** When the Moon is unconnected to the Sun and the Hour-marker, they happen to be impossible to

---

[562] *Prodēlon*. Or, "in front" (meaning somewhat unclear).

[563] That is, in the eighth.

[564] I am not sure of the rationale for these days, nor for the 50 days mentioned in **81**.

[565] *Epidontōn*, from *ephoraō*.

[566] *Katalēphtheisa* (from *katalambanō*). That is, the ninth acts as an upper limit to her, constraining her from being higher than the eighth. I am not sure why Hephaistion refers to this in the plural.

discover at the time of the flight; if she is configured, or in a phase,[567] and in harmony with the Hour, it shows that the finding will be without harm to anyone. **88** If she is in the assembling sign, waning, and not yet running along with[568] the Sun's rays, unconnected with the Hour, it causes the running away to be without [his] return; likewise, when she has made an eclipse on the Nodes, for the most part it indicates that the runaways will be imprisoned. **89** One should also include [the examination of] the signs that hear and see: for when she comes to pass through those, she makes someone hear or see about them.

90 And if nothing[569] is lacking (of the figures given before), they are taken within the first square;[570] if the smallest part is lacking, within the second (that is to say, within the diameter of the inception); if more is lacking, around the third square, or else the return of these to the initial position, the completion of the circle. **91** The Sun supplies their coming into visibility[571] when he is in a square (in the squares of the Full Moon), and in a triangle (in the triangles of the assembly). **92** As regards those inceptions that indicate slow finding, it is useful to divide into months the movement made by the Sun in the triangles.

93 In relation to the nativities of slaves, the matter of running away is comprehended from the star of Mercury. He[572] being unfavorably placed or beheld[573] by malefics, or else obtaining the place or bounds <belonging to them>, especially with Mars, [then] when the god is found in the setting [places] and the underground pivot, and away from the malefics, this produces running away. **94** One should also take into consideration his movement towards the Sun: for when he happens to be under the rays, the runaway will immediately hide; when fleeing from the rays and arising,[574] he will be made

---

[567] I take this to mean that she is coming out of or going under the rays.

[568] *Sunekdramousēs* (from *sunektrechō*). That is, she is not yet under them.

[569] *Mēden.* I have slightly edited a couple of words in this sentence for easier comprehension.

[570] That is, in about a week. In this awkward sentence, Hephaistion is saying that if the figure shows all of the indications of being found, they will be found very quickly; but the more the figure lacks these indications, the longer it will take.

[571] *Emphaneian.* This seems to mean it makes the *runaway* visible.

[572] In what follows, we refer to the star as "he" to more easily identify it with Mercury.

[573] *Theōroumenou.*

[574] *Anateilantos.* That is, while retrograding out of the Sun's rays so as to rise before the Sun.

evident; and turned additive,[575] will be made come back. **95** When Mars is in the sign in which he makes the rising, and makes an assembly with an evil decan, it cuts the throat; if the benefics look upon [him],[576] <they[577] preserve from death, but throw around him both fetters and evils.

96 It is necessary to watch the twelfth-parts of the stars in power:[578] for when it falls in agreement with[579] the Hour-marker, in every inception the matters turn out to have an easy ending.

97 Some say that when the Moon is with the Sun, the runaway will hide for some time, on which account such a man, having been immediately sought, will be found; though if he is not sought straightaway, he will become difficult to locate.

98 These things about running away, flight and theft.>

---

[575] That is, after stationing and then moving direct towards the Sun. It seems to me that this could also be taken in the other way: that when Mercury moves *forward* out of the Sun's rays, he is made evident, while then *retrograding* towards the Sun after his station, he will turn back.

[576] *Epitheōreō.*

[577] Up to the end of **98**, added by Pingree from two Epitomes.

[578] *Kratountōn.* This seems to be a reference to some kind of victor.

[579] *Sunekpesē.* Meaning unclear.

APPENDIX A: ON EASY & PAINFUL DELIVERY

Comment by Dykes. Appendices A-C represent three passages of Hephaistion material, which Pingree himself put in an Appendix of his edition (pp. 330-33), with a Latin title reading, "Certain chapters omitted from the third Book of Hephaistio."

1 The Sun, the Hour-marker, and the Moon being in masculine signs at the time of childbirth, affords an easy delivery when the children born are male, since bringing them to birth will be easy. **2** When they are female, if the Sun and the Hour-marker, but especially the Moon, chance to be in feminine signs, the delivery will proceed equally swiftly and unharmed.

3 On the other hand, the delivery proceeds, contrariwise, in a crooked and incongruous way when Saturn happens to be pivotal, and particularly if the place in which he is contains a feminine sign: for it brings on danger to those in labor. **4** In the same way, when Mars is pivotal, especially if the sign that he occupies chances to be feminine, the delivery is made easy, so that the pregnant one delivers all of a sudden and on the roads or in bathing places.

5 It[1] is also needful to examine whether the signs are straight or crooked: from Cancer through Sagittarius are the straight ones; from Capricorn through Gemini the crooked ones.[2] **6** If the Moon is found in straight signs, the childbirth becomes easy, since the fetus makes a straight way out; in crooked signs the delivery becomes crooked.

7 And Manetho says thusly: if the Moon is enclosed[3] by Saturn and Mars, it is painful for the woman in labor, particularly when these stars (Saturn and Mars) also happen to be in crooked signs, and the Moon is pivotal; in a similar way if these two were pivotal as well.

---

[1] See also Heph. III.1, **1,** *Excerpt* LIII, and *Frag.* V.1, **5**—V.4, **1** (sentences **5-6**).
[2] This is in the northern hemisphere; in the southern hemisphere these roles are reversed.
[3] *Emperischetheisa.* That is, besieged (see Greek-English glossary).

APPENDIX B: ON [THE DISPOSITION OF PROPERTY BY] A WILL, AND OTHERWISE

1 When someone wishes to seal up[1] an already-written testament for the purpose of credibility, observe carefully whether the Hour-marker and the Moon are in tropical signs: because if this happens, there will eventually be a change of the inception, since the testator will dispose of the property in a different manner, and obviously he will not die upon the first disposition of the will. **2** In addition, let the Moon be also increasing in light, lifted high in latitude, and subtractive in numbers as regards longitude,[2] connecting with any star having its station, and let her not be under the rays (for if she is under the rays the testator will quickly die).

3 Mars should perforce be closely watched, so that he does not mark the Hour nor is with the Moon, nor makes a square to her, nor is he in [her] diameter: since, this being so, not only will the testator die, but also the testament will be made to disappear (for instance, by being stolen or by accepting another fake will instead of it). **4** Mercury being maltreated, either being with the malefics or configured to them, becomes a cause of treacheries and disputes. **5** If Saturn marks the Hour, death will occur after some time, but the testament will be executed. **6** If Jupiter or Venus marks the Hour, it causes the testator not to die, [and] to make the will again.

7 The Hour-marker means the power[3] of the writing of the will, and the testator; the Midheaven, the completion of it; the setting, whether it is of high repute, or disreputable, true or counterfeit; the underground, of what sort are they who will receive the inheritance.

8 If Saturn marks the Hour in the inception, the testator will be old, knavish, and unjust; he will have treachery and lies, and the maker[4] will be ignoble, mean, or an emancipated slave. **9** If Mars, the testament will be [written] hastily from anger, without reasoning power, so that those to whom the inheritance belongs are considered out of it, and the maker is young, military, and inclined to anger. **10** If Jupiter, the will is shown as being just and opulent, and the testator also as such. **11** If Venus, especially when she is in the solstices, the testament will be good and manifold, the maker equally of

---

[1] *Sphragizō*, to authenticate a document or certify an object, by attaching a seal to it (**EG**).
[2] This must mean that she is slowing down in speed, or perhaps simply going at a speed slower than average.
[3] *Dunamis*. Or, "strength, force, quality."
[4] *Poiōn*. That is, the testator, here and below.

good and varied disposition. **12** If the majority of stars are in feminine signs, the testator will be a woman. **13** If Mercury, the testament will be diversified, talkative, and light, and the one who makes it will be [involved with] words[5] or household management. **14** If the Sun or the Moon, [the latter being] largest and conspicuous,[6] according to the manner in which they would chance to be testified to.

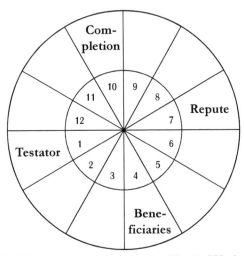

Figure 37: Houses for making wills (Heph. III, App. II, 7)

15 Saturn happening to be on the Midheaven means an ancient will, and the end of the testator according to the quality of the testimonies of the stars which look upon the Midheaven. **16** Mars would indicate that the will is empty and hasty.[7] **17** Jupiter on the other hand reveals that the testament is changed with additions in relation to wealth, and that the testator will live; in a similar way, Venus. **18** Mercury forecasts a quick opening of the will, plus a public statement of great loquacity, in relation to which it is good to examine the testimonies in the same manner. **19** The Sun and the Moon, along with indicating someone well-born, also show mighty individuals.

20 Saturn setting shows the will to be full of insulting treatment, accusation and wickedness. **21** Mars shows that it will not be treated as valid, and that the property will be plundered with violence. **22** Jupiter [indicates that

---

[5] *En logois.* That is, any activities involving words, argumentation, law, accounting, and so on (**EG**).
[6] *Episēmos.* Or, "significant, meaningful."
[7] *Oxeia.* Or, "sharp, acute."

the document] will be carefully observed, and held in high esteem, as being of good faith; similarly Venus. **23** On the other hand, Mercury shows forth that the will is spurious and forged: receiving testimony from benefics, it remains unnoticed; from malefics, it will be revealed to be invalid and dangerous. **24** The Sun and the Moon work the same things, according to the commixture of their figures.

25 Found in the underground, Saturn means taking possession [of the inheritance] by slaves, emancipated slaves and their grandsons; Mars, by the sons of emancipated slaves, and soldiers; Jupiter, siblings and relatives; Venus, by the wife, or young girl, or son, or by him who partakes of the mysteries; Mercury, by children, grandsons, rearers, and those worthy of mention; the Sun or the Moon, by the distinguished and the great.[8] **26** And if testified to by benefics, the inheritances will be profitable; if by malefics, loss-inducing.[9]

---

[8] Or perhaps, "the greatest" people (*megistois*).
[9] *Epizēmioi.*

APPENDIX C: ON THE HANDING DOWN OF THE ARTS

1 We shall learn whether the ones to whom an art[1] is handed down will be ready to learn it, or if they will turn out to be neglectful, and in relation to what there will be attention and successful accomplishment, or else laziness.

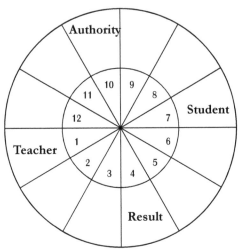

Figure 38: Houses for teaching (Heph. III, App. III, 2)

2 The Hour-marker gives indications on the things related to the teacher; the Midheaven, the one associated with him, such as the master, father or trustee;[2] the setting, the one who will be taught; the underground, the result of the teaching and of the imparting of knowledge—the consideration according to the combined proportion [of planetary testimonies] being taken in a manner similar to what was said above.[3]

3 Knowing in this manner about the trustees of the knowledge of the crafts, we shall keep an eye on the Moon: when she is full, and well placed with Mercury, he himself being well placed too, eastern,[4] and both being in signs of human shape, and configured towards each other—and then we shall hand down the knowledge for instruction.

---

[1] *Technē.* Any art or craft.
[2] That is, the employer who is ordering the education.
[3] Perhaps referring to Appendix II, on crafting a will.
[4] *Anatolikou.*

APPENDIX D: DOROTHEUS *EXCERPTS*

Comment by Dykes. The following *Excerpts* of material by Dorotheus were identified in Greek by David Pingree in *Vaticanus Graecus* 1056, ff. 238-41. Pingree and Burnett printed them as Appendix II of the Latin *Book of Aristotle* (1997), recently translated by me into English as *The Book of Aristotle* (BA), in *Persian Nativities III* (2009). The *Excerpts* were translated from Greek by Eduardo Gramaglia (2013), and edited by me.[1]

A great many of the sentences here may be traced back to known Dorothean material, in five sources:

- *Carmen*, the prose Arabic translation of the Pahlavi version, by 'Umar al-Tabarī. This was edited, translated into English, and published by David Pingree in 1976.[2]
- Greek and Latin *Fragments*, which were listed at the end of Pingree's edition of *Carmen* (see App. E below).
- *The Book of Aristotle* (see above), translated into Latin by Hugo of Santalla from the Arabic (now lost, but existing almost verbatim as a book on nativities by Sahl).
- Hephaistion of Thebes's Greek *Apotelesmatica*.
- Rhetorius of Egypt's Greek *Compendium*, translated into English by Holden in 2009.

The *Excerpts* are almost all in prose, except for XVII, **3**. As Gramaglia points out, every one also begins with *hoti* ("that," the equivalent of the English "he said *that*..."), and the syntax and use of particles such as *gar* ("since") indicates clearly that the writer has taken his material directly from a more complete source—though whether it was from a copy of the original Greek poem or something else, we do not know.

ဢ ဢ ဢ

III 1 Also,[3] the Sun making a diameter to the Moon means a marriage full of strife.

---

[1] I have included only those obviously related to Heph. III and *Carmen* V.

[2] In the next couple of years I will produce my own translation, in anticipation of a future reconstruction of Dorotheus from Greek, Latin, and Arabic.

[3] Cf. *Carmen* V.17, **7**; also Heph. III.9, **25**.

V 1 When eastern,[4] the stars make the matters manifest; western, they cover and conceal. **2** If the star is eastern and the Sun testifies, the scrutiny[5] and the disclosure[6] will be more certain, since the Sun is the cause of visible affairs, and of those which are made public, and he brings everything to light.

VI 1 The stars which are lords over[7] certain persons,[8] matters, and Lots, some of them falling into the setting or the underground, are indicative of a liability to quick change, and early dying, especially if malefics are also looking.

IX 1 The[9] quadrant from the Hour-marker up to the Midheaven is analogous to one's own country; the one from Midheaven up to setting, to other lands.

XI 1 The[10] star which is in another [star's] place, causes the operation[11] to be mixed.

XVI 1 One[12] should become friends with those people who are analogous to those stars which are well-posited as regards both phase and place. **2** For Jupiter, when he is well-posited, and not [in] a square or diameter by Saturn and Mars, makes friends of kings and wealthy people.

3 Venus means friendship from illustrious women, and more strongly so in Pisces (since it is her own exaltation); though if she is in Saturn's house he would care for those women advanced in age; if in Mercury's house, secret conversation with them, and sleeping [with them] in a hidden, easy [way].[13]

---

4 *Anatolikos...dutikos.* This adjective more specifically means "pertaining to" arising or sinking, and here probably means arising out of, or sinking under, the Sun's rays. See for instance Heph. III.47, **94**.

5 *Elegchos (elenchos).*

6 *Phanerōsis.* This word usually refers to the appearance of a star itself, but the author is using it here for the *effects* (**EG**).

7 *Kurieuontes.*

8 *Prosōpōn.* But this can also mean "faces," i.e., decans (**EG**).

9 See Heph. III.30, **1** and **8**.

10 See the Introduction §5 for "mixing"; also Heph. III.45, **6-7** and Rhetorius Ch. 82, **8**.

11 *Energeia.* That is, the active, "working" force which brings things about.

12 See *Excerpt* XIX, **2** below; also *Frag.* II.E, **13-14** (not in this volume) and Heph. III.20, **7**.

13 *Lathraios, euodos hupnos* (lit., "hidden, easy sleep"). Here Hephaistion is drawing on the relationship between *lathraios* (hidden, treacherous), and *Lathria*, an epithet of Aphrodite herself (who is linked with clandestine and treacherous love affairs). So, "hidden...sleep" is equivalent to "undiscovered/secret love affair" (**EG**).

4 [With] Mercury being well-posited, and unharmed by Saturn and Mars, but testified to by Jupiter and Venus, they will become friends with learned and intelligent people, scholars, merchants, bankers, and those who pursue the arts of Mercury: such as athletes, wrestlers, and teachers of the law; and if Mercury is in the house of Saturn, then the elder ones of these; in the house of Mars, the younger ones, and also soldiers and leaders of state.

5 The malefics also give occasional friendships when they are well-placed, in their own places, and seeing the benefics, except that they are not steadfast nor safe.

6 One[14] should also take into account the Lot of friendship (which is from the Moon up to Mercury, and the same [interval projected] from the Hour-marker), and the Lot of Eros (which is by day, from the Lot of Fortune up to the Lot of Spirit, and the same from the Hour Marker; by night, the reverse); the lords of these will indicate the persons.

XVII 1 Mars[15] overcoming Mercury arouses disturbances, harm, and insolence from friends, and for the most part the friends have a hostile disposition towards him. **2** If, contrariwise, Mercury overcomes Mars, he hurts his friends [by] using up and destroying what belongs to them, and surrounding them with debts and false promises in regard to the things in which they have trust.[16]

3 *These are the nativities that fit well with friendship,*[17]

…when the Moon is in the same sign, and a benefic is on the Moon of the other [person] or sees her by triangle; and when the Lots of Fortune [of both people] are in the same place, or the Lot of one is on the Moon of the other, or sees the Lot or the Moon of the other by triangle; also when the Suns are in the same sign, or the Sun of one lies on the Moon of the other, or is in a triangle [to it]; when the Midheaven of one is on the Moon of the other; likewise also the Moon of one on the Midheaven of the other; and[18] when

---

[14] Cf. Dorotheus *Frag.* II.E, **3** (not in this volume).

[15] For this whole *Excerpt*, cf. Dorotheus *Frag.* II.E, **12** (not in this volume).

[16] *Empisteuomena.* Or, things which they believe in (or perhaps things entrusted to them).

[17] This is a single line from Dorotheus's original poem. For the material on the Moon in the 6th and 12th later in this sentence, cf. Heph. III.9, **24-25**.

[18] I believe there is an error in the Greek here. The Moons being in the 6th and 12th is an indication of subjection in marriage (Heph. III.9, **24-25**), and would logically apply to

the Moons occupy each other's 12th place or the 6th; or if the Moon of one is in the 6th place [of the other], and the Moon of the other is in the 12th place of the first; and also when the two Lights are in the signs that see [each other] (or better, in the signs that hear).

XVIII 1 The[19] signs that see are those which lie at an equal distance from each of the tropics; signs that hear are those that stand equally apart from the equinoxes. **2** The malefics in the aforesaid places bring on hatred and want of affection.

3 Besides, those being in the same belt[20] are also sympathetic, as are the signs of equal ascensions.[21]

4 From[22] Aries until Virgo the days grow longer, from Libra until Pisces they decrease. **5** The one having the Moon in the signs which increase the light is better for friendship. **6** Such a one commands, whereas the one having the Moon in the signs that decrease in light, is commanded.

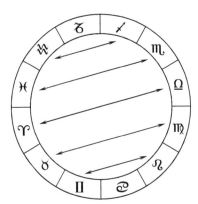

Figure 39: Seeing signs
(Dor. *Excerpt* XVIII, 1)

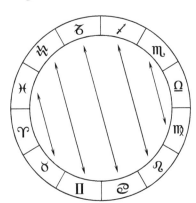

Figure 40: Hearing signs
(Dor. *Excerpt* XVIII, 1)

---

friendship. I propose that this should read, "*but not* when the Moons occupy…". The last part of the sentence (seeing and hearing signs) should resume the good indications for friendship.

19 Cf. Dorotheus *Frag.* II.E, **13-14** (not in this volume), and my Introduction.

20 *Homozôna.* That is, signs which are ruled by the same planet: thus planets in Aries and Scorpio will be sympathetic.

21 These are: Aries-Pisces, Taurus-Aquarius, Gemini-Capricorn, Cancer-Sagittarius, Leo-Scorpio, Virgo-Libra.

22 Cf. Dorotheus *Frag.* II.E, **15, 17** (not in this volume).

On an inception of friendship:[23]

XIX 1 When[24] someone is about to make an inception of friendship, it is necessary to have the luminaries be well-connected with each other, and only the benefics bear witness to them.

2 One[25] must make the person correspond with the stars. **3** For if he whom one wants to befriend is a soldier, Mars must be paid attention to (since he must be in a good phase, position, and testimony); if he is a ruler of people, the Sun must be observed; if a king, Jupiter; if a tiller of the soil, Saturn.

4 When[26] the year circling from the Hour-marker[27] falls in the sign in which the one with whom one makes friendship has the Moon, in one and the same sign (or in a different one, if the signs chance to be of those hearing or seeing each other),[28] then it is in that year that one should attempt the greatest[29] friendship.

On traveling abroad[30]

XXII 1 The[31] ancients knew the things pertaining to the body from the Moon, and those pertaining to the soul, from the Hour-marker, Venus, and Mercury. **2** If then in an inception you are asked about the sick, and find the Hour-marker, Venus, and Mercury harmed, declare that the sick one suffers from inflammation of the brain.[32]

XXVII 1 The[33] phase under the rays causes [one] to meet with entrapment, treachery, and concealment, in the same way as the phase out of the rays [causes it to be] with visibility, and with what does not escape detection.

---

[23] Title as given in f. 239v.

[24] Dorotheus *Frag.* II.F, **5** (not in this volume). See also Heph. III.20, **3-5**.

[25] For this sentence and the next, see Heph. III.20, **7** and *Frag.* II.F, **7** (not in this volume).

[26] See Dorotheus *Frag.* II.F, **3-4** (not in this volume), and Heph. III.3.

[27] This must be the profection of the Ascendant, to the year in question.

[28] See *Excerpt* XVIII, **1**.

[29] *Megistēn philian.* **EG**: The connotation is probably, "friendship with the powerful." **BD**: But perhaps it also means the best or greatest *type* of friendship.

[30] Title as given in f. 239v.

[31] Read with Heph. III.30 (on illness).

[32] *Phrenitis.* In ancient medicine this was a general term that applied to many types of disorders in thinking: delirium, madness, *etc.*

[33] Read with Heph. III.42 and III.47.

XXVIII 1 The[34] retrograde stars are a cause of returning.

XXXI 1 Every[35] star which by transit is diametrical to its natal position, is difficult. **2** And[36] if it comes to its natal place, it is malefic. **3** And[37] more so if Saturn or Mars is the star which in its transit is diametrical either to the Sun or to Jupiter, it becomes a cause of many terrible things; similarly when Saturn does that to the Moon in the fixing.[38] **4** When the Sun or Jupiter come to their natal places, or are diametrical to themselves, and it is a chart[39] of the day, and they are harmed by Mars, either by transit or at the fixing, the figure is bad; similarly when Saturn [harms] the Moon by night.

XXXII 1 Not only is transiting Mars evil [when] approaching[40] Sun and Jupiter [by body] according to [their places] in the fixing,[41] or being diametrical [to those places], but also if it occurs contrariwise: the transiting Sun and Jupiter approaching Mars [according to his place] in the fixing, or being diametrical, spoil the nativity, and more strongly so when they are stationary. **2** For[42] indeed, in the above-said approaches,[43] if the malefic were in a triangle to the sign where the damage occurred, from out of the beginning[44] or by approach, the terrible things will be lighter. **3** And if both then and now the figure is not harmonious, it will be found extremely difficult.

XXXV 1 The benefics found in unfavorable places at the fixing or by transit, are weak.

---

[34] *Palindromia.* See Heph. III.47, **53**.

[35] See *Carmen* IV.1, **186**. I have retained this and the following two *Excerpts* (XXXII, XXXV) as support for Hephaistio's material on transits, even though they more directly apply to annual techniques.

[36] See *Carmen* IV.1, **187**.

[37] See *Carmen* IV.1, **188**, which however makes more sense: that it would be Mars transiting the natal Jupiter or Sun in a *diurnal* nativity, but Saturn doing it to the Moon in a *nocturnal* nativity.

[38] That is, to the natal Moon.

[39] *Thema.*

[40] Throughout this paragraph, this is the same verb (*epembainô*) is the same one used for ingresses (*epembasis*), and so this probably refers as well to an ingress into the sign where the planet is, and not just to its body by degree.

[41] See *Excerpt* XXXI and its parallel in *Carmen* IV.1, **188**, which specifies that the Sun/Jupiter combination pertains to diurnal nativities.

[42] Cf. *Carmen* IV.1, **190**.

[43] Again, this can equally be read as "ingresses."

[44] The nativity.

XXXVII 1 The[45] Moon going towards the Midheaven causes matters to become visible. **2** One should observe this figure in inceptions about theft[46] and runaways.

XLII 1 The approach of the Sun to Venus arouses to venereal[47] affairs.

XLV 1 The[48] Moon being in the sign of a malefic at [the time of] laying down,[49] if that sign happens to contain a benefic at the fixing, announces that the patient will fall severely sick, but he will equally be drawn out from danger eventually. **2** But on the contrary it indicates the worst whenever the Moon at the lying-down chanced to be in the sixth, or twelfth, or eighth, or fourth place,[50] or in the place she was according to the fixing, and she would then be harmed by a malefic.

XLVI 1 Mercury[51] harmed by Saturn is cause of knavery and treachery. **2** In addition, one must watch out for this figure for those who borrow, since Mercury is at home with exchange, security, partnership, and business.

XLVII 1 The squares and diameters of the Moon, [even when] they contain a benefic, are unprofitable. **2** When the Moon comes to be in these places, good activities follow, since these are analogous to every opportune time of an inception.

XLVIII 1 The[52] Moon being connected with Saturn is not only indicative of sluggishness and hindrance, but also damage and loss; if, in addition to this figure, no benefic sees the Moon, there will be no return. **2** If[53] it comes to pass that Saturn and Mercury harm the Moon, then there will be trickery and treachery, and they will become a cause of imprisonment and sickness.

---

[45] See *Carmen* IV.1, **207**; and generally Heph. III.42 and III.47.
[46] *Klopē.*
[47] *Aphrodisiaka.* This word typically refers to pleasures, namely Venusian ones (especially sexual pleasures).
[48] Cf. *Carmen* V.31, **1-2**.
[49] *Kataklisis.* In Latin- and English-language astrology, this is a "decumbiture" (from Lat. *decumbo,* "to lay down").
[50] I take all of these to be places in the nativity, not in the decumbiture chart.
[51] Read with Heph. III.28-29.
[52] See *Carmen* V.22, **14**. See also generally Heph. III.30, **51ff**.
[53] See *Carmen* V.22, **16**. See also generally Heph. III.30, **51ff**.

XLIX 1 When[54] the Moon is with Mercury, and is seen by Jupiter by triangle or square, she becomes a cause of welfare, swiftness, favors, and gifts.

L 1 The sign following that of the Moon is said to be perilous and flowing with blood. **2** It is precisely from this sign—and from the squares and diameters to it—that one should examine the connections of the Moon, to form a judgment about future affairs.

LII 1 The outcomes,[55] either favorable or evil, commonly take place when the stars make a square to the Hour-marker or to the Moon, or they approach the place of the Hour-marker or the Moon: benefics in the case of good outcomes, and malefics [for] bad ones; sometimes they convey a similar meaning when transiting or squaring that star which shows the matter under inquiry.

LIII 1 The[56] tropical signs are unstable; the signs of straight ascension are of quick completion,[57] lucky,[58] and steady;[59] the crooked ones [are], secret, violent, long-lasting, and suffering hardship; the bicorporeal ones reveal that the result of the matters inquired about will be bipartite.

LIV 1 The[60] Moon coming to the diameter of the Sun causes dissension, dispute, and battle.

LV 1 The Moon has been allotted the word on every activity, and in addition to the Midheaven she certainly holds the word on doing. **2** It[61] is necessary that the Moon is not in aversion to the Midheaven, otherwise the resulting [events] will be incomplete and finish early, especially when the benefics are not pivotal. **3** This has been observed for a long time.

---

54 See *Carmen* V.22, **21**. See also generally Heph. III.30, **51ff**.

55 *Apotelesmata.*

56 Compare with *Carmen* V.2, which has opposite indications. But see Heph. III.1, **1**; Appendix A, **5-6**; *Frag.* V.1, **5**—V.4, **1** (**5-6**).

57 *Tachutelestos.*

58 *Eubolos*, lit. "throwing luckily at darts."

59 *Aplanēs*, lit. "not wandering."

60 See *Carmen* V.5, **5**; also Heph. III.1, **6**.

61 Cf. *Carmen* V.5, **9**.

LVI 1 The[62] Moon will indicate the first things of the inception; her lord, the last ones.

LVII 1 At all times,[63] the lord of the Moon being found in the post-ascensions makes the activities slower, and especially if it makes an evening phase in relation to the Sun.

LVIII 1 The[64] Moon flowing away from malefic, and connecting with a benefic, [is useful] only for runaway slaves.

LIX 1 If the lord of the Moon sees the Moon, both the runaway and what has been lost, is found; and the lender will recover the loan.

LX 1 The[65] straight signs indicate that the [legal] adversary[66] is simple and honest; the crooked ones, that he is treacherous and wicked. **2** It is also necessary to observe the testimonies of the stars: whether the benefics or malefics are seeing.

LXI 1 The[67] Midheaven always indicates the doing[68] of the subject that is sought. **2** As a result, should it or its lord be found to be testified to, it will show of what kind the action will be.

On sales and purchases

LXII 1 The[69] [star] having[70] the flowing-away of the Moon, is the seller; the [one having her] connection, the buyer; the Moon herself, the thing sold. **2** From[71] another point of view, the Hour-marker is the buyer, the setting the seller, the Midheaven the price, the underground the thing sold.

---

[62] See *Carmen* V.5, **18**; also Heph. III.2, **8**.

[63] See *Carmen* V.5, **23**.

[64] See *Carmen* V.5, **28**. Or rather, it is good for runaways *but not* for those pursuing them.

[65] Read with Heph. III.37-38.

[66] *Prosionta.* This probably indicates a prosecutor, or at least one bringing charges.

[67] Cf. Heph. III.2, **8**, and III.4, **2-4**.

[68] *Praxis.*

[69] See *Carmen* V.9, **1**; also Heph. III.16, **1-2**.

[70] *Epechō,* lit. "holding onto."

[71] See *Carmen* V.9, **6**; also Heph. III.16, **3**.

LXIII 1 The[72] Moon transiting the last [degrees] of the signs, is indicative of changes of places and affairs.

LXIV 1 The stars being in their own exaltations, or culminating, indicate that the matters or people are more honorable and of higher repute, especially Jupiter and Venus; Saturn would show them to be honorable, but also sordid or old. **2** In the depressions or declines, they disparage[73] the affairs.

LXVI 1 The[74] retrograde stars and the tropical signs make returns [from a journey] well-disposed.

LXVII 1 The assemblies of the Moon [show] whether the first things of the inception, or the last ones, will be better: for if she connects first with the good ones and then the malefics, the first things will be more agreeable and the things that follow will be distressing.

2 On the other hand, when the Moon marks the Hour, and is found within the first fifteen degrees, she accomplishes her business quickly; within the second [fifteen], slowly.

LXVIII 1 The[75] Moon being under the rays is suitable for thieves and runaways, because of her hiddenness.

LXIX 1 When[76] [the inception] is at the assembly or the Full Moon, the figures of the malefics are more destructive, due to which those who then run away will not be found, but will perish.

---

[72] Cf. *Carmen* V.5, **8**; also Heph. III.42, **34**.

[73] *Euteliz̄o*. This verb derives more especially from the notion of cheapening, making something shabby (*euteleia*).

[74] See *Excerpt* XXVIII above.

[75] See *Carmen* V.5, **3**; read also with Heph. III.42 and III.47.

[76] See *Carmen* V.36, **79c-80**; read also with Heph. III.42 and III.47.

APPENDIX E: DOROTHEUS *FRAGMENTS*

Comment by Dykes. In his 1976 translation of Dorotheus from 'Umar al-Tabari's Arabic, Pingree appended numerous other passages (pp. 323-437). The first set of passages (pp. 323-427) were *Fragments*: ancient passages known to be Dorothean, and numbered by Pingree according to what Book, Chapter, and Sentence of *Carmen* they corresponded to. Some of these were from Hephaistion. Following these were three Appendices (pp. 427-37), which included a short reference to Dorotheus by Firmicus Maternus, some other Greek passages from Hephaistio, and a few other ancient citations of Dorotheus.

Below I have included several of the *Fragments* which correspond to *Carmen* V (on elections and event charts), especially when they amplify Hephaistion's text. Again, they were translated by Eduardo Gramaglia and edited by me; a full listing will appear in my future reconstruction of Dorotheus. In the footnotes, I provide both the source of the *Fragment* (as given by Pingree) and relationships to the *Excerpts* and Heph. III.

ಬಿ ಬಿ ಞ

Fragment V.1, 5 – V.4, 1[1]

From the [treatise] on apotelesmatics by Dorotheus:
On the straight and crooked signs

1 Make[2] your inquiry about any activity, beginning this way: [by asking] whether the end will be good or bad. **2** Therefore it is necessary, they say, to know the nature of the straight and the crooked signs. **3** For straight are indeed Cancer, Leo, <Virgo>, Libra, Scorpio, and Sagittarius: for each of them, in its being borne upwards from the invisible to the visible sky for over two equinoctial hours, rules over 30 times. **4** The remaining six are crooked, for they rise in less than two equinoctial hours, and less than 30 times; they are Capricorn, Aquarius, Pisces, Aries, Taurus, and Gemini.

---

[1] See *CCAG* V.1, p. 240 (= Stegemann 64a). Cf. Also *CCAG* 11.2, p. 184. This corresponds roughly to Heph. III.1, **1**.
[2] For **1-4**, see *Carmen* V.1, **5-9**.

5 For[3] indeed when the straight signs mark the Hour, everything comes out quickly; if crooked, they produce long-lasting hardships and difficulties. **6** If any of the benefics looks upon the crooked signs, while they either mark the Hour or contain the Moon, then the maltreatment will have help. **7** If any looks upon the straight signs, or has power over[4] the Moon, while the malefic stars are looking on,[5] this harms the inception. **8** If[6] both benefics and malefics look upon the above-said signs while they mark the Hour, declare that in every inception the result of the matter is unsafe and idle, and take another inception at a different time.

9 When[7] the bicorporeal signs mark the Hour, it indicates that someone will not act as he proposed to, but he will do something else; let these things be equally common for you in every inception.

---

[3] For **5-6**, see *Carmen* V.2, **1-3**; also Heph. III.1, **1**, Appendix A, **5-6**, and *Excerpt* LIII.

[4] **EG/BD:** There are two problems here. In **6**, the verb *epechō* ("contain") was neuter plural, and necessarily referred to the signs; but in **7** it is in the third person singular, and so must indicate a planet (which we have taken to be a benefic). This is confusing, because planets do not contain other planets as signs do: thus it seems that *epechō* has two different meanings here. *Epechō* more generally means to hold something, and can mean to rule or have dominion over (in the sense of "holding territory"): but signs do not rule planets. To address these problems, we translate *epechō* as "contain" in **6** (so that the crooked signs are containing the Moon) and as "have power over" in **7** (so that the benefic is in some sense controlling the Moon). **BD:** I believe that this passage is the victim of bad editing or scribal confusion. Dorotheus is clearly trying to compare two combinations of signs and planets, to show how they mitigate an otherwise good inception, or bring benefit to an otherwise bad one. In this case, he wants to combine crooked signs (bad) which are rising or contain the Moon, with aspecting benefics (good); and straight signs (good) which are rising or contain the Moon, with aspecting malefics (bad). If the Moon is really meant to be included here (see below), I propose that what Dorotheus *intends* is the following, which also lets us out of the confusion over *epechō*: "**6** If any of the benefics looks upon the crooked signs, while they either mark the Hour or contain the Moon, then the corruption will have help. **7** If any of the malefics looks upon the straight signs while they either mark the Hour or contain the Moon, this harms the inception." This can be compared with *Carmen* V.2, **3-4**, which however omits the Moon. There, Dorotheus has a crooked sign rising, with a benefic in it or aspecting it (**3**), and then a straight sign rising, with a malefic in it or aspecting it (**4**).

[5] *Epiblepō.*

[6] Cf. *Carmen* V.2, **5**.

[7] Cf. *Carmen* V.4, **1**.

Fragment V.5, 16-17[8]

1 How to elude them,[9] is dealt with in a chapter by Dorotheus:

2 *Look at the great Helios and the swift Selēnē,*
and the lords of the houses which both Lights occupy,
[the one] on which the Hour-divider is, and also the sign
of the highest ether, which touches the mid-sky, passing through;
[see also] which of these places[10] Mēnē has, and who
is her lord. If her lord is in the declines
while she is on the pivots, the work met with
will appear bright at the beginning, but thereafter,
he will be disappointed,[11] [and] the result for him will be utterly destroyed.

Fragment V.9, 1-7[12]

On purchasing, by Julianus

1 Inquire about purchasing like this. **2** Let the Moon be the item to be bought, [the star] from which the Moon flows away, the seller; the one with which the Moon connects, the buyer. **3** If the Moon is brought from a malefic, the seller will be harmed, or he is not honest; if she is brought from a benefic towards another benefic, then it will be profitable for both the buyer and the seller.

4 As regards the subject of purchasing, you can also inquire like this. **5** Let the Hour-marker be the buyer, the setting the seller, the Midheaven the price, the underground the object sold. **6** If a good one testifies, announce that good things are indicated in each heading. **7** Search for the remaining ones in the book by Julianus.

---

[8] Edited by Cumont in *CCAG* I, p. 108, and Kroll in *CCAG* 6, p. 67 (= Stegemann 66a); see the prose version in Heph. III.2, **6-9**.

[9] That is, the unwanted configurations.

[10] **EG** That is, either the Hour-marker of the Midheaven. Thus Dorotheus is suggesting that the inception should have the Moon in one of those pivots (**EG**).

[11] *Pseusetai.* Or, "deceived." Pingree has filled a lacuna in this line with *horion* ("bound, limit"), which does not makes sense to us.

[12] Edited by Kroll in *CCAG* 6, p. 80. This corresponds to Heph. III.16, **1-3**.

Fragment V.38, 1- 2[13]

On vomiting and purgation

1 When the Moon is in Aries and Taurus, it is befitting for him who wills, to [cause to] vomit, as long as the Moon is waning and flowing towards a sign that is leading upwards,[14] while the benefics are looking on.[15] **2** But if she chanced to be [moving] towards a sign that is leading downwards,[16] there is need of enemas and the drawing out of feces; if the benefic stars testify, greater the help.

Fragment V.41, 1-41[17]

The 2nd by Dorotheus, on the sick

1 Assign[18] the sick one to the Hour-marker; the place where he has fallen ill and the kind of illness that he will have, to the setting; the physician to the Midheaven; the result of the illness, to the underground. In a like manner, the Moon indicates which illness, of what kind, and its cause.

2 When[19] the Hour-marker is seen by malefics, and the setting by benefics, it means that the illness will be heavy to bear, and will last for a long time. **3** If the Midheaven is corrupted, it means that the sick one will meet with a bad physician, and there will be complaints about that physician. **4** When the underground is beheld[20] by malefics, this indicates unambiguous danger for the sick one; if by benefics, it means salvation.

5 But make sure to see which star caused the illness: that is, the one that becomes western[21] or under the rays a few days before the illness, and

---

13 This *Fragment* is from Pingree's manuscript **L** for his edition of Hephaistio, corresponding to Heph. III.34, **1-3**.

14 This are the signs of northern declination (Aries through Virgo), or else those which are *becoming* more northern (Aries through Gemini), and likewise for **2**; see Heph. III.34, **2-3**.

15 *Epitheōreō.*

16 This might indicate the signs of southern declination, or else signs moving down from the MC towards the IC.

17 For the manuscript sources, see Pingree's **C** (Marcianus Graecus 334), ff. 143v-44; **S** (Oxioniensis Savilianus 51), f. 88-88v; **I** (Laurentianus 28), ff. 236v-237.

18 Cf. *Carmen* V.41, **36**.

19 Cf. *Carmen* V.41, **41**.

20 *Theōreō.*

21 *Dutikos.* This may mean going under the rays.

squares or is diametrical to the Moon; and also see when the figure changes to being eastern[22] and the remaining figures, and then the sick one will have health.

By the same man

6 As[23] regards those who are weak, one must take a look at the Hour-marker and the Moon, as well as their rulers and twelfth-parts, and the stars that look on,[24] and the assembly of the Moon: for then you will observe whether the illness will be dangerous or light and small. **7** Since[25] only the benefics looking on[26] indicate a quick and harmless release from the sickness; Mars [makes it] aggressive, harsh and perilous, Saturn, long-lasting and dangerous.

8 Also, the Hour-marker of the illness and its lord indicate the spirit,[27] and the Moon the body. **9** If the Moon is maltreated, the body will be sufficiently harmed as well; if the Hour-marker or its lord, or even both of them, is maltreated, without any benefic looking on,[28] the danger is evident. **10** The sign in which the Hour-marker or the Moon is, or even their diameters, indicate what the sickness is about: that is to say, the part of the body with which the sign has dealings,[29] is said to be in danger. **11** [The subject of] being sick will be known from the above-explained contemplation[30] of the stars.

12 Since[31] the illness's symptoms and abatement stand in relation to the course of the Moon, therefore I take the crisis of the 3rd day from the sign from which the Moon, changing her position, moves towards the next sign; of the 4th day when she comes <to> the hexagon of the sign from which she started; of the 7th day when she comes to a square with the place from which she departed; of the 9th day when to a triangle; of the 14th day when she comes to the diameter; of the 21st day when she comes to the other square, standing in a tenth-place relationship with herself. **13** Those that go beyond

---

[22] *Anatolē.* I.e., coming out of the rays.
[23] For **6-10**, cf. *Carmen* V.41, **1-9**.
[24] *Ephoraō.*
[25] See also below, *Frag.* V.41, **1-34** below, sentence 2.
[26] *Epitheōreō.*
[27] *Pneuma* (lit. "breath, wind").
[28] *Epiblepō.*
[29] *Chrēmatizei.* That is, the part of the body it rules.
[30] *Theōria.*
[31] For **12-14**, cf. *Carmen* V.41, **14-18**.

these figures remain without danger, but are established for a longer period of time. **14** If indeed the Moon, going from one figure to another, is contemplated[32] by a malefic, or comes to the bound of a malefic, she will prolong the weakness; but if she is not seen by a destructive one, [she produces] an abatement [of the illness].

Fragment V.41, 1-34[33]

On taking to bed, and illnesses

1 When examining with respect to diseases, look at the Hour-marker at [the moment of] taking to bed, the position of the Moon, and their rulers; also their connections and the twelfth-part of the Moon. **2** For if the benefics chance to be allotted to them,[34] no harm will occur, but the illness will be alleviated quickly and health will come as a result; if malefics on the other hand, harm and maltreatment are commonly shown; though more specifically, if Mars is allotted to them the illness will be acute and dangerous; if Saturn, the illness becomes chronic and difficult at the same time. **3** But if only the Moon appears [as] maltreated by Saturn and Mars, the harm will only fall upon the body of the man; if only the Hour-marker is harmed, there will be derangement and damage of the mind, as well as frenzy; if both places (that of the Moon and the Hour-marker) are harmed by the malefics, and if no benefic is looking on,[35] it is an evil sign, and a prelude of dangers and death. **4** From the natural sympathy and familiarity of the twelve signs, you should know around which place of the body the illness is.

5 If Saturn or Mars are either marking the Hour or diametrical to the Hour-marker, or assembled with or diametrical to the Moon, this is a sign of great danger and difficulty; if, these things being so, the benefics look upon the figure, there will be help for the sick one; if malefics, the evils will linger on.

6 The distress of the sick one is known according to the periods,[36] and sense of well-being[37] from the circumambulation[38] of the Moon and the daily

---

[32] *Theōreō.*
[33] Previously edited by Olivieri in *CCAG* I, pp. 122-24.
[34] This seems to mean that the benefics are in or rule these places (**EG**).
[35] *Epitheōreō.*
[36] *Periodos.* Or, a cycle, periodic recurrence, or revolution.

record [of motions].[39] **7** For when she connects to a malefic, there will be distress and an intensification of the pains, and especially if it happens in the bounds of a malefic; whenever she connects with a benefic, a sense of well-being comes to be and an abatement of the pains, and especially if in the bounds of a benefic.

8 One should also investigate as follows. **9** Taking the position of the Moon at the time of taking to bed, look at the Moon in the daily records,[40] when she has moved to her own square figure after 7 days; after 9 days she goes to the triangular figure of the inception; after 14 days she will clearly oppose herself; after 19, she moves into her right triangle; after 21 days she will advance to her own square figure. **10** Indeed, it is necessary to accurately examine the five figures of the Moon, and to which of the stars she is about to connect after being in configuration with the Moon of the inception. **11** For if she connects with the benefics, a sense of well-being follows; if malefics, distress and harm.

12 The illnesses which start during the day are judged by[41] 7 or by 14 days; those beginning at night by 10 or 20 days.[42] **13** So, examining these things, not only will you foreknow the day of well-being and distress, but also the hour. **14** For if at the critical [days][43] the benefics encounter the Moon, they produce well-being on the hour of their looking upon[44] [her] by degree, while the malefics [cause] distress and pain. **15** Saturn becomes more harmful for those who begin to be ill at night; Mars for those in the day.

16 The Moon and the Hour-marker being in the tropical signs make the illnesses return again. **17** The two luminaries being found under the earth at

---

[37] This word (*euphoria*) is paired with "distress" (*dusphoria*) here and below. Literally, they mean "easy to bear" and "difficult to bear."

[38] *Peripatos*. In this case, the text means her transit around the chart, not a primary direction: see **17** below.

[39] *Ephēmeridōn*. An *ephēmeris* is a log of daily values, whether for accounting or anything else—hence an astrological ephemeris is a record of daily planetary motions. But we cannot be sure that the author is speaking of an ephemeris in our sense, which calculates positions for specific days: most astrologers would have used tables of mean daily motions, and calculated forward to the day in question from an epoch date for which a planet's position was already known. Thus we have rendered this more literally as a "daily record."

[40] *Ephēmeridōn*. See above.

[41] *Dia*. This seems to mean, "on those days."

[42] This seems to mean one day before reaching the trines, as described in **7** above.

[43] *Krisesin*. This word literally means "decision, judgment," *etc.*, thus days of judgment.

[44] *Epitheōreō*.

the [time of] taking to bed indicate an evil sign for the sick one, and if[45] the maltreatment also emerges from any other signs: for one should not draw conclusions by inferring headlong from only one sign, but from many, [and preferred] in the direction of what is called "reckoned as the most numerous."[46]

18 Once the Moon has accomplished the aforesaid five figures by circumambulation, as it is said, if Saturn testifies to or is assembled with her, it causes frost, coolings, rheum,[47] nerve spasms, and pains; if Mars is allotted these [configurations], it brings about heat, fevers, and thirst, as well as dryness. **19** When Mars chances to be in such a condition, having caused a hemorrhage, he frequently brought the illness to a crisis and helped the sick one.[48]

20 If in the inception of the illness the Moon is found [to be] additive in numbers and configured to the Sun and Mars, know that on the 7th day or the 14th (that is, when she has squared or made a diameter to herself), the matters will be highly dangerous and unstable for the sick one, and death will not be far away. **21** Of the others, if Saturn testifies in this way to her and to the Sun, it becomes helpful. [But] if, the Moon being subtractive in numbers in the inception, Saturn assumes a figure with her, it becomes harmful to the sick one; if Mars looks on with the Moon being this way, it becomes helpful. **22** Once the Moon, in the succession of figures by transit, has come to her own square or diametrical figure, if Saturn looks upon[49] her (if the inception were at a time of good indications) it becomes a cause of salvation for the sick one; but if at a time of indications showing distress,[50] and Saturn maltreated[51] the Moon in a square or diameter to herself,[52] it becomes a cause of death to the sick person, and destroys.

---

[45] We should probably add "especially" here, since the text is saying that one indication is not enough to predict the worst possibilities.

[46] *Pleionopsēphia.* The lexicon defines this as the "dominant astrological influence." That is true so far as it goes, but we have used the more literal rendition of the word to illustrate how such dominance might be determined: most likely through a greater number of indications, but as is well known later medievals would have assigned weighted points to different kinds of indications and rulerships. See my *Search of the Heart* for a discussion of these.

[47] That is, a discharge of fluids.

[48] This may refer to bloodletting, in which case it suggests that the loss of blood might be helpful.

[49] *Epitheōreō.*

[50] *Kakōsis.*

[51] *Epikakoō.*

[52] Reading *heautēn* with the **L** manuscript, against Pingree's *heauton* ("himself") (**EG**).

Fragment V.41, 36-68[53]

Another examination

1 Let[54] the Hour-marker be the physician, the Midheaven the sick one, the setting the illness, the underground the therapy. **2** If[55] indeed a malefic should mark the Hour, the physician will not help the sick one, but he will be harmed by him. But if a benefic marks the Hour, the physician will be of benefit to the sick one. **3** If[56] a benefic is setting,[57] ...the illness will automatically grow easier without the physician. **4** If[58] a malefic marked the Hour, but a benefic were in the underground pivot, it would show that the first physician, though very wise, will be of no help to the sick one, but some other physician will later help him.

5 Observing the underground pivot, examine whether the star following it is in its throne[59] or not: for should it be in its own triangle or house, the physician will be native and not foreign; if in the places of others,[60] the physician will be foreign.

6 Dorotheus also says that, among the climacteric [points],[61] such figures as the seventh and the ninth days are dangerous. **7** Since if, he says, the total days from the birth of the sick one to the moment of taking to his bed, divided by 7, should leave off at 7 (or, divided by 9, they should leave off at 9), there will be a climacteric [point] for that birth: for which reason, should he fall sick, he will become dangerously ill.

---

[53] Edited by Olivieri in *CCAG* I, pp. 124-25.

[54] See *Carmen* V.41, **36**.

[55] See *Carmen* V.41, **37-38**.

[56] See *Carmen* V.41, **40**.

[57] Pingree indicates a lacuna here but does not explain how large it is.

[58] See *Carmen* V.41, **41**.

[59] *Idiothronei.* Ptolemy (*Tet.* I.23) says that to be in its own throne, a planet must be in at least two of its dignities (house, exaltation, triplicity, bound). Hephaistion himself, perhaps thinking of Ptolemy's use of phases, adds that a planet could also be rising out of the rays (Heph. I.19).

[60] That is, peregrine.

[61] *Klimaktēr.* Ptolemy's use of this term is general and non-technical (*Tet.* III.11, lines 340 and 348, Hübner edition), translated by Schmidt as "critical moments" and "crises." Valens uses the term in several ways: for example, to identify certain critical days through numerical procedures (*Anth.* III.8) or as critical times marked by certain profections (*Anth.* III.12). Increments of seven days roughly follow the Moon's quarters; increments of nine days roughly follow her trines to herself.

8 The same [writer] also says thus: **9** Taking the number of the interval of the signs themselves from the Sun at birth to the Moon at birth (also including into the reckoning the very signs in which the lights are placed at the beginning), and having then, as has been said, such a quantity of signs, take the days from the beginning of the birth up to the time of taking to one's bed, and divide these by the quantity of the signs, as has been indicated. Should this number equal the quantity of days, the one who has taken to bed will be dangerously ill.[62]

10 He also speaks in a different way: consider the Moon at the time of taking to bed. **11** If she should happen to be either in the 4th place of the nativity, or in the 6th place, or in the 8th, or the Moon herself was there at the fixing, these also reveal that the sickness is dangerous.

12 He also says that it is necessary to examine the two Suns (the one at the fixing and the one by transit), and even the transiting Moon of the taking-to-bed. **13** And if the Moon should connect with one of the Suns before coming to a square from herself, it indicates that the disease is mild. But should she square herself before connecting with one of the Suns, the indication[63] is evil.

---

[62] This procedure is obviously based on the concept of the Lot of Fortune, which pertains especially to the body and is determined by the distance between the natal Sun and Moon. But here, the number of days elapsed since birth is divided by the number of signs between the natal luminaries, to see if there is any remainder. Hephaistion speaks of this division being "equal" to the days, but what he really seems to mean is that there is no remainder. Thus if 10,000 days have elapsed from birth to going to bed (the decumbiture), and there are natally 5 signs between the Sun and Moon, then the division yields an integer number (10,000 / 5 = 2,000) and the illness will be worse.

[63] Sēmeion, lit. "sign."

Appendix F: Hephaistion III – *Carmen* Correspondence

The following table represents correspondences between Hephaistion Book III and other authors, principally as found in Pingree's critical apparatus. The primary purpose of Pingree's notes was to identify passages from Dorotheus: the *Carmen* column shows passages in his translation of the Arabic *Carmen*, and *Steg.* shows fragments of Dorotheus as catalogued by Stegemann (1939). The *Other* column lists other sources, such as Dorotheus *Fragments*, Manetho (Koechly 1858), and Nechepso-Petosiris (Riess 1892). This table will be superseded by my own reconstructed Dorotheus, to be released in a few years.

Hephaistion III	*Carmen*	Steg.	Other
1, **1-2**		64b	
1, **1**	V.1, **6-9**, V.2, **1-2**, V.3, **1**		
1, **2**	Cf. V.4, **2-5**		
1, **3-7**		65a	
1, **3-4**	V.5, **2-3**		
1, **5-7**	V.5, **5-8**		
2, **4-12**		66b	
2, **6-9**	V.5, **16-23**		*Frag.* V.5, **16-17**
4, **12**		73a	
7, **9-11**		81a	
7, **9-10**	V.6, **1-3**		
9, **1-5**		86a	
9, **1-21**	V.16, **1-26**		
9, **24-29**		86a	
9, **24**	V.16, **30-32**		
9, **25**	V.16, **39**		
9, **26**	V.16, **38**		
9, **27**	Cf. V.16, **40**		
9, **28**	V.16, **34-35**		
10, **5**			Nech. 10c
11, **1-5**		87a	
11, **1-2**	V.17, **1-2**		
11, **3**	V.17, **7-8**		
12, **1-2**	V.18, **1-2**		
16, **1-2**	V.9, **6-7**		
16, **3-4**	V.9, **1-4**		

16, **5**	V.11, **1-12**		
16, **9**	V.10, **1-3**		
16, **11-17**	V.43, **2-8**	80a	
17, **2**	V.23, **1-4**		
19, **1**	V.12, **1-4**		
20, **1-4**		95	
20, **5-7**		96	
21, **1**	V.13, **6**		
21, **5-8**		82a	
21, **5**	V.13, **3**		
21, **8**	V.13, **8**		
25, **1-2**	V.14, **1-4**		
26, **1**		78	
27, **1**	V.15, **1**		
28, **1**	V.20, **1**		
28, **4-6**	V.20, **6-8**		
28, **5-6**		79a	
28, **5**	Cf. V.20, **3**		
30, **1-2**		90a	
30, **1**	V.21, **1**		
30, **2**	Cf. V.21, **2, 4**		
30, **5**	Cf. V.21, **2**		
30, **8-12**		90a	
30, **8**	V.21, **5-7**		
30, **9-10**	V.21, **2-3**		
30, **10**	V.21, **8**		
30, **12**[1]			
30, **12-13**	V.21, **8-10**		
30, **37-62**		91a	
30, **38-65**	V.25, **1-37**		
30, **66-67**	V.22, **7-13**		
30, **68**	V.22, **2-3**		
30, **71**	V.22, **17**		
31, **12-15**	V.31, **1-5**		
31, **14**	Cf. V.29, **2, 4**		
32, **5**	V.40, **1**		
32, **7-8**	V.39, **9**		
33, **1-8**		114	
38, **10-34**	V.33, **1-41**		
38, **10-11**		112a	
38, **33-34**		112a	

---

[1] See **10** in the previous row.

40, **1-32**	V.27, **1-32**		
40, **1-24**		113a	
41, **1-4**	V.32, **1-5**		
42, **2-35**	V.35, **1-42**		
43, **1-11**	V.35, **45-74**		
44, **1-2**	V.35, **75-85**		
45, **1-16**	V.35, **86-129**		
45, **20**	V.35, **132-33**		
46, **1**	V.35, **134-38**		
47, **1-51**	V.36, **1-77**		
App. A, **1-6**	I.3, **1-6**		
App. A, **7**			Man. VI (III), **237-39, 244-45**
App. B, **1-6**	V.42, **1-7**		

GLOSSARY

This glossary is an expanded version of the one in my 2010 *Introductions to Traditional Astrology* (*ITA*), with the addition of other terms from my translations since then. After most definitions is a reference to sections and Appendices of *ITA* (including my introduction to it) for further reading—for the most part, they do *not* refer to passages in this book (and if so, are labeled as such).

- **Accident** (Lat. *accidens*, Ar. *ḥādith*). An event which "befalls" or "happens" to someone, though not necessarily something bad.
- **Adding in course.** See **Course**.
- **Advancing**. When a planet is in an **angle** or succeedent. See III.3 and the Introduction §6.
- **Advantageous places.** One of two schemes of **houses** which indicate affairs/planets which are more busy or good in the context of the chart (III.4). The seven-place scheme according to Timaeus and reported in *Carmen* includes only certain signs which **aspect** the **Ascendant** by whole-sign, and suggests that these places are advantageous for the *native* because they aspect the Ascendant. The eight-place scheme according to Nechepso (III.4) lists all of the **angular** and **succeedent** places, suggesting places which are stimulating and advantageous for a planet *in itself*.
- **Ages of man.** Ptolemy's division of a typical human life span into periods ruled by planets as **time lords**. See VII.3.
- **Agreeing signs.** Groups of signs which share some kind of harmonious quality. See I.9.5-6.
- *Alcochoden*. Latin transliteration for *Kadukḫudhāh*.
- **Alien** (Lat. *alienus*). See **Peregrine**.
- *Almuten*. A Latin transliteration for *mubtazz*: see **Victor**.
- **Angles, succeedents, cadents.** A division of houses into three groups which show how powerfully and directly a planet acts. The angles are the 1st, 10th, 7th and 4th houses; the succeedents are the 2nd, 11th, 8th and 5th; the cadents are the 12th, 9th, 6th and 3rd (but see **cadent** below). But the exact regions in question will depend upon whether and how one uses **whole-sign** and **quadrant houses**, especially since traditional texts refer to an angle or pivot (Gr. *kentron*, Ar. *watad*) as either (1) equivalent to the **whole-sign** angles from the **Ascendant**, or (2) the degrees of the **Ascendant-**

Midheaven axes themselves, or (3) **quadrant houses** (and their associated strengths) as measured from the degrees of the axes. See I.12-13 and III.3-4, and the Introduction §6.

- **Antiscia** (sing. *antiscion*), "throwing shadows." Refers to a degree mirrored across an axis drawn from 0° Capricorn to 0° Cancer. For example, 10° Cancer has 20° Gemini as its antiscion. See I.9.2.

- **Apogee**. Typically, the furthest point a planet can be from the earth on the circle of the **deferent**. See II.0-1.

- **Applying, application**. When a planet is in a state of **connection**, moving so as to make the connection exact. Planets **assembled** together or in **aspect** by sign and not yet connected by the relevant degrees, are only "wanting" to be connected.

- **Arisings**. See **Ascensions**.

- **Ascendant**. Usually the entire rising sign, but often specified as the exact rising degree. In **quadrant houses**, a space following the exact rising degree up to the cusp of the 2nd house.

- **Ascensions**. Degrees on the celestial equator, measured in terms of how many degrees pass the meridian as an entire sign or **bound** (or other spans of zodiacal degrees) passes across the horizon. They are often used in the predictive technique of ascensional times, as an approximation for **directions**. See Appendix E.

- **Aspect/regard**. One planet aspects or regards another if they are in signs which are configured to each other by a **sextile**, **square**, **trine**, or **opposition**. See III.6 and **Whole signs**. A connection by degrees or orbs is a much more intense of an aspect.

- **Assembly**. When two or more planets are in the same sign, and more intensely if within 15°. (It is occasionally used in Arabic to indicate the conjunction of the Sun and Moon at the New Moon, but the more common word for that is **meeting**). See III.5.

- **Aversion**. Being in the second, sixth, eighth, or twelfth sign from a place. For instance, a planet in Gemini is in the twelfth from, and therefore in aversion to, Cancer. Such places are in aversion because they cannot **aspect** it by the classical scheme of aspects. See III.6.1.

- *Azamene*. Equivalent to **Chronic illness**.

- **Bad ones**. See **Benefic/malefic**.

- **Barring**. See **Blocking**.

- **Bearing** (Lat. *habitude*). Hugo's term for any of the many possible planetary conditions and relationships. These may be found in III and IV.
- **Benefic/malefic.** A division of the planets into groups that cause or signify typically "good" things (Jupiter, Venus, usually the Sun and Moon) or "bad" things (Mars, Saturn). Mercury is considered variable. See V.9.
- **Benevolents.** See **Benefic/malefic.**
- **Besieging.** Equivalent to **Enclosure.**
- **Bicorporeal signs.** Equivalent to "common" signs. See **Quadruplicity.**
- **Blocking** (sometimes called "prohibition"). When a planet bars another planet from completing a **connection**, either through its own body or ray. See III.14.
- **Bodyguarding.** Planetary relationships in which some planet protects another, used in determining social eminence and prosperity. See III.28.
- **Bounds.** Unequal divisions of the zodiac in each sign, each bound being ruled by one of the five non-**luminaries**. Sometimes called "terms," they are one of the five classical **dignities.** See VII.4.
- **Bright, smoky, empty, dark degrees.** Certain degrees of the zodiac said to affect how conspicuous or obscure the significations of planets or the Ascendant are. See VII.7.
- **Burned up** (or "combust," Lat. *combustus*). Normally, when a planet is between about 1° and 7.5° away from the Sun. See II.9-10, and **In the heart.**
- **Burnt path** (Lat. *via combusta*). A span of degrees in Libra and Scorpio in which a planet (especially the Moon) is considered to be harmed or less able to effect its significations. Some astrologers identify it as between 15° Libra and 15° Scorpio; others between the exact degree of the **fall** of the Sun in 19° Libra and the exact degree of the fall of the Moon in 3° Scorpio. See IV.3.
- *Bust*. Certain hours measured from the New Moon, in which it is considered favorable or unfavorable to undertake an action or perform an **election.** See VIII.4.
- **Busy places.** Equivalent to the **Advantageous places.**
- **Cadent** (Lat. *cadens*, "falling"). This is used in two ways: a planet or place may be cadent from the **angles** (being in the 3rd, 6th, 9th, or 12th), or else cadent from the **Ascendant** (namely, in **aversion** to it, being in the 12th, 8th, 6th, or 2nd). See I.12, III.4, and III.6.1.
- **Cardinal.** Equivalent to "movable" signs. See **Quadruplicity.**
- **Cazimi:** see **In the heart.**

- **Celestial equator.** The projection of earth's equator out into the universe, forming one of the three principal celestial coordinate systems.
- **Centers of the Moon.** Also called the "posts" or "foundations" of the Moon. Angular distances between the Sun and Moon throughout the lunar month, indicating possible times of weather changes and rain. See *AW1*.
- **Choleric.** See **Humor**.
- **Chronic illness (degrees of).** Degrees which are especially said to indicate chronic illness, due to their association with certain fixed stars. See VII.10.
- **Cleansed.** Normally, when a planet is not in an **assembly** or **square** or **opposition** with a **malefic** planet, but possibly indicating being free of *any* **aspect** with a malefic.
- **Clime.** In general, a "region" of the earth which is ruled by some planet or sign; but in more mathematical accounts (such as in Ptolemy or al-Bīrūnī), it refers to a line or band of latitude on the earth, likewise ruled by some planet or sign. See *AW1*, Part IV.
- **Clothed.** Equivalent to one planet being in an **assembly** or **aspect/regard** with another, and therefore partaking in (being "clothed in") the other planet's characteristics.
- **Collection.** When two planets **aspecting** each other but not in an applying **connection**, each apply to a third planet. See III.12.
- **Combust.** See **Burned up**.
- **Commanding/obeying.** A division of the signs into those which command or obey each other (used sometimes in **synastry**). See I.9.
- **Common signs.** See **Quadruplicity**.
- **Complexion.** Primarily, a mixture of elements and their qualities so as to indicate or produce some effect. Secondarily it refers to planetary combinations, following the naturalistic theory that planets have elemental qualities with causal power, which can interact with each other.
- **Confer.** See **Pushing**.
- **Configured.** To be in a whole-sign **aspect**, though not necessarily by degree.
- **Conjunction (of planets).** See **Assembly** and **Connection**.
- **Conjunction/prevention.** The position of the New (conjunction) or Full (prevention) Moon most immediately prior to a **nativity** or other chart. For the prevention, some astrologers use the degree of the Moon, others

the degree of the luminary which was above the earth at the time of the prevention. See VIII.1.2.

• **Connection**. When a planet applies to another planet (by body in the same sign, or by ray in **aspecting** signs), within a particular number of degrees up to exactness. See III.7.

• **Convertible**. Equivalent to the movable signs. See **Quadruplicity**. But sometimes planets (especially Mercury) are called convertible because their **gender** is affected by their placement in the chart.

• **Convey**. See **Pushing**.

• **Corruption**. Normally, the harming of a planet (see IV.3-4), such as being in a **square** with a **malefic** planet. But sometimes, equivalent to **Detriment**.

• **Counsel** (Lat. *consilium*). A term used by Hugo and other Latin translators of Arabic, for "management" (III.18). An **applying** planet **pushes** or gifts or grants its counsel or management to another planet, and that other planet **receives** or gathers it.

• **Course, increasing/decreasing in**. For practical purposes, this means a planet is quicker than average in motion. But in geometric astronomy, it refers to what **sector** of the **deferent** the center of a planet's **epicycle** is. (The planet's position within the four sectors of the epicycle itself will also affect its apparent speed.) In the two sectors that are closest to the planet's **perigee**, the planet will apparently be moving faster; in the two sectors closest to the **apogee**, it will apparently be moving slower. See II.0-1.

• **Crooked/straight**. A division of the signs into those which rise quickly and are more parallel to the horizon (crooked), and those which arise more slowly and closer to a right angle from the horizon (straight or direct). In the northern hemisphere, the signs from Capricorn to Gemini are crooked (but in the southern one, straight); those from Cancer to Sagittarius are straight (but in the southern one, crooked).

• **Crossing over**. When a planet begins to **separate** from an exact **connection**. See III.7-8.

• **Cutting of light**. Three ways in which a **connection** is prevented: either by **obstruction** from the following sign, **escape** within the same sign, or by **barring**. See III.23.

• *Darījān*. An alternative **face** system attributed to the Indians. See VII.6.

• **Decan**. Equivalent to **face**.

- **Declination**. The equivalent on the celestial **equator**, of geographical latitude. The signs of northern declination (Aries through Virgo) stretch northward of the **ecliptic**, while those of southern declination (Libra through Pisces) stretch southward.
- **Decline** (Gr. *apoklima*). Equivalent to being **cadent** from the angles.
- **Deferent**. The circle on which a planet's **epicycle** travels. See II.0-1.
- **Descension**. Equivalent to **fall**.
- **Detriment** (or Ar. "corruption," "unhealthiness," "harm."). More broadly (as "corruption"), it refers to any way in which a planet is harmed or its operation thwarted (such as by being **burned up**). But it also (as "harm") refers specifically to the sign opposite a planet's **domicile**. Libra is the detriment of Mars. See I.6 and I.8.
- **Dexter**. "Right": see **Right/left**.
- **Diameter**. Equivalent to **Opposition**.
- **Dignity** (Lat. "worthiness"; Ar. *ḥazz*, "good fortune, allotment"). Any of five ways of assigning rulership or responsibility to a planet (or sometimes, to a **Node**) over some portion of the zodiac. They are often listed in the following order: **domicile, exaltation, triplicity, bound, face/decan**. Each dignity has its own meaning and effect and use, and two of them have opposites: the opposite of domicile is **detriment**, the opposite of exaltation is **fall**. See I.3, I.4, I.6-7, VII.4 for the assignments; I.8 for some descriptive analogies; VIII.2.1 and VIII.2.2*f* for some predictive uses of domiciles and bounds.
- **Directions**. A predictive technique which is more precise than using **ascensions**, and defined by Ptolemy in terms of proportional semi-arcs. There is some confusion in how directing works, because of the difference between the astronomical method of directions and how astrologers look at charts. Astronomically, a point in the chart (the significator) is considered as stationary, and other planets and their **aspects** by degree (or even the **bounds**) are sent forth (promittors) as though the heavens keep turning by **primary motion**, until they come to the significator. The degrees between the significator and promittor are converted into years of life. But when looking at the chart, it seems as though the significator is being **released** counterclockwise in the order of signs, so that it **distributes** through the bounds or comes to the bodies or aspects of promittors. Direction by **ascensions** takes the latter perspective, though the result is the same. Some later astrologers allow the distance between a significa-

tor/releaser and the promittor to be measured in either direction, yielding "converse" directions in addition to the classical "direct" directions. See VIII.2.2, Appendix E, and Gansten.

- **Disregard**. Equivalent to **Separation**.
- **Distribution**. The **direction** of a **releaser** (often the degree of the **Ascendant**) through the **bounds**. The bound **lord** of the distribution is the "distributor," and any body or ray which the **releaser** encounters is the "**partner**." See VIII.2.2f, and *PN3*.
- **Distributor**. The **bound lord** of a **directed releaser**. See **Distribution**.
- **Diurnal**. See **Sect**.
- **Domain**. A **sect** and **gender**-based planetary condition. See III.2.
- **Domicile**. One of the five **dignities**. A sign of the zodiac, insofar as it is owned or managed by one of the planets. For example, Aries is the domicile of Mars, and so Mars is its domicile **lord**. See I.6.
- **Doryphory** (Gr. *doruphoria*). Equivalent to **Bodyguarding**.
- **Double-bodied**. Equivalent to the common signs. See **Quadruplicity**.
- **Dragon**: see **Node**.
- **Drawn back** (Lat. *reductus*). Equivalent to being **cadent** from an **angle**.
- **Dodecametorion**. Equivalent to **Twelfth-part**.
- *Duodecima*. Equivalent to **Twelfth-part**.
- *Dustūrīyyah*. Equivalent to **Bodyguarding**.
- **East** (Lat. *oriens*). The Ascendant: normally the rising sign, but sometimes the degree of the Ascendant itself.
- **Eastern/western (by quadrant)**. When a planet is in one any of the **quadrants** as defined by the axial degrees. The eastern quadrants are between the degrees of the **Ascendant** and **Midheaven**, and between those of the **Descendant** and *Imum Caeli*. The western quadrants are between the degrees of the Midheaven and Descendant, and between those of the *Imum Caeli* and the Ascendant.
- **Eastern/western (of the Sun)**. A position relative to the Sun, often called "oriental" or "occidental," respectively. These terms are used in two major ways: (1) when a planet is in a position to rise before the Sun by being in an early degree (eastern) or is in a position to set after the Sun by being in a later degree (western). But in ancient languages, these words also refer mean "arising" or "setting/sinking," on an analogy with the Sun rising and setting: so sometimes they refer to (2) a planet arising out of, or sinking under, the **Sun's rays**, no matter what side of the Sun it is on (in

some of my translations I call this "pertaining to arising" and "pertaining to sinking"). Astrological authors do not always clarify what sense is meant, and different astronomers and astrologers have different definitions for exactly what positions count as being eastern or western. See II.10.

- **Ecliptic.** The path defined by the Sun's motion through the zodiac, defined as having 0° ecliptical latitude. In tropical astrology, the ecliptic (and therefore the zodiacal signs) begins at the intersection of the ecliptic and the celestial equator.

- **Election** (lit. "choice"). The deliberate choosing of an appropriate time to undertake an action, or determining when to avoid an action; but astrologers normally refer to the chart of the time itself as an election.

- **Element**. One of the four basic qualities. fire, air, water, earth) describing how matter and energy operate, and used to describe the significations and operations of planets and signs. They are usually described by pairs of four other basic qualities (hot, cold, wet, dry). For example, Aries is a fiery sign, and hot and dry; Mercury is typically treated as cold and dry (earthy). See I.3, I.7, and Book V.

- **Emptiness of the course.** Medievally, when a planet does not complete a **connection** for as long as it is in its current sign. In Hellenistic astrology, when a planet does not complete a connection within the next 30°. See III.9.

- **Enclosure.** When a planet has the rays or bodies of the **malefics** (or alternatively, the **benefics**) on either side of it, by degree or sign. See IV.4.2.

- **Epicycle.** A circle on the **deferent**, on which a planet turns. See II.0-1.

- **Equant.** A circle used to measure the average position of a planet. See II.0-1.

- **Equator (celestial).** The projection of the earth's equator into space, forming a great circle. Its equivalent of latitude is called **declination**, while its equivalent of longitude is called **right ascension** (and is measured from the beginning of Aries, from the intersection of it and the **ecliptic**).

- **Escape.** When a planet wants to **connect** with a second one, but the second one moves into the next sign before it is completed, and the first planet makes a **connection** with a different, unrelated one instead. See III.22.

- **Essence** (Lat. *substantia*). Deriving ultimately from Aristotelian philosophy, the fundamental nature or character of a planet or sign, which allows it to indicate or cause certain phenomena (such as the essence of Mars being responsible for indicating fire, iron, war, *etc.*). This word has often been translated as "substance," which is a less accurate term.

- **Essential/accidental.** A common way of distinguishing a planet's conditions, usually according to **dignity** (essential, I.2) and some other condition such as its **aspects** (accidental). See IV.1-5 for many accidental conditions.

- **Exaltation.** One of the five **dignities.** A sign in which a planet (or sometimes, a **Node**) signifies its matter in a particularly authoritative and refined way. The exaltation is sometimes identified with a particular degree in that sign. See I.6.

- **Face.** One of the five **dignities.** The zodiac is divided into 36 faces of 10° each, starting with the beginning of Aries. See I.5.

- **Facing.** A relationship between a planet and a **luminary**, if their respective signs are configured at the same distance as their **domiciles** are. For example, Leo (ruled by the Sun) is two signs to the **right** of Libra (ruled by Venus). When Venus is **western** and two signs away from wherever the Sun is, she will be in the facing of the Sun. See II.11.

- **Fall.** The sign opposite a planet's **exaltation.** See I.6.

- **Familiar** (Lat. *familiaris*). A hard-to-define term which suggests a sense of belonging and close relationship. (1) Sometimes it is contrasted with being **peregrine,** suggesting that a familiar planet is one which is a **lord** over a degree or **place** (that is, it has a **dignity** in it): for a dignity suggests belonging. (2) At other times, it refers to a familiar **aspect** (and probably the **sextile** or **trine** in particular): all of the family houses in a chart have a **whole-sign** aspect to the **Ascendant.**

- *Fardār.* See *Firdārīyyah.*

- **Feminine.** See **Gender.**

- **Feral.** Equivalent to **Wildness.**

- **Figure.** One of several polygons implied by an **aspect.** For example, a planet in Aries and one in Capricorn do not actually form a **square,** but they imply one because Aries and Capricorn, together with Libra and Cancer, form a square amongst themselves. See III.8.

- *Firdārīyyah* (pl. *firdārīyyāt*). A **time lord** method in which planets rule different periods of life, with each period broken down into sub-periods (there are also mundane versions). See VII.1.

- **Firm.** In terms of signs, the **fixed** signs: see **Quadruplicity.** For houses, equivalent to the **Angles.**

- **Fixed.** See **Quadruplicity.**
- **Foreign** (Lat. *extraneus*). Usually equivalent to **peregrine.**
- **Fortunate.** Normally, a planet whose condition is made better by one of the **bearings** described in IV.
- **Fortunes.** See **Benefic/malefic.**
- **Foundations of the Moon.** See **Centers of the Moon.**
- **Free.** Sometimes, being **cleansed** of the **malefics**; at other times, being out of the **Sun's rays.**
- **Gender.** The division of signs, degrees, planets and hours into masculine and feminine groups. See I.3, V.10, V.14, VII.8.
- **Generosity and benefits.** Favorable relationships between signs and planets, as defined in III.26.
- **Good ones.** See **Benefic/malefic.**
- **Good places.** Equivalent to **Advantageous places.**
- **Governor** (Ar. *mustawlī*). A planet which has preeminence or rulership over some topic or indication (such as the governor over an eclipse); normally, it is a kind of **victor.**
- **Greater, middle, lesser years.** See **Planetary years.**
- *Ḥalb.* Unknown as a native Arabic word, but probably Pahlavi for "sect." It normally describes a sect-related rejoicing condition (see III.2): when a diurnal planet is above the horizon in a diurnal chart (and below it in a nocturnal one), or a nocturnal planet is below the horizon in a diurnal chart (and above it in a nocturnal one). It may be a later misunderstanding for the Ar. *ghalab*, the act of conquering, triumphing, *etc.*, from the verb *ghalaba* (to conquer, be victorious).
- *Ḥayyiz.* Arabic for "domain," and definitely a translation of the Gr. *hairesis* ("sect"), but often used to denote a gender-intensified condition of *ḥalb*: when a planet in its *ḥalb* and also in a sign of its own gender (see III.2).
- **Hexagon.** Equivalent to **Sextile.**
- *Hīlāj* (From the Pahlavi for "releaser"). Equivalent to **Releaser.**
- **Hold onto.** Hugo's synonym for a planet being in or **transiting** a **sign.**
- **Horary astrology.** A late historical designation for **Questions.**
- **Hour** (Gr. *hōra*). In Hellenistic astrology, equivalent to **Hour-marker** or **Ascendant**, when something is said to "mark the Hour."
- **Hour-marker** (Gr. *hōroskopos*). Equivalent to **Ascendant.**
- **Hours (planetary).** The assigning of rulership over hours of the day and night to planets. The hours of daylight (and night, respectively) are divided by 12, and each period is ruled first by the planet ruling that day, then the

rest in descending planetary order. For example, on Sunday the Sun rules the first planetary "hour" from daybreak, then Venus, then Mercury, the Moon, Saturn, and so on. See V.13.

- **House.** A twelve-fold spatial division of a chart, in which each house signifies one or more areas of life. Two basic schemes are (1) **whole-sign** houses, in which the **signs** are equivalent to the houses, and (2) **quadrant houses.** But in the context of dignities and rulerships, "house" is the equivalent of **domicile.**

- **House-master.** Often called the *alcochoden* in Latin, from **kadukhudhāh** (the Pahlavi for "house-master"). One of the lords of the longevity **releaser**, preferably the **bound lord**. See VIII.1.3. But the Greek equivalent of this word (*oikodespotēs*, "house-master") is used in various ways in Hellenistic Greek texts, sometimes indicating the **lord** of a **domicile**, at other times the same longevity planet just mentioned, and at other times a kind of **victor** over the whole **nativity.**

- **Humor.** Any one of four fluids in the body (according to traditional medicine), the balance between which determines one's health and **temperament** (outlook and energy level). Choler or yellow bile is associated with fire and the choleric temperament; blood is associated with air and the sanguine temperament; phlegm is associated with water and the phlegmatic temperament; black bile is associated with earth and the melancholic temperament. See I.3.

- **IC.** See *Imum Caeli.*

- *Imum Caeli* (Lat., "lowest part of heaven"). The degree of the zodiac on which the lower half of the meridian circle falls; in **quadrant house** systems, it marks the beginning of the fourth **house.**

- **In the heart.** Often called *cazimi* in English texts, from the Ar. *kaṣmīmī.* A planet is in the heart of the Sun when it is either in the same degree as the Sun (according to Sahl ibn Bishr and Rhetorius), or within 16' of longitude from him. See II.9.

- **Indicator.** A degree which is supposed to indicate the approximate position of the degree of the natal **Ascendant**, in cases where the time of birth is uncertain. See VIII.1.2.

- **Inferior.** The planets lower than the Sun: Venus, Mercury, Moon.

- **Infortunes.** See **Benefic/malefic.**

- *ʾIttiṣāl.* Equivalent to **Connection.**

- **Joys.** Places in which the planets are said to "rejoice" in acting or signifying their natures. Joys by house are found in I.16; by sign in I.10.7.
- *Jārbakhtār* (From the Pahlavi for "distributor of time"). Equivalent to **Distributor**; see **Distribution.**
- *Kadukhudhāh* (From the Pahlavi for "house-master"), often called the *alcochoden* in Latin transliteration. See **House-master.**
- *Kardaja* (Ar. *kardajah*, from Sanskrit *kramajyā*). An interval used in the rows of astronomical tables such as in the *Almagest*. Each row begins with a value (called an "argument"), and one reads across to find the corresponding value used to correct such things as planetary positions. The increment or interval between each argument is a *kardaja*. A single table may use different increments based on theoretical considerations, levels of accuracy needed, *etc.* Some books of tables defined the *kardajas* in terms of sine functions. According to al-Hāshimī (1981, p. 143), the lower **sectors** of a planet's epicycle (closer to the earth, where it is retrograde) are the "fast" *kardajas*. But this probably also refers to the lower sectors of the eccentric or deferent circle, closer to a planet's **perigee.**
- *Kaṣmīmī*: see **In the heart.**
- **Kingdom.** Equivalent to **exaltation.**
- **Largesse and recompense.** A reciprocal relation in which one planet is rescued from being in its own **fall** or a **well**, and then returns the favor when the other planet is in its fall or well. See III.24.
- **Leader** (Lat. *dux*). Equivalent to a **significator** for some topic. The Arabic word for "significator" means to indicate something by pointing the way toward something: thus the significator for a topic or matter "leads" the astrologer to some answer. Used by some less popular Latin translators (such as Hugo of Santalla and Hermann of Carinthia).
- **Linger in** (Lat. *commoror*). Hugo's synonym for a planet being in or **transiting** through a **sign.**
- **Lodging-place** (Lat. *hospitium*). Hugo's synonym for a **house**, particularly the **sign** which occupies a house.
- **Lord of the year.** Natally, the **domicile lord** of a **profection**. The Sun and Moon are not allowed to be primary lords of the year, according to Persian doctrine. See VIII.2.1 and VIII.3.2, and Appendix F. But in mundane ingress charts, it is the planet that is the **victor** over the chart, indicating the general meanings of the year.

- **Lord.** A designation for the planet which has a particular **dignity**, but when used alone it usually means the **domicile** lord. For example, Mars is the lord of Aries.
- **Lord of the question.** In questions, the lord of the **house** of the **quaesited** matter. But sometimes, it refers to the client or **querent** whose question it is.
- **Lot.** Sometimes called "Parts." A place (often treated as equivalent to an entire sign) expressing a ratio derived from the position of three other parts of a chart. Normally, the distance between two places is measured in zodiacal order from one to the other, and this distance is projected forward from some other place (usually the Ascendant): where the counting stops, is the Lot. Lots are used both interpretively and predictively. See Book VI.
- **Lucky/unlucky.** See **Benefic/malefic.**
- **Luminary.** The Sun or Moon.
- **Malefic.** See **Benefic/malefic.**
- **Malevolents.** See **Benefic/malefic.**
- **Masculine.** See **Gender.**
- **Meeting** (Ar. *ʾijtimāʿ*). The conjunction of the Sun and Moon at the New Moon, which makes it a **connection** by body.
- **Melancholic.** See **Humor.**
- **Midheaven.** Either the tenth sign from the **Ascendant**, or the zodiacal degree on which the celestial meridian falls.
- **Minister.** A synonym for **Governor.**
- **Movable signs.** See **Quadruplicity.**
- *Mubtazz.* See **Victor.**
- **Mutable signs.** Equivalent to "common" signs. See **Quadruplicity.**
- *Namūdār.* Equivalent to **Indicator.**
- **Native.** The person whose birth chart it is.
- **Nativity.** Technically, a birth itself, but used by astrologers to describe the chart cast for the moment of a birth.
- **Ninth-parts.** Divisions of each sign into 9 equal parts of 3° 20' apiece, each ruled by a planet. Used predictively by some astrologers as part of the suite of **revolution** techniques. See VII.5.
- **Nobility.** Equivalent to **exaltation.**
- **Nocturnal.** See **Sect.**

- **Node.** The point on the ecliptic where a planet passes into northward latitude (its North Node or Head of the Dragon) or into southern latitude (its South Node or Tail of the Dragon). Normally only the Moon's Nodes are considered. See II.5 and V.8.
- **Northern/southern.** Either planets in northern or southern latitude in the zodiac (relative to the ecliptic), or in northern or southern declination relative to the celestial equator. See I.10.1.
- **Not-reception.** When an **applying** planet is in the **fall** of the planet being applied to.
- **Oblique ascensions.** The **ascensions** used in making predictions by ascensional times or primary **directions**.
- **Obstruction.** When one planet is moving towards a second (wanting to be **connected** to it), but a third one in a later degrees goes **retrograde**, connects with the second one, and then with the first one. See III.21.
- **Occidental.** See **Eastern/western**.
- **Opening of the portals/doors.** Times of likely weather changes and rain, determined by certain **transits**. See VIII.3.4, and *AW1*.
- **Opposition.** An **aspect** either by **whole sign** or degree, in which the signs have a 180° relation to each other: for example, a planet in Aries is opposed to one in Libra.
- **Optimal place.** Also called "good" and "the best" places. These are probably a subset of the **advantageous places**, and probably only those houses which **aspect** the **Ascendant**. They definitely include the Ascendant, tenth, and eleventh houses, but may also include the ninth. They are probably also restricted only to houses above the horizon.
- **Orbs/bodies.** Called "orb" by the Latins, and "body" (*jirm*) by Arabic astrologers. A space of power or influence on each side of a planet's body or position, used to determine the intensity of interaction between different planets. See II.6.
- **Oriental.** See **Eastern/western**.
- **Overcoming.** When a planet is in the eleventh, tenth, or ninth sign from another planet (i.e., in a superior **sextile**, **square**, or **trine aspect**), though being in the tenth sign is considered a more dominant or even domineering position. (But Heph. III.2, **1** also allows it by the **opposition**.) See IV.4.1 and *PN3*'s Introduction, §15.
- **Own light.** This refers either to (1) a planet being a member of the **sect** of the chart (see V.9), or (2) a planet being out of the **Sun's rays** and not yet

connected to another planet, so that it shines on its own without being **clothed** in another's influence (see II.9).

- **Part.** See **Lot.**
- **Partner.** The body or ray of any planet which a **directed releaser** encounters while being **distributed** through the **bounds.** But in some translations from Arabic, any of the **lords** of a place.
- **Peregrine.** When a planet is not in one of its five **dignities.** See I.9.
- **Perigee.** The position on a planet's **deferent** circle which is closest to the earth; it is opposite the **apogee.** See II.0-1.
- **Perverse** (Lat. *perversus*). Hugo's occasional term for (1) **malefic** planets, and (2) **places** in **aversion** to the **Ascendant** by **whole-sign**: definitely the twelfth and sixth, probably the eighth, and possibly the second.
- **Phlegmatic.** See **Humor.**
- **Pitted degrees.** Equivalent to **Welled degrees.**
- **Pivot.** Equivalent to **Angle.**
- **Place.** Equivalent to a **house,** and more often (and more anciently) a **whole-sign** house, namely a **sign.**
- **Planetary years.** Periods of years which the planets signify according to various conditions. See VII.2.
- **Possess.** Hugo's synonym for a planet being in or **transiting** a **sign.**
- **Post-ascension** (Gr. *epanaphoros*). Equivalent to being **succeedent.**
- **Posts of the Moon.** See **Centers of the Moon.**
- **Pre-ascension** (Gr. *proanaphoros*). Equivalent to being **cadent** from the angles, or a **place** that rises by **primary motion.**
- **Prevention.** See **Conjunction/prevention.**
- **Primary directions.** See **Directions.**
- **Primary motion.** The clockwise or east-to-west motion of the heavens.
- **Profection** (Lat. *profectio*, "advancement, setting out"). A predictive technique in which some part of a chart (usually the **Ascendant**) is advanced either by an entire sign or in 30° increments for each year of life. See VIII.2.1 and VIII.3.2, and the sources in Appendix F.
- **Prohibition.** Equivalent to **Blocking.**
- **Promittor** (lit., something "sent forward"). A point which is **directed** to a **significator,** or to which a significator is **released** or directed (depending on how one views the mechanics of directions).
- **Pushing.** What a planet making an **applying connection** does to the one **receiving** it. See III.15-18.

- *Qasim/qismah*: Arabic terms for **distributor** and **distribution**.
- **Quadrant**. A division of the heavens into four parts, defined by the circles of the horizon and meridian, also known as the axes of the **Ascendant-Descendant**, and **Midheaven-IC**.
- **Quadrant houses.** A division of the heavens into twelve spaces which overlap the **whole signs**, and are assigned to topics of life and ways of measuring strength (such as Porphyry, Alchabitius Semi-Arc, or Regiomontanus houses). For example, if the Midheaven fell into the eleventh sign, the space between the Midheaven and the Ascendant would be divided into sections that overlap and are not coincident with the signs. See I.12 and the Introduction §6.
- **Quadruplicity.** A "fourfold" group of signs indicating certain shared patterns of behavior. The movable (or cardinal or convertible) signs are those through which new states of being are quickly formed (including the seasons): Aries, Cancer, Libra, Capricorn. The fixed (sometimes "firm") signs are those through which matters are fixed and lasting in their character: Taurus, Leo, Scorpio, Aquarius. The common (or mutable or bicorporeal) signs are those which make a transition and partake both of quick change and fixed qualities: Gemini, Virgo, Sagittarius, Pisces. See I.10.5.
- **Quaesited/quesited**. In **horary** astrology, the matter asked about.
- **Querent**. In **horary** astrology, the person asking the question (or the person on behalf of whom one asks).
- **Questions**. The branch of astrology dealing with inquiries about individual matters, for which a chart is cast.
- **Reception.** What one planet does when another planet **pushes** or **applies** to it, and especially when they are related by **dignity** or by a **trine** or **sextile** from an **agreeing** sign of various types. For example, if the Moon applies to Mars, Mars will get or receive her application. See III.15-18 and III.25.
- **Reflection**. When two planets are in **aversion** to each other, but a third planet either **collects** or **transfers** their light. If it collects, it reflects the light elsewhere. See III.13.
- **Refrenation**. See **Revoking**.
- **Regard**. Equivalent to **Aspect**.
- **Releaser**. The point which is the focus of a **direction**. In determining longevity, it is the one among a standard set of possible points which has certain qualifications (see VIII.1.3). In annual predictions one either directs

or **distributes** the longevity releaser, or any one of a number of points for particular topics, or else the degree of the **Ascendant** as a default releaser. Many astrologers direct the degree of the Ascendant of the **revolution** chart itself as a releaser.

- **Remote** (Lat. *remotus*, prob. a translation of Ar. *zāyīl*). Equivalent to **cadent**: see **Angle**. But see also *Judges* §7.73, where 'Umar (or Hugo) distinguishes being **cadent** from being **remote**, probably translating the Ar. *zāyīl* and *sāqiṭ* ("withdrawn/removed" and "fallen").

- **Render.** When a planet **pushes** to another planet or place.

- **Retreating.** When a planet is in a cadent place. See III.4 and the Introduction §6, and **Angle**.

- **Retrograde.** When a planet seems to move backwards or clockwise relative to the signs and fixed stars. See II.8 and II.10.

- **Return, Solar/Lunar.** Equivalent to **Revolution.**

- **Returning.** What a **burned up** or **retrograde** planet does when another planet **pushes** to it. See III.19.

- **Revoking.** When a planet making an applying **connection** stations and turns **retrograde**, not completing the connection. See III.20.

- **Revolution.** Sometimes called the "cycle" or "transfer" or "change-over" of a year. Technically, the **transiting** position of planets and the **Ascendant** at the moment the Sun returns to a particular place in the zodiac: in the case of nativities, when he returns to his exact natal position; in mundane astrology, usually when he makes his ingress into 0° Aries. But the revolution is also understood to involve an entire suite of predictive techniques, including **distribution**, **profections**, and *firdārīyyāt*. See *PN3*.

- **Right ascensions.** Degrees on the celestial **equator** (its equivalent of geographical longitude), particularly those which move across the meridian when calculating arcs for **ascensions** and **directions**.

- **Right/left.** Right (or "dexter") degrees and **aspects** are those earlier in the zodiac relative to a planet or sign, up to the **opposition**; left (or "sinister") degrees and aspects are those later in the zodiac. For example, if a planet is in Capricorn, its right aspects will be towards Scorpio, Libra, and Virgo; its left aspects will be towards Pisces, Aries, and Taurus. See III.6.

- **Root.** A chart used as a basis for another chart; a root particularly describes something considered to have concrete being of its own. For example, a **nativity** acts as a root for an **election**, so that when planning an election one must make it harmonize with the nativity.

- **Safe.** When a planet is not being harmed, particularly by an **assembly** or **square** or **opposition** with the **malefics**. See **Cleansed**.
- *Sālkhudhāy* (from Pahlavi, "lord of the year"). Equivalent to the **lord of the year**.
- **Sanguine.** See **Humor**.
- **Scorched.** See **Burned up**.
- **Secondary motion.** The counter-clockwise motion of planets forward in the zodiac.
- **Sect.** A division of charts, planets, and signs into "diurnal/day" and "nocturnal/night." Charts are diurnal if the Sun is above the horizon, else they are nocturnal. Planets are divided into sects as shown in V.11. Masculine signs (Aries, Gemini, *etc.*) are diurnal, the feminine signs (Taurus, Cancer, *etc.*) are nocturnal.
- **Sector** (Ar. *niṭāq*). A division of the **deferent** circle or **epicycle** into four parts, used to determine the position, speed, visibility, and other features of a planet. See II.0-1.
- **Seeing, hearing, listening signs.** A way of associating signs similar to **commanding/obeying**. See Paul of Alexandria's version in the two figures attached to I.9.6.
- **Separation.** When planets have completed a **connection** by **assembly** or **aspect**, and move away from one another. See III.8.
- **Sextile.** An **aspect** either by **whole sign** or degree, in which the signs have a 60° relation to each other: for example, Aries and Gemini.
- **Shift** (Ar. *nawbah*). Equivalent to **Sect**, and refers not only to the alternation between day and night, but also to the period of night or day itself. The Sun is the lord of the diurnal shift or sect, and the Moon is the lord of the nocturnal shift or sect.
- **Sign.** One of the twelve 30° divisions of the **ecliptic**, named after the constellations which they used to be roughly congruent to. In tropical astrology, the signs start from the intersection of the ecliptic with the celestial equator (the position of the Sun at the equinoxes). In sidereal astrology, the signs begin from some other point identified according to other principles.
- **Significator.** Either (1) a planet or point in a chart which indicates or signifies something for a topic (either through its own character, or house position, or rulerships, *etc.*), or (2) the point which is **released** in primary **directions**.

- **Significator of the king**. In mundane ingress charts, the **victor** planet which indicates the king or government.
- **Sinister**. "Left": see **Right/left.**
- **Slavery.** Equivalent to **fall.**
- **Sovereignty** (Lat. *regnum*). Equivalent to **Exaltation.**
- **Spearbearing.** Equivalent to **Bodyguarding.**
- **Square.** An **aspect** either by **whole sign** or degree, in which the signs have a 90° relation to each other: for example, Aries and Cancer.
- **Stake.** Equivalent to **Angle.**
- **Sublunar world.** The world of the four **elements** below the sphere of the Moon, in classical cosmology.
- **Substance** (Lat. *substantia*). Sometimes, indicating the real **essence** of a planet or sign. But often it refers to financial assets (perhaps because coins are physical objects indicating real value).
- **Succeedent.** See **Angle.**
- **Sun's rays** (or Sun's beams). In earlier astrology, equivalent to a regularized distance of 15° away from the Sun, so that a planet under the rays is not visible at dawn or dusk. But a later distinction was made between being **burned up** (about 1° - 7.5° away from the Sun) and merely being under the rays (about 7.5° - 15° away).
- **Superior.** The planets higher than the Sun: Saturn, Jupiter, Mars.
- **Supremacy** (Lat. *regnum*). Hugo's word for **Exaltation**, sometimes used in translations by Dykes instead of the slightly more accurate **Sovereignty.**
- **Synastry.** The comparison of two or more charts to determine compatibility, usually in romantic relationships or friendships. See *BA* Appendix C for a discussion and references for friendship, and *BA* III.7.11 and III.12.7.
- *Tasyīr* (Ar. "dispatching, sending out"). Equivalent to primary **directions.**
- **Temperament.** The particular mixture (sometimes, "complexion") of **elements** or **humors** which determines a person's or planet's typical behavior, outlook, and energy level.
- **Testimony.** From Arabic astrology onwards, a little-defined term which can mean (1) the planets which have **dignity** in a place or degree, or (2) the number of dignities a planet has in its own place (or as compared with other planets), or (3) a planet's **assembly** or **aspect** to a place of interest, or (4) generally *any* way in which planets may make themselves relevant to the inquiry at hand. For example, a planet which is the **exalted** lord of the

Ascendant but also **aspects** it, may be said to present two testimonies supporting its relevance to an inquiry about the Ascendant.

- **Tetragon.** Equivalent to **Square.**
- **Thought-interpretation.** The practice of identifying a theme or topic in a **querent's** mind, often using a **victor**, before answering the specific **question.** See *Search.*
- **Time lord.** A planet ruling over some period of time according to one of the classical predictive techniques. For example, the **lord of the year** is the time lord over a **profection.**
- **Transfer.** When one planet **separates** from one planet, and **connects** to another. See III.11.
- **Transit.** The passing of one planet across another planet or point (by body or **aspect** by exact degree), or through a particular sign (even in a **whole-sign** relation to some point of interest). In traditional astrology, not every transit is significant; for example, transits of **time lords** or of planets in the **whole-sign angles** of a **profection** might be preferred to others. See VIII.2.4 and *PN3.*
- **Translation.** Equivalent to **Transfer.**
- **Traverse** (Lat. *discurro*). Hugo's synonym for a planet being in or **transiting** through a **sign.**
- **Trigon.** Equivalent to **Trine.**
- **Trine.** An **aspect** either by **whole sign** or degree, in which the signs have a 120° relation to each other: for example, Aries and Leo.
- **Turn** (Ar. *dawr*). A predictive technique in which responsibilities for being a **time lord** rotates between different planets. See VIII.2.3 for one use of the turn. But it can occasionally refer more generally to how the planets may equally play a certain *role* in a chart: for example, if the lord of the Ascendant is Saturn, it means X; but if Jupiter, Y; but if Mars, Z; and so on.
- **Turned away.** Equivalent to **Aversion.**
- **Turning signs.** For Hugo of Santalla, equivalent to the movable signs: see **Quadruplicity.** But *tropicus* more specifically refers to the tropical signs Cancer and Capricorn, in which the Sun turns back from its most extreme declinations.
- **Twelfth-parts.** Signs of the zodiac defined by 2.5° divisions of other signs. For example, the twelfth-part of 4° Gemini is Cancer. See IV.6.
- **Two-parted signs.** Equivalent to the double-bodied or common signs: see **Quadruplicity.**

- **Under rays.** When a planet is between approximately 7.5° and 15° from the Sun, and not visible either when rising before the Sun or setting after him. Some astrologers distinguish the distances for individual planets (which is more astronomically accurate). See II.10.
- **Unfortunate.** Normally, when a planet's condition is made more difficult through one of the **bearings** in IV.
- **Unlucky.** See **Benefic/malefic.**
- *Via combusta.* See **Burnt path.**
- **Victor** (Ar. *mubtazz*). A planet identified as being the most authoritative either for a particular topic or **house** (I.18), or for a chart as a whole (VIII.1.4). See also *Search.*
- **Void in course.** Equivalent to **Emptiness of the course.**
- **Well.** A degree in which a planet is said to be more obscure in its operation. See VII.9.
- **Western.** See **Eastern/western.**
- **Whole signs.** The oldest system of assigning house topics and **aspects.** The entire sign on the horizon (the **Ascendant**) is the first house, the entire second sign is the second house, and so on. Likewise, aspects are considered first of all according to signs: planets in Aries aspect or regard Gemini as a whole, even if aspects by exact degree are more intense. See I.12, III.6, and the Introduction §6.
- **Wildness.** When a planet is not **aspected** by any other planet, for as long as it is in its current sign. See III.10.
- **Withdrawal.** Equivalent to **separation.**

BIBLIOGRAPHY

Brennan, Chris, "The Katarchē of Horary," *Geocosmic Journal* (New York: NCGR, Summer Solstice 2007), pp. 23-34.

Brennan, Chris, "The Planetary Joys and the Origins of the Significations of the Houses and Triplicities," *International Society for Astrological Research Journal* Vol. 42, No. 1 (2013), pp. 27-42.

Copenhaver, Brian, *Hermetica* (Cambridge: Cambridge University Press, 1992)

Dorotheus of Sidon, *Carmen Astrologicum*, trans. David Pingree (Abingdon, MD: The Astrology Center of America, 2005)

Dykes, Benjamin trans. and ed., *Works of Sahl & Māshā'allāh* (Golden Valley, MN: The Cazimi Press, 2008)

Dykes, Benjamin trans. and ed., *Persian Nativities* vols. I-III (Minneapolis, MN: The Cazimi Press, 2009-10)

Dykes, Benjamin trans. and ed., *Introductions to Traditional Astrology: Abū Ma'shar & al-Qabīsī* (Minneapolis, MN: The Cazimi Press, 2010)

Dykes, Benjamin trans. and ed., *The Book of the Nine Judges* (Minneapolis, MN: The Cazimi Press, 2011)

Dykes, Benjamin trans. and ed., *The Forty Chapters of al-Kindī* (Minneapolis, MN: The Cazimi Press, 2011)

Dykes, Benjamin, trans. and ed., *Choices & Inceptions: Traditional Electional Astrology* (Minneapolis, MN: The Cazimi Press, 2012)

Dykes, Benjamin, trans. and ed., *Astrology of the World I: The Ptolemaic Inheritance* (Minneapolis, MN: The Cazimi Press, 2013)

Dykes, Benjamin and Jayne Gibson, *Astrological Magic: Basic Rituals & Meditations* (Minneapolis, MN: The Cazimi Press, 2012)

Hephaistio of Thebes, *Apotelesmaticorum Libri Tres*, ed. David Pingree, vols. I-II (Leipzig: Teubner Verlagsgesellschaft, 1973)

Hephaistio of Thebes, *Apotelesmatics* vol. II, trans. and ed. Robert H. Schmidt (Berkeley Springs, WV: The Golden Hind Press, 1994)

Hephaistio of Thebes, *Apotelesmatics* vol. II, trans. and ed. Robert H. Schmidt (Cumberland, MD: The Golden Hind Press, 1998)

Hermann of Carinthia, Benjamin Dykes trans. and ed., *The Search of the Heart* (Minneapolis, MN: The Cazimi Press, 2011)

Jiménez, Aurelio P., "Περὶ Δείπνου: A propósito de Heph., III 36," MHNH, 2 (2002), pp. 237-54.

Jiménez, Aurelio P., "Hephaestio and the Consecration of Statues," MHNH, 11 (2007), nos. 1 and 2, pp. 111-34.

Koechly, Arminius, *Corpus Poetarum Epicorum Graecorum*, vol. 7: *Manethoniana* (Leipzig: B. G. Teubner, 1858)

Liddell & Scott, *A Greek-English Lexicon* (Oxford: The Clarendon Press, 1968)

Maternus, Firmicus, *Mathesis*, trans. and ed. James H. Holden (Tempe, AZ: American Federation of Astrologers, Inc., 2011)

Paulus Alexandrinus, *Late Classical Astrology: Paulus Alexandrinus and Olympiodorus*, trans. Dorian Gieseler Greenbaum, ed. Robert Hand (Reston, VA: ARHAT Publications, 2001)

Pingree, David, trans. and ed., *The Yavanajātaka of Sphujidhvaja* vols. I-II (Cambridge, MA and London: Harvard University Press, 1978)

Ptolemy, Claudius, *Tetrabiblos* vols. 1, 2, 4, trans. Robert Schmidt, ed. Robert Hand (Berkeley Springs, WV: The Golden Hind Press, 1994-98)

Rhetorius of Egypt, trans. James H. Holden, *Astrological Compendium* (Tempe, AZ: American Federation of Astrologers, Inc., 2009)

Riess, Ernst, "Nechepsonis et Petosiridis Fragmenta Magica," in *Zeitschrift für das classische Alterthum*, vol. 6, Suppl. 1, pp. 325-94.

Schmidt, Robert trans., Robert Hand ed., *The Astrological Record of the Early Sages in Greek* (Berkeley Springs, WV: The Golden Hind Press, 1995)

Stegemann, Viktor, *Die Fragmente des Dorotheos von Sidon* (Heidelberg: F. Bilabel, 1939)

Valens, Vettius, *The Anthology*, vols. I-VII, ed. Robert Hand, trans. Robert Schmidt (Berkeley Springs, WV: The Golden Hind Press, 1993-2001)

CPSIA information can be obtained
at www.ICGtesting.com
Printed in the USA
LVHW021327191218
600903LV00003B/317/P

9 781934 586402